ECOLOGY,
ECONOMICS,
ETHICS

ECOLOGY,
ECONOMICS,
ETHICS
The Broken Circle

EDITED BY
F. HERBERT BORMANN
STEPHEN R. KELLERT

Yale University Press New Haven & London

Designed by Sonia L. Scanlon.
Set in Palatino type by Keystone Typesetting, Inc.,
Orwigsburg, Pennsylvania.
Printed in the United States of America by
Vail-Ballou Press, Binghamton, New York.

Printed on recycled paper.
The paper in this book meets the guidelines for
permanence and durability of the Committee on
Production Guidelines for Book Longevity of
the Council on Library Resources.

Library of Congress Cataloging-in-Publication Data
Ecology, economics, ethics : the broken circle / edited
by F. Herbert Bormann and Stephen R. Kellert.
p.   cm.
Includes bibliographical references and index.
ISBN 0-300-04976-5 (cloth)
0-300-05751-2 (pbk.)
1. Ecology. 2. Environmental policy—Moral and
ethical aspects. I. Bormann, F. Herbert, 1922–   .
II. Kellert, Stephen R.
QH541.E31934   1991
179'.1—dc20   91-15191

A catalogue record for this book is available from the
British Library.

10 9 8 7 6 5 4 3

To our students,
our constant source of renewal

CONTENTS

PREFACE THE
GLOBAL
ENVIRONMENTAL
DEFICIT

In our contemporary society there is great concern for the earth and for the future human condition. For many people, the realization that we are the cause of the deterioration of our planet is a recent discovery. Our problems are related to growth in human numbers, to our voracious use of natural resources, and to economic decisions seeking short-term gains that do not carefully consider social and environmental implications. Changing directions involves making ethical and economic decisions that create enormous problems for all of us. Answers are required to such fundamental questions as "What is our responsibility to future generations of humans, to our own generation, and to other earth-bound organisms?"

If we view ecology, economics, and ethics as parts of a whole, of an interconnected circle, then the current linkage seems weak and the circle seems broken. We are apparently faced with choices that further rip the circle asunder: jobs or environment; population control or right to life; tropical forests or economic viability of tropical nations; economic recession or toxification of air, land, and water; conspicuous consumption or drab uniformity. None of these problems and controversies are really new (Bormann, 1972).

Twenty years ago, the first editor and a colleague, Garth Voigt, put together a lecture series designed to examine what appeared to be a newly recognized and apparently unyielding paradox. Humanity seemed to be approaching

F. Herbert
Bormann
and
Stephen R.
Kellert

at lightning speed the pinnacle of technological accomplishments with an extraordinary list of achievements and more coming daily. Our ability to control and shape the human environment-first to human needs seemed to be without limit. Yet we were beginning to discern all about us signs of a steady and seemingly inexorable deterioration of both human and natural environments. Evidence was easy to find: Streams and rivers were polluted; palls of smog shrouded our cities; garbage and ugliness were commonplace, as were urban decay and associated violence. Scientists were busy documenting more subtle effects on food chains polluted with biocides and on air masses contaminated with an array of waste products generated by society.

We wondered if these evidences were symptoms of a deeper and more pervasive malady: a dominating involvement with the here and now, and a resultant loss of harmony between the goals of our species and the laws of nature. Humankind might be subtly but cumulatively destroying the very life-support systems upon whose function all humans are ultimately dependent.

On the brighter side, the younger generation's fumbling but perceptive rebellion was forcing a reexamination of our philosophy toward natural and human resources. Questions were being raised about our future, our failure to appreciate the interrelatedness of our species to all other organisms and to natural cycles, and our failure to calculate the real costs we must pay for altering our environment. Did not environmental alterations made for the presumed good of humankind often lead to a withering of the very amenities necessary for a dignified life?

To examine these fateful questions, the first editor and Garth Voigt brought together in 1969 a distinguished group of scholars and citizens. They examined the science underlying environmental problems, technology as friend and foe, conflicts of interest, and the social, philosophical, and moral implications of current environmental trends. These contributions were published in a small book entitled *The Environmental Crisis* (Helfrich, 1970).

In 1989 these issues were reexamined as the basis for the current book, but under changed circumstances. About a billion and a half people have been added to the world's population since 1969, and several billion more are expected by the mid-twenty-first century. Since 1969 we have seen a continuation of our species' remarkable ability to utilize renewable and nonrenewable resources of the earth in the service of humankind. The production of coal, oil, steel, fertilizers, and many chemicals has increased exponentially. Agricultural production has risen apace with human population. Our use of forests, soils, fisheries, and water supplies has grown immensely.

Throughout the world, societies have made concerted efforts to lessen human impacts on the environment. Through legislation, international agreements, and individual and corporate actions, a massive effort has been made to improve the quality of our air, water, food, and life in general. Environmental awareness and sophistication have grown; the achievements have been impressive.

Unfortunately, despite this welcome progress, environmental and social problems now appear more grave. The gap between wealthy and poor countries has widened, world hunger has grown. In many countries crime and drug use are major concerns. A spate of environmental problems are viewed as being out of control.

In many of the less developed areas of the world, population growth and increased expectations have brought about more contacts with the developed world, greater pressure on limited natural resources, and more pollution, with little improvement in the general quality of life. Even in wealthy countries, economics geared toward profit and satisfaction of personal wants is too often coupled with deterioration of both human and natural environments. Life is less satisfying for many people even in the United States and in Japan.

Most important, what in 1969 appeared to be a patchwork of environmental problems restricted to individual regions or countries has coalesced into serious global trends. Nowhere is this more evident than in the threat of pollution-induced global warming, a problem to which all nations contribute and to which all are subject.

Yet greenhouse gases are but one of an array of factors contributing to the deterioration of the global atmosphere. Acid rain, a mixture of pollutants, now falls on substantial portions of North America, Europe, and Asia. In many areas, there is grave concern about the effects of acid rain on lakes, forests, and manmade structures. The stratospheric ozone layer, particularly at higher latitudes, appears to be thinning because of chlorofluorocarbon pollutants. Scientists fear that decreases in the ozone layer will increase the amount of biologically destructive ultraviolet radiation reaching the earth's surface, with unknown consequences.

Recently, a synoptic study of the chemistry of clouds and fog that impinge on North American vegetation found them to be more heavily contaminated than acid rain. The same is true over areas of Europe and

Asia. While ozone in the upper atmosphere is decreasing, ozone from manmade pollution in the lower atmosphere is increasing over several continents and is known to cause major damage to crop plants and to natural vegetation. As our analytical ability improves, we are finding more and more evidence of long-range transport of air pollutants; for example, pesticides sprayed on cotton in Alabama are found in Lake Superior. The spread of radioactive fallout from Chernobyl dramatized the fact that air pollutants do not respect national borders.

How are humans to think about this bewildering array of environmental insults? We might gain focus by borrowing from economics. In the United States, the 1980s was a decade of both trade and budget deficits. Americans were deeply concerned about how borrowing would affect future generations. Other nations were concerned about the effect of the U.S. deficit on the stability of global economics.

There is another and more important deficit, however, that is deeper, longer-lasting, and more potent in its implications for humankind: the global environmental deficit (Bormann, 1990). This deficit has arisen from a wide diversity of economic activities and ethical choices. It results from the collective and mostly unanticipated impact of humankind's alteration of the earth's atmosphere, water, soil, biota, ecological systems, and landscapes. The global environmental deficit exists because the longer-term ecological, social, and economic costs to human welfare are greater than the shorter-term benefits flowing from these alterations. Anthropogenic alteration of global life-support systems produces not only climate change and toxification of air, water, land, and food but also an extraordinary loss of species, as well as appalling soil loss, forest destruction, and desertification. These changes, in turn, will certainly have long-term negative impacts on the development of human societies and on humankind's aspirations and well-being. Judging by indicators like global soil erosion rates and the flow of greenhouse gases to the atmosphere, the global environmental deficit is rising at an alarming rate.

The global environmental deficit, like its economic counterpart, also borrows from the future but differs from trade and budget deficits in that its implications are far greater and not easily reversed. The causes of the global environmental deficit are rooted in the seemingly inexorable growth of human numbers and in the development and implementation of technology designed to satisfy real and imagined human needs.

Human numbers have increased from about a half billion in the

Middle Ages to about a billion at the time of ratification of the U.S. Constitution two hundred years ago and to more than five billion today. Use of natural resources has grown apace with human numbers. In fact, the two are locked into a positive feedback: Growth in human numbers creates demand for natural resources, and successful utilization of resources makes greater human numbers possible. Of course, there are ultimate limits to this relationship, limits that we may be approaching.

Currently, growth in human numbers and the use of natural resources are not evenly distributed throughout the world. Rapid population growth is focused in the poorer, less developed countries, whereas the accelerated use of natural resources typifies wealthy developed nations.

The editors of this book believe that the global environmental deficit has grown to such proportions that it threatens the basic functions of our biosphere that are vital to human welfare. A few of the more important components that are exhibiting symptoms of large-scale environmental degradation are biogeochemical cycles that renew and maintain the atmosphere; the hydrologic cycle; global climate; the soil formation cycle; and the maintenance of species diversity. The exponential growth of human numbers and of exploitive technology suggests that we are entering a new phase of impact so profoundly powerful as to alter nature in ways inimical to human welfare and survival.

The biosphere is no fragile flower. It has huge self-correcting powers, but these are enacted with no regard for the human condition. Changes we have set in motion may result in a world in which humankind is but a minor component. Although study and documentation of these symptoms of environmental decline are important, such work by itself will not generate the necessary debate on the ethics of what humankind is doing, nor will it generate the political and social will to make the extremely difficult decisions necessary to reduce the global environmental deficit. In many respects, we humans have made life more difficult for ourselves, and only our actions can reverse this trend.

To understand the enormity of the task, we must face the fact that the human population is expected to increase by three to five billion people by the year 2100, and that continued development of global resources will be necessary to meet the needs of new people and to improve the lot of existing populations. To meet this challenge, at least two strategies seem vital: (1) we must learn how to reduce the growth rate of human populations, and (2) we must devise development techniques for both developed and less developed countries that are energy- and materials-efficient, along with practical techniques that minimize increases in the global environmental deficit. To achieve these objectives, developing and developed countries have no choice but to work together to design and implement societies that meet human needs but at the same time work in harmony with nature.

For society to learn to act effectively, it must perceive the link between ecosystem function and human welfare. It will take an enormous feat of human ingenuity and cooperation to focus resource use in such a way as to sustain the human species over the long term. Economic policy based on short-term estimations of material return that discount future long-term negative environmental impacts needs to be viewed not only as bad economics but also as morally inconsistent with our sense of community membership and stewardship. Moral considerations should include more equitable living standards between rich and poor and between developed and less developed regions. We should also realize that uncontrolled development can only lead to bankruptcy for humanity. Until we mend the cleavage in our understanding of the relationships among ecology, economics, and ethics, our willingness to make changes to maintain the long-term integrity and quality of the biosphere will not develop.

In this book a number of experienced and creative scholars examine those relationships and address the problem of mending the broken circle. All of the contributors to this volume have, to various degrees, dealt with ecology, economics, and ethics. To provide more organization, the contributions are divided into five major subject areas. In addressing species diversity and extinction, Edward O. Wilson writes on biodiversity, prosperity, and value; Norman Myers contributes an essay on biological diversity and global security; and David Ehrenfeld discusses the "management" of diversity. On the subject of modern agriculture, Wes Jackson writes about nature as the measure for a sustainable agriculture, and David Pimentel offers thoughts on dimensions of the pesticide question. Holmes Rolston examines environmental values in his essay on environmental ethics, in which he considers values in and duties to the natural world. On the topic of pollution and waste, Paul H. Connett probes the disposable society, and William Goldfarb discusses the vulnerability of groundwater. Gene E. Likens examines the relationships among pollution, politics, and communication. Finally, three contributors explore market mechanisms for repairing the broken circle. Malcolm Gillis discusses tropical forests; William A. Butler suggests incentives for conservation; and Thomas Eisner offers a viewpoint about chemical prospecting.

We think these analyses provide significant insights and understandings. More important, we hope that this book will nurture our society's capacity to effect decisions of courage and vision.

ACKNOWLEDGMENTS

This volume is based on a lecture series at the Yale University School of Forestry and Environmental Studies during the spring of 1989. The success of the series, which attracted more attendees than any other series in the history of the school, was due to the efforts of many people. We are particularly indebted to Professor Jan Stolwijk for his participation in the early planning of the series. Our colleagues, Professors Clark S. Binkley, Gordon T. Geballe, Garry D. Brewer, John P. Wargo, Robert Mendelsohn, Richard Fern, and William R. Burch gave generously of their time to introduce and host the speakers. Dr. Joseph Miller prepared an extensive display of bibliographic material for each speaker. Students from the school contributed during the planning stage, and through their wholehearted participation made the discussion sessions following each talk lively and pertinent. Jill and Chip Isenhart contributed their equipment and expertise to videotape both lecture and discussion sessions. Roland C. Clement contributed many important editorial comments. John C. Gordon, dean of the School of Forestry and Environmental Studies, encouraged and supported the development of the series. Finally, Ann Hooker, the lecture series coordinator, is due special thanks for her full participation in the development and advertisement of the series and for the smooth and graceful operation of all of its phases.

We are particularly indebted to the Andrew W. Mellon

Foundation and to the Geraldine R. Dodge Foundation for making the series possible. This book is also a publication of the Hubbard Brook Ecosystem study. A deep appreciation is due our editor at Yale University Press, Jean Thomson Black.

SPECIES DIVERSITY AND EXTINCTION   I

1 BIODIVERSITY, PROSPERITY, AND VALUE

One errant Old World primate species is now changing the global environment more than that environment has changed at any previous time since the end of the Mesozoic Era sixty-five million years ago. Humanity has begun to understand the dire consequences of these actions; it may be that we are about to enter the century of the environment. The next hundred years will be a time when mankind will either make its home permanently livable or forfeit much of its future security and happiness.

Edward O. Wilson

The global scope of the change is what is new in environmental thinking. The impact of growing, industrializing populations is seen to be no longer composed of local events and hence just the concern of individual cities and countries. Now we see that all of the local events are coalescing to create planet-wide secular trends, none of which augurs well for humanity or the rest of life. The earth as a whole has begun to respond to human excess in a frightening way.

Until recently the attention of the public at large has focused almost exclusively on three major categories of environmental change: the accumulation of toxic wastes; the greenhouse effect, caused mainly by a steady rise in atmospheric carbon dioxide; and the depletion of the ozone layer, leading to increased ultraviolet irradiation of the earth's surface. Now there is increasing awareness of the fourth horseman in the environmental apocalypse, one that, unlike the first three, is neither reversible nor predictable in its consequences. This horseman is species extinction and other forms of genetic depletion due to the destruction of natural habitats. The metaphor is unfortunately very apt. The fourth horseman of Revelations was death, to which the other horsemen were ancillary.

This subject can be framed in a different, more constructive manner. It can be said that every country has three kinds of wealth: material, cultural, and biological. The first two, the basis of almost all of our visible economic and political life, we think about every day. The third, made up of the fauna and flora and the uses to which natural diversity is put, we take a lot less seriously. Biological wealth, however, is much more potent for long-term human welfare than is generally appreciated, and this wealth is declining steeply. The problem is exacerbated by the fact that the greatest variety of life now occurs in developing countries—especially in the tropics—where population growth and habitat destruction are also the greatest. For these reasons, many people recognize that industrialized countries would be wise to give the preservation and use of biological diversity a larger role in scientific and foreign policy and to make a greater effort to link conservation with the economic and political realities of our time.

How much biodiversity is there in the world? The answer is remarkable: No one knows the number of species even to the nearest order of magnitude. Aided by monographs, encyclopedias, and the generous help of specialists, I recently estimated the total number of described species (those given a scientific name) to be 1.4 million, a figure perhaps accurate to within the nearest 100,000. But most biologists agree that the actual number is at least 3 million and could easily be 30 million or more. In a majority of particular groups the actual amount of diversity is still a matter of guesswork.

An anecdote will illustrate the basis of that generalization. The ants are a reasonably well-known group, at least as far as insects are concerned. Yet from my ongoing taxonomic revision of *Pheidole*, the largest of the ant genera, I estimate the number of valid, described species in the New World alone to be about 300, the number of described and undescribed species in the collection at my disposal to be well over 500, and the number actually in existence in nature easily to exceed 1,000. In a 1.5-kilometer area of rain forest around the laboratory building at the La Selva biological reserve of Costa Rica, I have collected no fewer than 34 species of *Pheidole*, of which 16 were new to science. Terry Erwin has estimated that as many as 30 million insect species live in the canopies of tropical rain forests; I have identified 42 kinds of ants from a single tree in Peru (although few species are limited to one kind of tree, and the total number collected in the vicinity is 135).

When proper surveys are launched among the least-known groups of organisms and least-explored habitats, the prodigies of insect diversity may be approached if not matched. Mites and fungi, many of which are host-specific parasites of insects, are among the groups least explored, and the numbers of distinct species in each group could easily reach a million or more. Similarly, the invertebrate fauna of the deep seafloor has proved to be diverse beyond all expectations; the total number of echinoderms, mollusks, annelids, and members of other dominant groups is probably in the hundreds of thousands.

Another part of the living world yet to be plumbed is the bacterial flora. Some 3,000 species have been registered to date, but they certainly represent only a tiny fraction of the whole. Few localities in the world have been explored for their bacterial diversity, and when they are, the results are often surprising. An entire new flora of bacteria has recently been discovered living at depths of 350 meters beneath the ground surface at Hilton Head, South Carolina, for example. The great majority of bacterial forms are incommunicado: they exist as sparsely distributed, nearly invisible populations of slowly growing cells or spores until the right nutrients and microenvironment become available, and then they multiply and disperse rapidly for brief intervals of time. The detection of most bacterial diversity therefore awaits the invention of new culturing techniques combined with sophisticated biochemical diagnoses.

Many systematists familiar with global distributions agree that whatever the absolute number of living species, a majority live in the tropical rain forests, or closed moist tropical forests, as they are more technically called. Occupying just 6 percent of the land surface, these ecosystems exist only in warm regions with two hundred centimeters or more of rainfall a year, conditions that allow evergreen broad-leaved trees to flourish. The trees typically sort into three or more layers, with the canopy of the tallest rising thirty meters or more from the ground. Together, the tree crowns of the several layers filter out most of the sunlight before it reaches the forest floor, inhibiting the development of undergrowth, and leaving large open spaces near the ground through which it is relatively easy to walk.

Human activity has already reduced the area of tropical rain forest to about 55 percent of its original cover. The rate of destruction is increasing rapidly, with an estimated 100,000 square kilometers, or 1 percent of the total cover, being eliminated yearly. (This is approximately equal to the area of Switzerland and the Netherlands combined, or to an acre per second.) During four disastrous months in the dry season of 1987, an equivalent area was burned in the Brazilian Amazon alone. At this rate, most of the rain forest of the world will be gone within thirty years.

The rate of destruction is by far the greatest since the origin of this biome during the Jurassic period 150 million years ago. Once cleared, the rain forests return only very slowly, if at all. One reason is that about two-thirds of the land area underlying them is composed of highly acidic soils that are extremely poor in nutrients and have dense concentrations of iron and aluminum that bind phosphorus tightly. Unlike temperate forest, where a large fraction of organic material exists at any given moment in the humus layer and soil, rain forest keeps a very high fraction locked up in the living trees and undergrowth. The humus layer is thin, and the soil surface is bare in spots. When the vegetation is cut and burned, some of the ongoing capital is quickly washed away. Another reason for fragility of rain forest is that most seeds from remnant patches of the forest disperse poorly, greatly slowing the recovery of surrounding cleared land.

What is the effect of rain forest destruction on biodiversity? The answer lies in geography. Tropical forests, like natural environments everywhere, are being swiftly insularized by human activity. That is, people are chopping them into islandlike remnants of variable size and distance from each other, so that they look more like archipelagoes than continuous wilderness. Biogeographers have found that on conventional archipelagoes, such as the West Indies and Polynesia, the number of species of birds, reptiles, flowering plants, and other taxonomic groups usually increases somewhere between the fifth and third root of the area. The same relation between area and biodiversity occurs in "habitat islands," such as forests surrounded by pastures, and lakes in a "sea" of land. Translated into a rough rule of thumb, the number of species doubles with each tenfold increase in area. If island A is one hundred square miles in area and island B is one thousand square miles, island B will have about twice the number of bird species, ant species, and so on. Consider the effect of reducing rain forest in an individual case. The once-rich Atlantic forest of Brazil, centered on Rio de Janeiro, has been cleared to less than 1 percent of its original cover during the past 150 years. If no more damage is done, so that this forest is kept at its present size, we can expect an eventual decline in the number of plant and animal species to perhaps one-quarter the original number.

Using conservative island-biogeographic models, I have estimated that the ultimate loss due to rain forest clearing alone, at the present 1 percent annual global rate estimated in 1980, will be 0.2 to 0.3 percent of all species in the forests per year. That is, each year's clearing and burning dooms an additional 0.2 to 0.3 percent. Taking a very conservative estimate of two million species confined to the rain forests, the absolute loss due to this process alone could be four thousand to six thousand species a year. That in turn is as much as ten thousand times greater than the prehuman extinction rate.

Both theoretical extrapolations and field studies indicate that such losses are real, and the doomed species can disappear rapidly. In Central and South America, birds go extinct in reduced habitats at a readily observable rate. In newly created patches of forest between one and twenty square kilometers, a common size for reserves and parks in the tropics and elsewhere, 20 percent or more of the species disappear within fifty years. Some of the birds vanish quickly. Others linger on as the slowly declining "living dead."

The estimate of 0.2 to 0.3 percent of species per year doomed to extinction is in fact probably low, because it is based on an assumption that populations are widely distributed through the extant forests. Yet we know that many species are very local and can be eliminated immediately by the removal of a small portion of forest or other habitat. When a single ridge top in Ecuador was cleared recently, more than ninety species of plants known only from that locality were lost. Systematists and ecologists have begun to identify such hot spots around the world, habitats that are both rich in species and in imminent danger. Among the most familiar examples are the Brazilian Atlantic forest, most of Madagascar, and Lake Victoria and the other ancient great lakes of East Africa. Not all the hot spots are tropical. One of the more surprising exceptions is Lake Baikal in Siberia, where large numbers of endemic crustaceans, flatworms, and other invertebrates, as well as the Lake Baikal seal, are endangered by rising levels of pollution.

How are we to translate these losses into human terms? There can be no doubt that biological diversity is important to people, even if value is defined in the most narrow practical terms. The wild species of rain forests and other endangered habitats are among our most important physical resources and also the least utilized. We use fewer than one in ten thousand at present, while most of the rest remain untested and fallow. In the course of history, people have used about seven thousand plant species for food, but today they rely heavily on only about twenty species, such as wheat, rye, millet, and rice. These primary crop plants happen to be the ones whose ancestors grew near human populations at the dawn of agriculture. At least seventy-five thousand plant species have parts that are edible, out of a grand total of about a quarter million composing the world flora. At least some of the wild species are demonstrably superior in nutrition, taste, or productivity, whereas the quality of others could be brought to commercial levels with appropriate hybridization and selection.

Plant and animal species are also vast reservoirs of potential new pharmaceuticals, fibers, petroleum substitutes, and other products. The classic paradigm of opportunity gained through knowledge of the flora involves the rosy periwinkle (*Catharanthus roseus*), an inconspicuous roadside plant that originated in Madagascar. It yields two alkaloids, vinblastine and vincristine, that largely cure two previously deadly cancers, acute lymphocytic leukemia of children and Hodgkin's disease of young adults. These products are now the base of an industry yielding an income of more than $100 million annually. Five other species of *Catharanthus* live on Madagascar. None has been carefully studied, and one is in danger of extinction due to destruction of its habitat.

After discussing the problem of species extinction with many biologists, economists, forestry experts, policy analysts, and others with the greatest stake in biodiversity, I have concluded that the following steps should be taken:

- We need to explore the diversity of life on this planet in full. A complete biotic survey, with each species given a scientific name and the beginnings of a biological dossier, is needed to plan the preservation and use of biodiversity. Such an effort would be comparable in size to the human genome and supercollider projects, but it is ultimately more important for humanity.
- The social sciences should at last become aware of the natural environment and its importance to human welfare. Neoclassical economic models are still inadequate to the measurement of the value of biodiversity. Psychologists have virtually no research programs to assess the effect of the environment and other organisms on human

mental development. Sociologists and political scientists are largely devoid of concern for the issues created by this most profound of all environmental issues. In short, a vast new opportunity awaits the social sciences.

• We should tie conservation ever more closely to economic and social development in the Third World. Contrary to widespread opinion, the two goals are reinforcing, not antagonistic. Most of the problems of tropical countries, ranging from poor health and overpopulation to stalled economic growth, are ultimately biological in origin. These countries are endowed with most of the biological wealth of the world, and they should learn to use it to their best advantage.

In the end, decisions concerning the preservation and use of biodiversity turn on our values and ways of moral reasoning. A sound ethic of biodiversity will obviously take into account the immediate practical uses of wild species, translated into amounts of income and number of lives saved. But it must reach further and incorporate the very meaning of human existence. All life on earth is related to humans by common descent, in consequence of which we all share a large portion of DNA as well as fundamental molecular processes. The human species evolved a particular physiology and mode of cognition adapted to interaction with other organisms; it is not adapted to a sterile planet. The full diversity of life is part of the human heritage, and to dispose of it as we are now doing is a folly comparable to destroying our libraries and museums.

Once gone, species and the more genetically complex races cannot be called back. An important part of the earth's history is lost. Paleontologists estimate that the average clade, defined as a species and other species descended from it, lasts for an average of one to ten million years before going extinct. Thus the typical species encountered in a rain forest or a coral reef is likely to be hundreds of thousands or millions of years old. And it is likely to persist for a comparable span of time into the future unless destroyed by human activity.

The loss of any species should be considered a tragedy. Every organism—animal, plant, microorganism—contains a million to ten billion bits of information in its genetic code, hammered into existence by an astronomical number of mutations and episodes of natural selection. Biologists will soon be able to read off the complete genetic codes of species, but I doubt they will ever manufacture the equivalent of a wild species, simply because they cannot re-create the thousands or millions of years of history that went into its making. The power of evolution by natural selection may be too great even to conceive, let alone duplicate. In evidence is the circumstance that (to the best of my knowledge at least) no artificially selected genetic strain has ever outcompeted wild variants of the same species in the natural environment. Even if new species could be generated and brought together to create new synthetic ecosystems, they would only be an extension of the limited human imagination, a Disney World inferior in every respect to the real biota.

There is more involved in this controlled panic among biologists than just economic and political exigencies, more than we can fully imagine with our imperfect knowledge of the living world and limited moral and aesthetic sensibilities. Why have we become aware of biodiversity so slowly, and why do we disregard it so recklessly? The familiar argument is that people come first. After their problems are solved, we can enjoy the natural world as a luxury. If that is indeed the answer, the wrong question was asked. The question of importance concerns purpose. Solving practical problems is the means, not the purpose. Let us assume that human genius has the power to thread the needles of technology and politics, avoid nuclear war, and feed a stabilized population. What then? The answer is the same everywhere: Individuals will strive toward personal fulfillment and the realization of their full potential. But what is fulfillment, and for what purpose did potential evolve? How can we know without understanding our relation to the natural world?

The truth is that we never conquered the world, never understood it. We only think we have control. We don't know why we respond a certain way to other organisms and why we need them in diverse ways, so deeply. The prevailing myths about our relation to the environment are obsolete and destructive. The more the mind is fathomed in its own right, as an organ of survival, the greater will be the reverence for life for purely rational reasons. Similarly, the more we know of other forms of life, the more we will enjoy and respect ourselves as a species. Humanity is exalted not because we are so far above other living creatures but because knowing them well elevates the very concept of life.

2 BIOLOGICAL DIVERSITY AND GLOBAL SECURITY

As we grapple with the challenges posed by the mass extinction of species now under way, we need to be clear about our purposes. Why should we mount exceptional efforts to save the earth's species? What are the compelling arguments to deploy sizable resources in support of a global save-the-species campaign? Without a carefully developed rationale, our campaign may fall short.

Norman Myers

Three arguments are advanced to justify these efforts: ecological, economic, and ethical. It is artificial to consider these as distinct categories because each interweaves with the other two, each supports the other two, each has less validity when divorced from the other two. But for the sake of ready analysis, it is simpler for us to treat them at first separately, while bringing them together in an integrative appraisal at various points along the way.

I shall not consider economic justification but merely note that in terms of dollars and sense, at least in the impoverished countries of the Third World, wildlife that demonstrably pays its way in the marketplace is more likely to be vouchsafed a place in the future than wildlife perceived to be devoid of commercial value: price-less, far from connoting priceless, quickly comes to mean worthless (Myers, 1983).

The Ecological Rationale

First, there is a scientific reason we should seek to safeguard species for their ecological attributes: Species are the basic units of ecology and nature. If we lose a major proportion of extant species, will that not severely limit our options for studying determinants of diversity, population dynamics, ecosystem regulation, resource-sharing strategies, food-web structures, nutrient flows, and social systems—all of which are central to our understanding of how creatures live in relation to their environments, whether gophers in relation to their habitat or human-kind in relation to the biosphere?

Second, we must ask whether some species contribute more to healthy ecosystems than do others. Are certain species essential to the survival of their ecosystems, whereas other species can be considered superfluous to the vigorous workings of their ecosystems? Although the disappearance of any species must constitute an impoverishment of its ecosystem, the loss can range from "regrettable but marginal" to "critical if not worse." Can we yet establish a gradient of "loss significance" through comparative evaluation of different species' contributions to their ecosystems?

Biological Diversity and Ecological Stability

These questions of ecological attributes can be broached through the concept of energy flow—insofar as energy flow serves as a measure of a species' relative importance (Odum, 1969; Ehrlich and Roughgarden, 1987). If all bird species in a temperate-zone ecosystem amount to, say, 0.5 percent of animal biomass, and their contribution to energy flow can be measured only in hundredths of a percent, how is their role in an ecosystem's functioning to be evaluated in comparison with that of arthropod species that make up, say, 10 percent of the biomass and contribute a much larger proportion of energy flow? Similarly, do some species contribute more than others by virtue of their numbers rather than their biomass? Or by their status in their food pyramids? Or by their role in ecosystem regulation?

A related question concerns the theoretical relationship between biological diversity and ecological stability. It is sometimes proposed that the more numerous an ecosystem's species, the greater the ecosystem's stability. There is much evidence for an association between these two characteristics (Usher and Williamson, 1974; Goodman, 1975; Van Dobben and Lowe-McConnell, 1975). For one thing, more species can use the sun's energy more efficiently than can a few. For another, an ecosystem can probably withstand perturbations better if each species can depend on many rather than few food sources and can be regulated by many rather than few predators—whereupon the eggs-in-one-basket effect is reduced.

But the idea is not to be taken in the simple sense that variety is the essence of life. The relationship is far more complex. Diversity in this context refers to quality as well as quantity of difference among species, whereas stability can refer to numbers and relative abundance of species, or to dominance by a few species. So to assert that diversity equals stability is to overstate the case (May, 1973; Pimm, 1984, 1991). A more concise way to express the situation is to say that diversity and stability have had evolutionary relationships that run parallel without being causal. Alternatively, one can say that high environmental stability leads to higher community stability, which in turn permits, though is not determined by, high diversity of species.

Keystone Species and Mobile Links

An alternative way to think about the diversity-stability relationship is to look at the keystone role played by certain species in their ecosystems, notably tropical forest species (Gilbert and Raven, 1975; Janzen, 1975; Gilbert, 1980; Terborgh, 1986). Among the more important groups of species are bees, ants, bats, and hummingbirds. These species usually pollinate a number of obligate-outcrossing plants, or they may assist in dispersal of seed.

The ecological input of these species groups can be best perceived in the context of food webs. A patch of tropical forest features many parallel and host-restricted food webs. Though similar in their trophic organization, these food webs differ from each other in their taxonomic makeup. Existing as hundreds of food webs, in even a small patch of tropical forest, each of these subsystems may depend upon just a few keystone species that serve as link organisms.

An example of a keystone species is orchid bees, or euglossine bees, of Neotropical forests. Often these insects are intimately related to hundreds of plant species in a single locality. One species of bee may feed from plant species in all strata of the forest and in all stages of forest succession, linking the plants into a system of indirect mutualism. Female bees, for example, gather pollen from successional plants such as

Solanum and *Gassia,* in some cases being the primary pollinators—and they may travel great distances in foraging, thereby being important to the reproduction of many isolated plants. Male euglossines serve a similar specialist function by pollinating epiphytic species such as *Spathiphyllum* and *Anthurium.* Certain euglossine species rely on early successional plants for larval resources; at the same time, they are important, even necessary, pollinators of plants restricted to later successional stages of the forest ecosystem (which means, in turn, that certain categories of species, such as canopy orchids and aroids, may depend, via indirect resource relationships, upon early successional patches of forest). So multifaceted are the interdependency functions facilitated by these bees that proliferant arrays of plants and animals may owe their origin, in part, to an abundance of euglossine stocks (Williams and Dressler, 1976). Thus, euglossines could have played a major part in the emergence of entire communities in tropical forests—with all that implies for evolutionary patterns of the past and for the evolutionary potential of the future.

In short, a sector of primary forest with a variety of successional taxa can feature many specialization linkages between host plants and pollinator insects. In the case of euglossine bees, these linkages depend on the insects not having to fly too far to find their food supplies. Under human impact, however, a forest tract may be reduced to fragments, or parts of it may be protected in the form of too-small preserves, thus isolating habitats. In such circumstances, several successional plant species may become locally extinct. The euglossines then find that they can no longer commute the extended distances between their dispersed food stocks, whereupon they fade from the scene. The bees' demise leads to the decline of additional plant species. The process ends in a domino effect—a series of extinctions at all strata, stages, trophic levels, and community types of the forest.

There is thus a crucial role for these mobile links—a term that refers not only to euglossine bees but also to hummingbirds, bats, and other pollinators as well as to seed dispersers. Such mobile links may find sufficient support for themselves in just a few plant species—these being plants that, by supplying food to extensive associations of mobile links, can be termed keystone mutualists (Gilbert, 1980; Terborgh, 1986). If a single one of these keystone mutualists becomes extinct, the loss to the ecosystem may eventually prove severe. The initial decline of mobile links will precipitate, via breakdown in reproduction and dispersal mechanisms, multiple losses of interrelated plants. In turn, as host communities become impoverished, host-specialized insect species will steadily disappear. The upshot is a multitude of linked extinctions, by means of a ripple effect that spreads throughout the ecosystem (Futuyma, 1973).

Notable among keystone species are top predators, those that can regulate populations of their prey species (Eisenberg, 1980; Terborgh and Winter, 1980). The loss of a top predator in a rocky marine intertidal ecosystem, for example, has been shown to lead to drastic simplification of the residual community (Paine, 1966). So great can this regulatory function become, with its disproportionate repercussions for ecosystem stability, that the importance of top predators can hardly be overemphasized. Likewise, top predators tend to be unduly prone to extinction through overhunting, poisoning programs, and other activities on the part of man.

Although we tend to think of top predators in the form of the lion, the leopard, the jaguar, the cougar, and the wolf, we should also consider other types like the aardvark, the giant anteater, and the giant armadillo. All of these can exert a stabilizing influence on their ecosystems.

While exercising key functions in ecosystems, top predators exist at very low densities. They also tend to be large in body size and to breed slowly. Even the largest preserves can feature only small breeding populations of top predators. Because this means a limited gene pool, the result can be a loss of genetic variability, with subsequent decline in fecundity through inbreeding.

Indicator Species
Finally, consider indicator species. Certain species provide baseline monitoring of what is happening to natural environments. This serendipitous value of species, although often difficult to identify ahead of time, is becoming all the more important as we encounter the growing need to monitor the health of our environments.

Regrettably, indicator species tend to be threatened species. A species in trouble often signals malfunctions in an ecosystem that may thereby contain other threatened species. The cheetah, for example, is a highly specialized predator that plays an important role in regulating savannah ecosystems. By virtue of its susceptibility to more threats than seem to afflict the lion, the leopard, and other predators (threats such as changes in prey communities and vegetation patterns), the cheetah can give warning of environmental stress when its numbers decline markedly. Similarly, we have to thank the peregrine falcon, the brown pelican, and other birds of prey for drawing attention to DDT and other toxic pollutants that, when they reach excessive levels in the environment, prove poisonous to carnivores, including man. It is this role of indicator species that makes them especially useful to human society, in ways we do not anticipate until they flash a red light concerning new threats to our welfare. The most sensitive indicator species are often those at the ends of food chains, that is, species that concentrate contaminant materials in their tissues. At the same time, their position at the end of food chains usually means that they occur in small numbers as compared with, say, herbivores, a factor that makes such indicator species more susceptible to extinction.

The Ethical Argument

The ethical argument postulates that all forms of life on earth enjoy equal rights to existence (see, for example, Norton, 1986, 1987). Conversely, humankind has no right to exterminate a species. Even more to the point, humankind has no right to precipitate, through the elimination of large numbers of species, a fundamental and permanent shift in the course of evolution. So widespread is the perception of this ethical rationale, grounded in notions of humankind's stewardship for earth's other creatures, that it has become inherent in many religious and cultural traditions around the world.

Plausible as it seems, the ethical argument deserves close scrutiny. Do we wish to preserve all forms of life for their own intrinsic value? Would many people not be glad to see the end of the virus that causes the common cold? And would the same question apply to whatever organisms contribute to cancer? These are unique forms of life with just as much "right" to existence as the giraffe or the whooping crane. We have now reached a stage when the smallpox virus has been backed into a corner, to the extent that no human being suffers from the disease and the organism exists only in the laboratory. Should man, by conscious and rational decision, obliterate this manifestation of life's diversity?

Absolute and Relative Values
Similarly, is it realistic to postulate that a species represents an absolute value and must not be traded against other values on the ground that a

unique, irreplaceable entity is beyond measurement of worth? Virtually no value is considered by society to be absolute, not even human life. To be sure, an individual views his or her life as an untradable asset. But as members of the larger community, we seldom view human life in general as anywhere near an absolute value. The number of road-accident deaths each year—55,000 in the United States, 110,000 in Europe, and more than one-quarter of a million worldwide—is an appalling loss of life, yet it is apparently considered by society as an acceptable price for rapid transportation.

Presumably, there is only one value that represents an absolute, and that is the survival of life on earth. To this absolute value, each species makes an absolute contribution: when there are no more species left, there will be no more life. But, as was discussed above, not all species make the same contribution. Some are considered more important than others in the maintenance and function of their ecosystems. So the value of a species, far from being absolute, is relative.

Especially difficult is the question of relative value between humans and other species. Already the conflict is plain to see in many localities where people compete with wildlife for living space. This conflict is growing fast. True, in a few instances there is no clash; the blue whale encroaches on no human environment for its survival needs, and thus its demise would be all the more regrettable. For most species, however, the problem is basic: sufficient habitat for them means less habitat available for human communities with their growing numbers.

How is this conflict to be resolved? The problem raises complex ethical issues. Many conservationists could probably accept the elimination of a species if it could be demonstrated that the creature's habitat would produce crops to keep huge communities of people alive (and provided that the food could not be grown elsewhere, that the people could not find any other means to sustain themselves, that the species could not be translocated to an alternative location, and so forth). If the situation were reduced to bald terms of one species against one million people, it might well be viewed as a tolerable though regrettable trade-off.

But the prospect facing humankind in the coming decades is an altogether different affair. To allow expanding numbers of people the living space they seem to think they need, at least one-fifth, possibly one-third, conceivably one-half, of all species on earth may be driven to extinction. Would this be in the best interests of human communities even in the short run? From the merely utilitarian viewpoint of benefits for agriculture, medicine, and industrial materials that stem from the genetic resources of species, it is virtually certain that humankind would suffer greatly through the disappearance of, say, one million species.

Such is the nature and scale of the ethical conflict we now confront. It is a challenge that merits much more attention than it has hitherto received from conservationists, technologists, economic planners, political leaders, philosophers, and whoever else determines the future course of life on earth.

But the ethical conflict cannot wait to be resolved until we have engaged in sufficient fine-grained analysis of the issues involved. All too unwittingly, but effectively and increasingly, we are deciding that certain species are more deserving of a place on the planet than others. Even with a several-times increase in funding, we cannot save all the species that seem doomed to disappear: The processes of habitat disruption are too solidly under way to be halted quickly or completely. Because we are intervening in the evolutionary process with all the impact of a major glaciation, we should do it with as much conscious awareness of our activities as we can muster. Because we are committed to playing God and dooming large numbers of species to extinction, we might as well do it as selectively as possible. But how to accomplish this? Can we at least establish the right direction in which to move?

These are large questions. How do we decide which species shall be allowed to become extinct through our deliberate decision, and thereby concentrate our conservation efforts—limited as they are bound to be— on "better" species? This means that certain species would disappear because we have pulled the carpet out from under them. We might, for example, abandon the Mauritius kestrel to its all-but-inevitable fate and use the funds to proffer stronger support for any of the hundreds of other threatened bird species that are more likely to survive. In short, species would disappear through human design. As agonizing a prospect as this is, is it not better than allowing species to disappear by default?

A Triage Strategy?

Such an approach would amount to a triage strategy for species (Myers, 1983). The term derives from French medical practice in World War I, when battlefield doctors had more wounded than they could treat. So they assigned each soldier to one of three categories: first, those who could certainly be helped by medical attention; second, those who could probably survive without attention; and third, those who were likely to die no matter how much attention they received. The first category absorbed most of the medical services available, so the other two categories were ignored. If such a strategy were applied to threatened species, it would be systematic rather than haphazard, and it would enable conservationists to make maximum use of their finances and skills.

How would choices be made? How could we decide between the Bengal tiger and a crab in the Caribbean? Should we focus on remnant patches of rain forest in countries that have experienced decades of destruction, or should we try to lock away vast tracts of forest in regions that have been little touched? These will be difficult decisions. A start could be made through systematic analysis of factors that make some species more susceptible to extinction than others—for example, sensitivity to habitat disruption, reproductive capacity, and K-selection traits. In addition to these bioecological factors, there is need to consider economic, political, legal, and sociocultural aspects of the problem: The Bengal tiger requires large amounts of living space in a part of the world that is crowded with human beings, but it could stimulate more public support for conservation of its ecosystem (and thereby help save many other species) than could a less charismatic creature such as a crab. When we integrate all the various factors that tell for and against a species, we shall have a clearer idea of where best to apply our conservation muscle.

Nobody will like the challenge of deliberately consigning certain species to oblivion. But insofar as we are already consigning huge numbers to oblivion, we will do it better with some selective discretion.

Above all, let us recognize the urgent necessity of making choices among threatened species. This is not a formidable challenge to be confronted somewhere down the road, when we have had a chance to engage in sufficiently detailed consideration of the prospect. It is a challenge we already cope with by virtue of the funding allocation systems that we already employ—less than systematic and rational as some of those approaches are. Ever since the start of the save-species movement, we have been making choices between species. The expanded strategy proposed here is simply more methodical. The key issue is not whether we shall now attempt to apply triage but how we shall apply triage to better effect.

Regrettably, the term *triage* raises negative connotations in many minds. Yet a triage strategy applied to threatened species would be a better approach than that practiced hitherto. Those threatened species that for biological, economic, or sociocultural reasons present the most productive opportunities for investment of conservation resources should clearly be at the top of our shopping list of priorities. Equally clearly, other species may not, so far as we can discern, merit priority treatment. For lack of adequate conservation resources, and for no other reason, certain species will be low down on a hierarchical ranking of priorities. Still others will be placed so far down on the list that they will effectively be consigned to a category that we designate "We wish we could do something about them, but to our massive regret, we just do not have the means available."

This is not to say that we consign any species to a ragbag of "species that are not worth saving." All species are worth saving; we simply cannot save them all. No species is without intrinsic value or scientific interest. No species is without biological value. All species make a contribution of some sort to their ecosystems. We cannot possibly tell which species may offer economic potential to our society at some stage in the future. Any species may one day generate aesthetic appeal in ways that we do not yet suspect. Still further justifications may be advanced in favor of any species—any species at all. And as a bottom-line rationale, we can say that no species needs any justification for its survival, insofar as all species, being manifestations of life's diversity on earth, can be considered to possess ipso facto a right to live.

Species and Global Security

Finally, let us consider the mass extinction issue within a context of security—not so much security of the conventional sort (though that comes into it) but rather security of an unusual sort.

As noted, there is a question about the biosphere's capacity for continued functioning when it loses some of its biotic components. Not all species are essential to the healthy workings of their ecosystems. That is plain; otherwise we would be in trouble because of the elimination of the wolf, bear, cougar, bison, passenger pigeon, and the like from most if not all parts of the United States. Even more to the point, the global ecosystem has lost tens of thousands of species in the last few decades, yet it seems to have suffered no marked setbacks in its ecological stability, resilience, and other key attributes. But when do species losses shift from being marginal to becoming significant, serious, critical, crucial, and catastrophic?

We simply do not know the answers to these momentous questions.

Indeed we are very far from knowing even how to get to know them. Rather than learning to supply the right answers, we have yet to learn to ask the correct questions. In light of this gross uncertainty, is it not the path of prudence to err on the cautious side by safeguarding a maximum, rather than an optimum, number of species? And won't we ultimately find that from an ecological standpoint alone, an optimum number of species is always the same as a maximum number? Is it not axiomatic that a new form of security, ecological security, must lie in maintaining the full complement of planetary biodiversity?

More important still, we are testing these existential questions by conducting a global-scale experiment, entirely unplanned, with irreversible results and unknown outcome—and with the main impact of our experiment's repercussions left to fall on generations unborn. For the sake of present-day indulgences, such as consumerist life-styles that lead to habitat destruction, we are bequeathing a depauperized biosphere to generations extending into the distant future. Given what we can discern from the geological past, the recovery period—that is, the length of time before evolutionary processes can generate an array of new species with abundance and variety to match today's—will surely be ten million years and perhaps twenty-five million years. These periods of time represent 400,000 to 1,000,000 generations—or forty to one hundred times longer than the span of time since the emergence of *Homo sapiens*.

Here is an ethical challenge indeed. The nearest parallel in the contemporary world is the persistence of nuclear waste, a period of such protracted dimension that it is viewed as some kind of ultimate with respect to human responsibility. Yet it involves a span of a mere ten thousand years (four hundred generations), or one-thousandth of the shortest time envisaged before evolution's creativity can make good the damage likely to be wrought by present generations in a scant fifty years. The finest writings on intergenerational responsibility—Rawls (1971), Partridge (1980), and Weiss (1988), for example—do not begin to address the scope of this ethical challenge.

Put more succinctly, is there not here a key question of ethical security that concerns the whole of humankind, that is, a question of global security grounded in ethical issues? Is mass extinction not distinctively different from all the other assaults that our biosphere is currently subject to? Surely these environmental insults are more profound and pervasive than anything that has been visited upon the biosphere in such short order during human history. But none will impose so enduring an impact as the mass extinction of species. Through a combination of natural restorative processes and human interventions, large-scale pollution such as acid rain can be cleaned up in a matter of decades. Desertification can presumably be reversed within a century. Tropical forests can certainly be reestablished within a thousand years. Soil cover can be replenished in ten thousand years—just as the ozone layer can be restored and global climate returned to pre-greenhouse-effect equilibria within the same ten thousand years. But in the wake of mass extinction, a panoply of species to match today's will not appear before many millions of years have passed.

In its ethical import as well as its ecological impact, mass extinction is uniquely significant. Not that we need to engage in detailed discussion to assess the character of what we are doing. It is enough to ask whether we know what we are doing when we casually cause deep damage to the greatest celebration of nature to grace the planet in four billion years of life's history. All too unwittingly, we are dismantling the apogee of evolutionary processes, the culmination of nature's creativity—and we are doing it in the twinkling of a geological eye.

Our spiritual security is at stake in all this. The potential loss we shall experience through mass extinction has been encapsulated by Daniel Janzen (1982) so cogently that it is worth quoting in full:

If I told you that I was going to magically introduce a gene into the human population that would make all your grandchildren and all their descendants color blind, you would be less than pleased. The same is true of a gene that would eliminate all awareness of music. But what are color vision and music awareness? Traits that you would never know you had if the world was not colored and the air not filled with complex sonorous sounds. I maintain that you, dear reader, are an animal rich in mental and physical receptors for the complexity of nature; and by destroying that nature, you condemn your offspring to the sleep of never even knowing those receptors exist—and by destroying tropical nature, you destroy easily the majority of the signals those receptors are designed to receive. Of course, humans are good at generating mild complexity in their workings. But the level of complexity generated by humanity is to the complexity of a tropical forest as a mouse's squeak is to all of human music. The city-center dweller who feels no cultural and biological deprivation is simply unaware of what he is missing. If your response is, well, what he doesn't know won't hurt him, then I suppose that you won't mind if I eliminate color vision from your children at birth, and all their children after them. Humans have spent rather many millions of years inventing the ability to be very aware of what is around them. How ironic that just about the time they get themselves to where they can sit back and gawk rather than fear all of that, their quintessential human trait is removing the very thing that made them what they are. A human without senses is not even an animal.

Linkages to Conventional Security

Security as conventionally understood entails military prowess before all else. Capacity for violence overshadows capacity for ethical appreciation, let alone scientific inquiry. Ironically, there is a linkage between security in terms of weaponry and security in terms of biodiversity.

To safeguard the planetary spectrum of species will cost a lot of money. Although no specific budget has yet been proposed, it may well run into billions of dollars a year for at least ten years and more likely twenty years. Protection of species is far more than a matter of additional parks and reserves. It is a case of resisting and repelling the forces of habitat destruction that make it necessary for us to establish parks and reserves. As McNeely (1988) suggested, the year 2050 may well see a world with no protected areas. According to a downside scenario, all such areas will have been overrun by impoverished peasantry; or, according to a golden-age scenario, we shall be managing our world in such a rational manner that there will be no more need for protected areas, because wildlands and wildlife will be adequately cared for through alternative provisions.

What is entailed in rolling back the tide of habitat destruction? In much of the tropical world (which is, largely, the developing world), it means eliminating the land hunger motivating people to hack down forests, dig up savannahs, and cultivate hillsides. To eliminate that motivation means enabling people to make a sustainable livelihood on existing high-productivity farmlands, often far away from forests, savannahs, and hilly areas. In turn, that means enabling people to shift from extensive to intensive cultivation, from migratory to stabilized agriculture, and from wasteful to efficient use of farmland resources—whereupon many more people can be accommodated in existing farmlands.

This all means modernization of the agricultural sector—and in turn a shift in development policies, a radical reorientation of aid-and-trade patterns, a vigorous attack on population growth and associated problems of poverty, a resolution of the international debt problem, and the establishment of strategies for sustainable development throughout the Third World. Also pertinent is sustainable development throughout the developed world: Without moving beyond today's prodigal use of fossil fuel, there will be no avoiding the greenhouse effect, with all its adverse repercussions for climatic patterns, temperature bands, vegetation belts, and biotic communities from the equator to the poles.

What might such an ambitious effort cost? Lester Brown et al. (1985) proposed an annual budget of $170 billion per year, a sizable sum by any standards—except one. It is equivalent to less than six months of worldwide military spending. Would we not purchase more real and enduring security by diverting some military expenditures to safeguard our biosphere and thus the myriad communities of species at risk?

An analysis along these lines would have been dismissed until recently as impractical politics. But now these ideas are being advanced as a realistic proposition by leaders such as George Kennan, Robert McNamara, and Mikhail Gorbachev and are already being implemented by Third World countries such as China, Peru, and Argentina.

Thus the impending extinction spasm can be avoided without unacceptably high cost to the present generation. It ultimately depends on management of the planetary ecosystem in a manner that mobilizes earth's resources—soils, vegetation, water supplies, atmosphere, climate, and so forth—so as to provide sustainable benefits for humankind, with human population regulated in accord with the carrying capacity of the biosphere. Were we to engage in this efficient use of earth's resources, we would surely find sufficient living space for ourselves and our fellow species.

A Final Thought

These are some of the issues we should bear in mind as we impose a fundamental shift on evolution's course. The largest dilemma by far is that as we proceed on our disruptive path, we give scarcely a moment's thought to what we are doing. If we were to consider a mass extinction more deeply, would it be what we truly want? Unfortunately, we are making decisions with only the most superficial reflection—deciding all too unwittingly, yet effectively and increasingly. The impending upheaval in evolution's course could rank as one of the greatest biological revolutions of paleontological time. It might equal in scale and significance the development of aerobic respiration, the arrival of flowering plants, and the development of limbed animals. But of course the prospective degradation of many evolutionary capacities will be an impoverishing, not a creative, phenomenon.

The future of evolution should rank as one of the most challenging problems that humankind has ever encountered. We are the first species ever to look out upon nature's work and to decide whether we would remake part of it—to consciously determine evolution by what we do or don't do.

Fortunately there are a few glimmerings of a new spirit emerging. The mass extinction of species is beginning to be perceived as a vast rending of the fabric of life itself, with profound implications for scientists and citizens around the world. The message is being picked up by political leaders, notably by the government of the United States, as witness the plethora of biodiversity-related bills in Congress, the expanded mandate for the Agency for International Development to take explicit account of the needs of threatened species in the developing tropics, and, at American initiative, the World Bank's recent measure in the form of a biodiversity task force.

By comparison with the needs of the situation, this can all be viewed as far too little and far too late. But it is a start toward recognizing what many biologists perceive as the single most significant issue of our time. The first great waves of extinctions are only beginning to wash over the earth's biotas. We still have time—though barely time—to save species in their millions. Should we not consider ourselves fortunate that we alone among generations are being given the chance to support the right to life of a large share of our fellow species, even to safeguard the creative capacities of evolution itself? As Charles Dickens might have asserted, "It is the best of times, it is the worst of times." And as his co-patriot Charles Darwin would surely have asserted, this is an unprecedentedly challenging time to be a biologist—or, for that matter, to be a conservationist or a common citizen.

THE MANAGEMENT OF DIVERSITY: A CONSERVATION PARADOX

3

David Ehrenfeld

The paradox of conservation is that active management often reduces diversity—conservationists can learn from the example of industrial accidents.

I begin this examination of a conservation paradox with some words from the preface to Aldo Leopold's justly celebrated book *Game Management* (1933), which was first presented as a historic series of lectures at the University of Wisconsin in 1929: "Control comes from the co-ordination of science and use. This book attempts to explore the possibilities of such co-ordination in a single, limited field—the conservation of game by management. Its detail applies to game alone, *but the principles are of general import to all fields of conservation*" (italics added).

Leopold worked out a comprehensive management system for maintaining, year after year, comfortably high population levels of a comparatively few exploited vertebrate species: selected waterfowl, grouse, pheasant, bobwhite quail, and deer, to mention the important ones. In the passage just quoted, Leopold made quite clear that the principles of game management could someday be applied not just to animals that are hunted but to all animals and plants everywhere.

My purpose in this chapter is to question whether the

principles and scientific approach of game management—intensive management—can in fact be generalized to all parts of conservation, as Leopold claimed, and to find out whether there are fundamental theoretical and practical objections to doing this. If there are objections, as I believe there are, I will then consider the modified role that management might realistically be expected to play in the conservation of all nature, not just game species.

Generality and Specificity

The quest for generality governs the scientific mentality of our time (Ehrenfeld, 1986). There is a dichotomy between those who look for general laws and those who seek to add to our knowledge of the specific—the finders of new species, for example. Those who achieve generality, who make and use general discoveries during the course of their scientific research, can win fame and power. Those who do not, those who are unsuccessful in their quest for generality or who never look for it at all, who prefer to stick to the specificities that we associate with such fields as natural history, may achieve happiness but not dominance in the scientific hierarchy. It was once common for biology graduate students to pick a taxonomic group of plants or animals to work on, for example; now a student is much more likely to select a general hypothesis and test it using any organism that seems appropriate and convenient.

In the first half of this century, generality belonged to physicists and, to a lesser extent, chemists who produced testable hypotheses and laws—such as relativity and the uncertainty principle—that seemed to sweep from one end of the universe to the other, and from atoms all the way to celestial bodies. In biology the only comparable generality, prior to the 1950s, was the evolutionary theory of Darwin and Wallace, of which the field of ecology was an important by-product. Not until Watson and Crick's discoveries, however, did biology gain a modern generality that rivaled the earlier discoveries of Einstein and Heisenberg. And like the theoretical breakthroughs of physics and chemistry, the central dogma of molecular biology has led to all kinds of practical applications, has brought in research money in unprecedented amounts from government and industry, has allowed molecular biology to dominate most university biology departments, and has taken over the biology news that reaches television and newspapers. After all, what could be more general than a universal genetic code?

Of course, some clouds of specificity hang over the bioengineering landscape, gathering clouds that few people noticed four or five years ago. Bacterial and mammalian cells do not necessarily fold proteins the same way, for example. And genes can vary remarkably in their expression, depending on their genetic, intracellular, and external physical environments. Some of these specificities may ultimately limit the achievements of genetic engineering, but that remains to be seen.

What matters here is that since the early days of Watson, Crick, Jacob, and Monod, ecologists have also been looking for a special, simple generality of their own—preferably something more useful and more purely ecological than the theory of evolution, something with which that theory could be supplemented. In 1963 many of my fellow graduate students and I thought we had found it in Ramon Margalef's *American Naturalist* paper titled "On Certain Unifying Principles in Ecology." But that hope faded in a few years. Then there was the idea of diversity and stability, and soon, thanks to theoreticians like Robert May (1973), that generality also faded. After that came the generality of competition, but it too was not the grail. Yet the appeal of generality persists; a passion for patterns is part of the twentieth-century mind-set.

Now, as we enter the last decade of the century, I don't hear many people calling for simple, general laws of ecology. Instead, complex generalities are the order of the day. It is as if, mindful of the enormous number of unique specificities that make up ecology, we are still determined to sweep them all in under the umbrella of a general theory. In a recent article, Robert Ricklefs (1987) noted, "Ecologists must broaden their concepts of community processes and incorporate data from systematics, biogeography, and paleontology into analyses of ecological patterns and tests of community theory." That is a reasonable statement. I agree with it. But I wonder what kind of patterns will emerge from all that welter of information, much of it in the form of unique bits. Paleoecologists are asserting, for example, that most or all of today's biome-scale patterns of North America are less than six thousand to eight thousand years old (Hunter et al., 1988). How does one work that into a general theory of community structure?

Another complex generality has been provided by Urban et al. (1987), who applied hierarchy theory to try to make sense out of landscape patterns, incorporating a multitude of events at varying levels on both spatial and temporal scales. Their goal was to produce eventually a single conceptual and analytic model to delineate and explain the patterns of entire landscapes.

One obvious question to ask is, How much power and utility can such models have? A less obvious question is, When and where are models useful in ecology? I am not going to try to answer either question now. My point here is that the biosphere is a system, or a set of systems, with many millions of elements that are changing in time and are affected by myriad local irregularities and discontinuities and by countless historical singularities. As yet, there is no single comprehensive theory besides evolution that takes it all in. Quite possibly there never will be. Atomic physicists, who seem to discover a new subatomic particle daily, may have similar problems. Lewis Carroll, who enjoyed situations of this sort, gave a beautiful example of an all-embracing but worthless model. In his book *Sylvie and Bruno Concluded*, he tells of a marvelous map of the entire German countryside, drawn on a scale of one inch to the inch. It showed every detail, but it could never be used because when it was unfolded, it kept sunlight from reaching the crops.

In ecology, we have an incredibly complex system with no central dogma like that of molecular biology to let us even pretend that we have control. Nowhere is this more apparent than in conservation, where we have persuaded ourselves that some degree of control is really necessary. Consider the following quotation from a paper by White and Bratton (1980), who were referring to conservation management: "Management can be approached on two levels: (1) an ecosystem-community ('process-oriented') level and (2) a species-population ('species-oriented') level. Management on these two levels sometimes conflicts." As the authors point out, this conflict leads to all kinds of dilemmas: "Should all natural disturbances be allowed free rein if they conflict with other resources . . . ? In cases where succession is eliminating disturbance-dependent species, should natural disturbances be mimicked to maintain such species or should there be an attempt to arrest succession and hold the landscape in a mosaic of static states of varying maturity? . . . Should we reintroduce species lost through local catastrophe? . . . Should we attempt to manage long-term climatic, geologic, or successional trends?" Those are questions concerning natural areas. For cultural landscapes, other equally difficult choices are needed. Wouldn't it be nice, or at least easier, if there were some comprehensive rule or theory to tell us what to do in each case?

In game management there are far fewer elements—only a handful of primary species to worry about at a time—and the goal is sharply defined in terms of game abundance. It is possible to achieve control by the "co-ordination of science and use," as Leopold put it. In the case of entire ecosystems or cultural landscapes, things are not so simple. I have previously discussed (Ehrenfeld, 1981: 112, 113, 126) the von Neumann and Morgenstern theorem presented in *Theory of Games and Economic Behavior* (1953), in which the authors showed that it is mathematically impossible to maximize more than one variable at a time in an interlinked system. In a classic paper, P. A. Larkin (1977) indirectly supported this theorem by pointing out that because of the complexity of oceanic fisheries systems, "a wide variety of unexpected consequences can flow from what seem to be simple management strategies."

Indeed, juggling everything at once when things are so complex inevitably creates dissension, opposing strategies, confusion, and conflict. A good example in contemporary conservation biology is the corridor debate. Should we put scarce conservation resources into creating safe corridors between existing patches of protected land, linking them in one continuous sanctuary, or should we use the money to expand existing parks and reserves and to create buffers around them? Simberloff and Cox (1987) argued that corridors have costs as well as benefits. They may transmit contagious diseases and fires, they expose the wild animals using them to poachers, predators, and domestic animals, and they are very expensive. On the other hand, Noss (1987) responded that the benefits of corridors outweigh their costs by ameliorating some of the most important problems of habitat fragmentation, and that the alternatives to corridors, such as moving animals from one reserve to another, are impractical.

The complexity of natural and mixed natural-human ecosystems makes it difficult to know what questions to ask, what goals to set, and what strategies to employ in their study and conservation. There are always unforeseen eventualities, specificities that mar the application of general rules. When Jennifer Jarvis captured male and female naked mole rats (*Heterocephalus glaber*) in 1974 to breed in her laboratory in Cape Town, she had no way of knowing that the reason she was having no success was that the society of these underground rodents is organized like that of honeybees, and she hadn't obtained a queen, which is usually one of the last to be captured (Gamlin, 1987). Her problems in breeding them were caused by not keeping the whole colony intact and together in the laboratory. But when some of the last black-footed ferrets were captured for breeding in Wyoming, only hindsight and tragic experience told us that they should have been caged separately rather than together, in case one or two individuals were incubating canine distemper (Thorne and Williams, 1988).

These simple examples each involve one species kept in controlled laboratory conditions. What about in situ management involving many species or whole communities? There are so many things to think of— the interactions are so numerous and often so counterintuitive. It is easy to create edge to benefit deer; a science has been made of it. But add the rest of the system and everything changes. The more edge, the more deer, true, but the fewer box turtles (*Terrapene carolina*), as Stanley Temple (1987) showed in Wisconsin. The farther the box turtles were from the edge of their habitat, the better their reproductive success. Predators that like edges, such as skunks and raccoons, also like box turtle eggs. The creation of edge to benefit one species can hurt another.

The conservation paradox, therefore, is that active management, the kind of management that involves decisions to manipulate environments, is inherently a destabilizing process. This paradox can be restated in the broader context that I introduced earlier: Active management needs rules; rules are based on generalities, simplifications, and assumptions; and generality is often the enemy of specificity, which is the same as diversity. To put it still another way, the more balls you juggle, the more likely you are to drop a few. At this point, I should state that I do not reject generality. Specificity without generality is chaos. But generality without specificity is nothingness. Scientific wisdom and insight are generated by a dialectic—a balanced interaction between the two. In recent decades, however, the balance in biology has been lost, and with the rejection of the specific has come a loss of wisdom.

There is a way around the conservation paradox, but to explain it, I must first introduce what may seem like a strange digression.

Normal Accidents

When I first began to prepare this chapter, I was coincidentally in the midst of reading a book called *Normal Accidents,* by sociologist Charles Perrow (1984). While reading the book and, no doubt, at the same time pursuing unconscious ideas about the conservation paradox, an unexpected fusion of the two trains of thought occurred.

In Perrow's book I came across an account of a relatively minor accident at the Dresden 2 nuclear power plant outside Chicago, which is considered an unusually well run nuclear plant. The account was originally from a book entitled *The Accident Hazards of Nuclear Power Plants*, by Richard E. Webb (1976), and Perrow introduces the following extract with this advice: "Do not try to understand the complex interactions, but let yourself be overwhelmed by the operators' frequent, uncomprehending attempts to cope with multiple equipment failures, false signals, and bewildering interactions." I urge the present readers to follow Perrow's advice and to put aside for a moment any conscious thoughts about conservation, generality, game management, and the like.

The steam valve began to malfunction and then closed. Fortunately, the reactor SCRAMmed automatically. The power dropped to the afterheat level, reducing the size of the steam bubbles in the core. This caused the water level in the reactor to drop, which caused the feedwater pumps to increase coolant flow into the reactor to avoid uncovering the core. As the water level rose, the operator noticed that the level indicator was reading a low level. Actually, however, the indicator was stuck and giving a false low-water-level reading. The operator reacted by manually increasing the feedwater flow still further, so that the water then filled the reactor and spilled over into the steam line. The feedwater-flow error was uncovered and corrected; but then the pressure began to rise, and two safety systems designed to cope with the problem and cool down the reactor were found inoperative. The operator then reduced pressure by opening a relief valve momentarily. At this point, water hammer occurred, produced by the water spill-over into the steam line, and this popped safety valves (pressure relief valves), which stuck open due to a design error. The relief valves then discharged reactor steam to the reactor containment atmosphere, which began to pressurize the containment. The loss of coolant through the stuck relief valves should have caused the ECCS to activate to inject replacement coolant; but one system was found inoperative, and the operators blocked the operation of the other system on the assumption that the loss-of-coolant problem was minor. However, they did not know the cause (stuck valve) and could not make a sound judgment (it could have been a leaky coolant pipe about to completely rupture). Meanwhile, the pressure in the containment rose beyond the range of the pressure gauge (5 psig). The containment is equipped with water sprays to quench the steam pressure whenever two psig pressure is exceeded, but the operators blocked this safety action because that would have cold-shocked some equipment and thereby damaged it. They did not, however, have sufficient knowledge of the events to justify their action. The containment reached 20 psig compared to 60 psig design pressure before the plant was finally brought under control.

That was an accident that did not have major consequences. The accident at Three Mile Island did, and Perrow's summary of the initial events may be instructive: "There was a false signal causing the condensate pumps to fail, two valves for emergency cooling out of position and the indicator obscured, a PORV [pilot-operated relief valve] that failed to reseat, and a failed indicator of its position. *The operators could have been aware of none of these.*" (At that point, they were only thirteen seconds into the accident.) Perrow continues: "Moreover, while all these parts are highly interdependent, so that one affects the other, they are *not* in direct operational sequence . . . as in a production line." (Perhaps the ecologists among the readers are beginning to get some familiar vibrations.) "Here," Perrow notes, "we have the essence of the normal accident: the interaction of multiple failures that are not in a direct operational sequence. . . . There is one other ingredient . . . incomprehensibility."

I have not described, nor will I, the major part of the accident, which began at zero plus two minutes. But there are two points I want to make about it. First, the operators had no way of knowing what was actually happening. As is true of any complex system, what is going on inside a nuclear power plant is learned indirectly from hundreds of dials, lights, and printouts that summarize and integrate the input from many sensors—some of them functioning correctly and some not. A given reading can be interpreted in many ways. At Three Mile Island, the operators had no particular reason to assume that the cause of the drop in core coolant pressure was a stuck valve, the notorious PORV, that was pouring one-third of the reactor coolant into a drain tank while two other valves controlling the relief water supply were stuck in the closed position. Nor did they assume that. What happens in such a case, says Perrow, is this: "You are actually creating a world that is congruent with your interpretation, even though it may be the wrong world. It may be too late before you find that out." This is the incomprehensibility factor. My second point is the difficulty about what to do with such a tightly coupled, complex system, even assuming one has perfect knowledge. Long after the accident at Three Mile Island was over, and with all the benefit of hindsight, experts were still arguing about which emergency system should have been used when. In this kind of situation, to talk about operator error is absurd.

Perrow describes two kinds of interactions in modern industrial systems: linear, which occur in familiar, observable sequences; and complex, which occur in unfamiliar, unexpected sequences and are either not visible or not immediately comprehensible. Information about the state of components and processes in complex systems, such as nuclear power plants, is always indirect and inferential. Perrow summarizes the attributes of complex systems as follows:

- proximity of parts or units that are not in a production sequence;
- many common mode connections between components . . . not in a production sequence;
- unfamiliar or unintended feedback loops;
- many control parameters with potential interactions;
- indirect or inferential information sources; and
- limited understanding of some processes.

By this point it may be obvious why I am devoting so much space in this chapter to a book about accidents in nuclear power plants, chemical factories, marine shipping lanes, and air traffic control systems, a book that makes no mention of natural systems except once, when the author briefly refers to accidents in complex systems as "eco-system" accidents. To me, there is a striking and unexpected correspondence between normal accidents in complex industrial systems and what we might call normal accidents in managed ecosystems—except that when there are accidents in ecosystems, nothing blows up. What happens in ecosystem accidents is that components disappear: Species become extinct, and habitat types are diminished in number. These consequences occur not in thirteen seconds but in a few months or years, which is an explosively fast rate compared with the normal extinction rates in undisturbed systems.

Before continuing with this analogy, I want to make plain that just as management of complex industrial systems does not lead to accidents most of the time, so ecosystem management for conservation does not usually lead to damage or extinctions. Nor am I saying that there is no such thing as wise conservation management. Of course, there is. Often management is the only sensible option. What I am saying is that the conservation management of ecosystems reminds me of the management of what Perrow calls complex systems in industry, and maybe there is something important to be learned from that.

What are some of the similarities between conditions in complex industrial systems and in managed ecosystems? Incomprehensibility is certainly one. What is the meaning of even reliable information? Take species diversity, for example. What does it indicate about the state of the system? The answer is, that depends. Monitored ecosystems often experience local increases in species diversity. Such increases, however, like the low core pressure at Three Mile Island, are not necessarily indicators of system health (although they may be). In Rutgers's Hutcheson Memorial Forest, a sixty-four-acre protected patch of mixed hardwoods that has been uncut since precolonial times, species diversity has increased in recent decades, but the increase is almost entirely attributable to invasive exotics such as the tree of heaven (*Ailanthus altissima*), bird cherry (*Prunus avium*), and the princess tree (*Paulownia tomentosa*) (Forman and Elfstrom, 1975; Steward T. A. Pickett, pers. com., 1989). In a study of thirty-two swamps in the New Jersey Pine Barrens, Joan Ehrenfeld (1983) found that the pristine, untouched swamps, which were half the total, had a significantly lower species diversity than the other sixteen swamps, which received runoff from suburban and agricultural development. With development, some of the characteristic herbaceous and shrub species of the Pine Barrens disappeared, to be replaced by a motley assortment of mostly herbaceous species and vines, with many exotics. Species diversity increased, and so did the variability of species composition from site to site. An increase in species diversity was thus associated with what many ecologists would consider degradation of the habitat.

Another example shows that even accurate measures of ecosystem parameters might lead managers to erroneous conclusions. Braithwaite and Lonsdale (1987) discussed the rarity of a shrewlike Australian marsupial insectivore, *Sminthopsis virginiae*. Populations of this mammal, which was quite scarce a few decades ago, have lately been found to be locally sizable again, in association with the invasion of an exotic shrub, mimosa. Braithwaite and Lonsdale reconstruct the story in this way: *Sminthopsis* was once common in areas covered by dense thickets of the native shrub *Pandanus*. When water buffalo were introduced, they opened up the *Pandanus* thickets, and *Sminthopsis* became rare. In recent years, overgrazing by the buffalo has favored the spread of mimosa, which has helped *Sminthopsis* by providing cover. But as mimosa spreads, it destroys the graminoid vegetation in which *Sminthopsis* forages, so *Sminthopsis*, the authors predict, will become rare again unless the water buffalo and mimosa are simultaneously brought under control. Does this sound a bit like the pressure and temperature relationships inside a nuclear power plant? It did to me. And keep in mind that we understand few relationships among the components of ecosystems as well as we appear to understand the *Sminthopsis* story.

Resolving the Conservation Paradox

Now we return briefly to the topic of game management. Game management, I suggest, corresponds in a number of ways to Perrow's linear system, the kind of system that rarely produces normal accidents. Two of the characteristics of such systems are fewer feedback loops and single-purpose, segregated controls. The timing of the various deer hunting seasons, such as doe season and bow hunting season, can be set independently of the brant goose season or the mallard season, for example. Also, there is more direct information in linear systems. What can be more direct than the sorts of data that come from a hunter check station during deer season? Finally, another characteristic of linear systems that we see in game management is extensive understanding. Thanks to Leopold and his successors, we understand the ecological relationships and population biology of game species far better than those aspects of most other organisms. So game management is linear rather than complex, in Perrow's terminology.

Unfortunately, most ecosystems—wilderness, seminatural, or cultural, and their conservation management strategies—are not linear. They are complex, with all the characteristics of complex systems. Incomprehensibility, for example, is an element of ecosystems. We know most of the critical elements of the system that produces deer. But suppose you were interested in conserving microbes? According to microbiologist Harlyn Halvorson (1988), we can identify about one percent of the species of soil microbes. For marine bacteria, the figure is two orders of magnitude lower. The manipulative maintenance or repair of any apparatus is limited if we cannot identify its various parts.

Does this mean that active management of ecosystems is impossible, that the conservation paradox of active management's leading to an overall loss of preexisting species is unavoidable? I do not think so. It is the application of general rules, not management per se, that opposes specificity or diversity. True, we cannot do anything to reduce the complexity of ecosystems (and thus perhaps make them less accident-prone) without violating the very conservation principles we are trying to uphold. But is system complexity the only cause of normal accidents? To answer this, we must return to Perrow.

Do any complex industrial systems seem to have a lower-than-expected number of normal accidents? Perrow says yes, and his major example is the air traffic control system. Air traffic control differs from a nuclear power plant, he asserts, in that the various parts of air traffic control are loosely coupled. The system is based on both redundancy and segregation of management components. Air traffic controllers can get information about planes by voice contact via radio, by radar, and by transponders. This redundancy is multiplied by backup radios in the aircraft and other backups. Furthermore, for purposes of management, potentially interactive parts of the system are segregated; jumbo jets and smaller, slower, less instrumented aircraft normally fly in different airspaces, for example. Similarly, different air traffic controllers manage different pieces of the action. Accidents occur and always will, but they occur infrequently enough to make an inherently hazardous form of transportation comparatively safe.

How does this relate to conservation management? I do not want to strain what is only an analogy past the breaking point, but I do think there may be some lessons to learn. The complexity of the ecological systems we manage is a given—we do not want to change it. Similarly, the degree of coupling, or linkage, inside the system is also a given and cannot be altered. But some kinds of management maximize the tight coupling that exists in the system, thus increasing the system's vulnerability to normal accidents; other types of management simulate loose coupling, which reduces the danger.

The former case, in which management amplifies the tight coupling within the ecosystem, would apply to those active, manipulative management plans that apply the same protocol over very large regions. This confronts management with both complexity and tight coupling, setting it up to experience normal accidents—extinctions and loss of habitat types. I hasten to say that this is not an argument against large preserves;

I believe that the larger they are, the better. It is an argument against any large, prioritized, single-protocol, single-theory, generalized management scheme, whether it is the management of very large blocks of contiguous land or the centralized, uniform management of a patchwork of smaller pieces scattered over a large area.

The alternative, which I think makes more sense, for the very large blocks of protected land, is the low-management option or even the no-management option in a few cases, because the more manipulation, the more the risk of normal accidents. On the other hand, for the fragmented landscapes that often require active management, the air traffic control model would have us managing the protected patches more actively, but according each patch, except perhaps for the very smallest, the maximum of independence for its management protocol. This way, if an accident occurred in the management of one part, the loose coupling would prevent it from becoming a system-wide problem. Such individualized management has the added virtue of automatically taking into account the singularities and uniqueness of each separate piece of land.

This kind of loosely coupled management is also similar to what Piore and Sabel (1984) refer to as a craft production system—as opposed to conventional mass production. Craft production systems, which Piore and Sabel see as having the potential to reinvigorate the economy of the developed world after the stagnation of a half century of mass production, are decentralized, flexible, capable of small-scale operation, information-sensitive, and composed of elements that are integrated yet independent. One example the authors give is the enormously successful textile district of Prato, in central Italy, which includes a network of highly autonomous small shops, coordinated into a single flexible production unit. This complex but loosely coupled system (to use Perrow's terminology) has made Italian cottage industry a power in the world textile market, has kept employment steady during a time of textile industry unemployment, and accounts for three-fourths of Italy's textile exports. It is a good model for the conservation management of multiple conservation units, with the potential of neatly sidestepping the conservation paradox and the conflict between generality and specificity.

Finally, what about human-dominated agricultural landscapes, especially those valuable ones in which the relationship between people and the land has evolved slowly? Such landscapes are often associated with a high level of desirable diversity. Here, because of the complexity and the unavoidable tight coupling, nonmanipulative management—the kind of management that protects, fosters, and facilitates the preservation of the cultural status quo—is the only acceptable alternative. In an article about peasant agriculture and conservation, Altieri et al. (1987) wrote: "We do not intend to romanticize subsistence agriculture or consider development per se as detrimental. We want, however, to stress the value of traditional agriculture in the preservation of native crop diversity and the adjacent vegetation communities. . . . Basing a rural development strategy on traditional farming and ethnobotanical knowledge not only assumes continual use and maintenance of valuable genetic resources but also allows for the diversification of peasant subsistence strategies."

I conclude with the idea that conservationists may have to learn to pay almost as much attention to developing a strategy of management as to producing a theory or theories of conservation ecology. We should take the lessons of normal accidents in nuclear power plants and other complex systems to heart so that we can create conservation management regimes that do not make analogous accidents more frequent in parks, reserves, other conservation lands, and cultural landscapes. Yet I would be less than honest if I failed to add that I believe that the true prospects for conservation ultimately depend not on the conservation manipulations of scientists but on the overarching consideration of how many people there will be in the world in the next century, the way they live, and the ways in which they come to regard and use nature. Proper management for conservation is necessary, but by itself it will not be enough.

MODERN AGRICULTURE

II

4 NATURE AS THE MEASURE FOR A SUSTAINABLE AGRICULTURE

At the Land Institute in Salina, Kansas, we use the prairie as our standard or measure in attempting to wed ecology and agriculture. When Wendell Berry dedicated our new greenhouse in March 1988, he traced the literary and scientific history of our work at the institute. To set the stage for understanding the institute's place in the grand scheme of things, I shall review the history he provided (Berry, 1990).

Berry first cited Job:

> . . . ask now the beasts, and they shall teach thee;
> and the fowls of the air, and they shall tell thee:
> Or speak to the earth, and it shall teach thee; and
> the fishes of the sea shall declare unto thee.

Later Berry mentioned other writings. At the beginning of *The Georgics* (36–29 B.C.), Virgil advised that

> . . . before we plow an unfamiliar patch
> It is well to be informed about the winds,
> About the variations in the sky,
> The native traits and habits of the place,
> What each locale permits, and what denies.

Toward the end of the 1500s, Edmund Spenser called nature "the equall mother" of all creatures, who "knittest each to each, as brother unto brother." Spenser also saw

Wes Jackson

nature as the instructor of creatures and the ultimate earthly judge of their behavior. Shakespeare, in *As You Like It*, put the forest in the role of teacher and judge; Touchstone remarks, "You have said; but whether wisely or no, let the forest judge."

Milton had the lady in *Comus* describe nature in this way:

> She, good cateress,
> Means her provision only to the good
> That live according to her sober laws
> And holy dictate of spare Temperance.

And Alexander Pope, in his *Epistle to Burlington*, counseled gardeners to "let Nature never be forgot" and to "consult the Genius of the Place in all."

"After Pope," Berry (1990) has stated, "so far as I know, this theme departs from English poetry. The later poets were inclined to see nature and humankind as radically divided, and were no longer much interested in the issues of a *practical* harmony between the land and its human inhabitants. The romantic poets, who subscribed to the modern doctrine of the preeminence of the human mind, tended to look upon nature, not as anything they might ever have practical dealings with, but as a reservoir of symbols."

In my own region of the prairies, I think of Virgil's admonition: "Before we plow an unfamiliar patch / It is well to be informed about the winds." What if the settlers and children of settlers who gave us the dust bowl on the Great Plains in the 1930s had heeded that two-thousand-year-old advice? What if they had heeded Milton's insight that nature "means her provision only to the good / That live according to her sober laws / And holy dictate of spare Temperance"? Virgil was writing about agricultural practices, whereas Milton was writing of the spare use of nature's fruits. It is interesting that the poets have spoken of both practice in nature and harvest of nature.

Berry pointed out that this theme surfaced again among the agricultural writers, first in 1905 in a book by Liberty Hyde Bailey entitled *The Outlook to Nature*. The grand old dean at Cornell wrote, "If nature is the norm then the necessity for correcting and amending abuses of civilization become baldly apparent by very contrast. The return to nature affords the very means of acquiring the incentive and energy for ambitious and constructive work of a high order." In *The Holy Earth* (1915)

Bailey advanced the notion that "most of our difficulty with the earth lies in the effort to do what perhaps ought not to be done." He continued, "A good part of agriculture is to learn how to adapt one's work to nature. . . . To live in right relation with his natural conditions is one of the first lessons that a wise farmer or any other wise man learns."

J. Russell Smith's *Tree Crops*, published in 1929, contributed to the tradition. Smith was disturbed with the destruction of the hills because "man has carried to the hills the agriculture of the flat plain." Smith too believed that "farming should fit the land."

In 1940 Sir Albert Howard's *An Agriculture Testament* was published. For Howard, nature was "the supreme farmer": "The main characteristic of Nature's farming can therefore be summed up in a few words. Mother earth never attempts to farm without live stock; she always raises mixed crops; great pains are taken to preserve the soil and to prevent erosion; the mixed vegetable and animal wastes are converted into humus; there is no waste; the processes of growth and the processes of decay balance one another; ample provision is made to maintain large reserves of fertility; the greatest care is taken to store the rainfall; both plants and animals are left to protect themselves against disease."

It may appear that our work at the Land Institute is part of a succession in a literary and scientific tradition, for we operate with the assumption that the best agriculture for any region is one that best mimics the region's natural ecosystems. That is why we are trying to build domestic prairies that will produce grain. We were ignorant of this literary and scientific tradition, however, when we began our work. I did have a background in botany and genetics and could see the difference between a prairie and a wheat field out my windows at the Land Institute, but as Berry said about the poets and scientists he quoted, understanding probably comes out of the familial and communal handing down of agrarian common culture rather than from any succession of teachers and students in the literary culture or in the schools. As far as the literary and scientific tradition is concerned, Berry pointed out that it is a series, not a succession. The succession is only in the agrarian common culture. I came off the farm out of a family of farmers, and apparently my "memory" of nature as measure is embedded in that agrarian common culture. George Bernard Shaw said that, "perfect memory is perfectful forgetfulness." To know something well is not to know where it came from. That is probably the nature of succession in the nonformal culture.

"Unwitting Accessibility to the World"

It is always easier to think of a better way to produce either food or a consumer item than it is to propose how to avoid using food or a gadget wastefully. Of all the poets mentioned here, Milton is the only one who wrote about human consumption. Yet if nature is to be our measure, we must be attentive to the "holy dictate of spare Temperance." This is where I see humankind's split with nature widening, and therefore an examination of what is at work is in order.

I believe that we live in a fallen world. By that, I mean that to meet our food and fiber needs, we have changed the face of the earth. We employed human cleverness to make the earth yield up an unbounded technological array that has produced even more countless things. In agriculture we have hot-wired the landscape, bypassing nature's numerous control devices. What drives us to do this in the face of the evidence all around that we are destroying our habitat? Carlos Castaneda's Don Juan called it our "unwitting accessibility to the world." I should explain my interpretation of that phrase.

A few years ago on the last page of *Life* I saw a memorable photograph of a near-naked and well-muscled tribesman of Indonesian New Guinea, staring at a parked airplane in a jungle clearing. The caption noted the Indonesian government's attempt to bring such "savages" into the money economy. A stand had been set up at the edge of the jungle and was reportedly doing a brisk business in beer, soda pop, and tennis shoes.

We can imagine what must have followed for the members of the tribe, what the wages of their "sin," their "fall," must have been—decaying teeth, anxiety in a money system, destruction of their social structure. If they were like most so-called primitive peoples, then in spite of having a hierarchical structure, their society was much more egalitarian than industrialized societies today.

Unlike Adam and Eve, who partook of the tree of knowledge, the New Guinea tribesmen did not receive an explicit commandment to avoid the goodies of civilization. They were simply given unwittingly accessibility to the worldly items of beer, soda pop, and tennis shoes. In the Genesis version, the sin involves disobedience, an exercise of free will. In the latter version, the "original sin" is our unwitting accessibility to the material things of the world. I perceive that to be the largest threat to our planet and to our ability to regard nature as the standard.

In *Beyond the Hundredth Meridian* (1953), Wallace Stegner described the breakdown of American Indian culture:

> For however sympathetically or even sentimentally a white American viewed the Indian, the industrial culture was certain to eat away at the tribal cultures like lye. One's attitude might vary, but the fact went on regardless. What destroyed the Indian was not primarily political greed, land hunger, or military power, not the white man's germs or the white man's rum. What destroyed him was the manufactured products of a culture, iron and steel, guns, needles, woolen cloth, *things that once possessed could not be done without* (italics added).
>
> It was not the continuity of the Indian race that failed; what failed was the continuity of the diverse tribal cultures. These exist now only in scattered, degenerated reservation fragments among such notably resistant peoples as the Pueblo and Navajo of the final, persistent Indian Country. And here what has protected them is aridity, the difficulties in the way of dense white settlement, the accident of relative isolation, as much as the stability of their own institutions. Even here a Hopi dancer with tortoise shells on his calves and turquoise on his neck and wrists and a kirtle of fine traditional weave around his loins may wear down his back as an amulet a nickel-plated Ingersoll watch, or a Purple Heart medal won in a white man's war. Even here, in Monument Valley where not one Navajo in ten speaks any English, squaws may herd their sheep through the shadscale and rabbitbrush in brown and white saddle shoes and Hollywood sunglasses, or gather under a juniper for gossip and bubblegum. The lye still corrodes even the resistant cultures.

This reality—things that once possessed cannot be done without—is so powerful that it occupies our unconscious, and yet we know that nature "means her provision only to the good / That live according to her sober laws / And holy dictate of spare Temperance."

Voluntary Poverty as a Path toward Insight

Lynn White (1967) has proposed Saint Francis of Assisi as the patron saint of ecologists. Francis held the radical position that all of creation was holy. Yet nothing in the record shows that he arrived at that position because he was initially endowed with the wilderness psyche of a Henry David Thoreau or a John Muir or an Aldo Leopold. In fact, his entry point was from a nearly opposite end of the spectrum—this son of a well-to-do man chose poverty. Apparently, Francis took seriously the words of Jesus of Nazareth, "If you have done it unto the least of these my brethren, you have done it unto Me." Francis's intimate identification with the least, his joining the least, must have prepared him psychologically to be sensitively tuned to all of creation—both the living and the nonliving world. He was a Christian pantheist who believed that birds, flowers, trees, and rocks had spiritual standing.

Francis, the founder of the most heretical brand of Christianity ever, began his journey with a marriage to poverty. This poverty, voluntarily chosen, apparently was the prerequisite for making what White (1967) called "the greatest spiritual revolutionary in Western history." His marriage to poverty and his sparing use of the earth's resources led to deep ecological insight. You may remember the legend of the famous wolf of Gubbio, which had been eating livestock and people. Francis approached the wolf and asked him, in the name of Jesus Christ, to behave himself. The wolf gave signs that he understood. Francis then launched into a description of all that the wolf had done, including all the livestock and people he had killed, and told him, "You, Friar Wolf, are a thief and a murderer" and therefore "fit for the gallows." The wolf made more signs of understanding, and Francis continued, stating in effect, "I see you have a contrite heart about this matter, and if you promise to behave, I'll see to it that you are fed." The wolf showed signs that he promised, and the legend has it that the wolf came to town, went in and out of people's houses as a kind of pet, and lived that way two years before he died. The townspeople all fed him, scratched his ears, and so on. It was life at the dog food bowls of Gubbio.

In light of that story, I once thought that Saint Francis might more properly be regarded as the patron saint of domesticators. Anyone able to encourage a wolf to quit acting like a wolf should act, given everything from its enzyme system to its fangs, is not likely to be regarded as an ecologist, let alone a patron saint for such.

A few weeks ago, at about three in the morning, the barking of our two dogs woke me up. Soon there was hissing and growling and more barking right on the back porch. I went outside and saw a raccoon cowering under a step stool by the dog food bowl. I chased it away with a stick, sicced our border collie Molly on him, and went back to bed. I confidently went to sleep. A few minutes later I heard more barking, more hissing, more growling. Once again I went outside, and the dogs and I ran the coon off. Back to bed, and sure enough the same story. This time, however, I left the porch light on for this nocturnal animal. I lay in bed and listened, and there was no more ruckus. I felt pleased with myself for having solved the problem with a light switch by means of my biological knowledge about nocturnal animals, and I went to sleep. The next morning, I headed out the back door to begin the day's work, and there in a box of tinder on a table was the coon, sleeping away. Both dogs were asleep under the table. Each time I returned to the house during the day, I expected to see that the coon had gone. But he didn't leave. And as he slept that day, the dogs would walk by, look up, and sniff, well on their way toward accepting their new fellow resident.

What was going on here? We are taught to consider recent changes when something unusual breaks a pattern. And so I might have an answer. Late in the afternoons this winter I have been going to my woods with a chain saw, some gasoline, and matches to burn brush. I am clearing out most of the box elder trees that have grown up there over the last forty years. They are early-stage succession trees that have mostly covered the area where the former tenant logged out all the walnuts and burr oaks. The box elders are the first trees to green up in the spring, and they accommodate woodpeckers. But they are no good for lumber, and though we burn them, they are very low in fuel value. I want to accelerate succession by planting some walnuts and oaks for my grandchildren. Nearly every box elder I took down was hollow. The woods are less than a quarter of a mile from my house along the Smoky Hill River, and I suspect that I destroyed the home of Friar Coon and that Friar Coon, looking for a new home, simply moved into mine.

Now back to Gubbio. Why was the thieving, murdering wolf forgiven and then given a life at the dog food bowls? I suspect that the ecological context necessary to accommodate proper wolfhood around Gubbio had been destroyed, that the usual predator-prey relationship had been somehow disrupted, and that Francis realized it. If so, Francis's deeper ecological insight was a derivative of his respect and love for nature. He could, after all, have organized a posse to eliminate the killer wolf, but instead his love and respect for nature—in turn at least partly derived from his identification with poverty—made him forgiving and compassionate.

But there is still an item on our agenda for discussion. Was Saint

Francis engaged in an act of domestication? It appears so, but if harmony with nature is what we seek, should we not be willing to be in harmony any way we can? The wolf's tame behavior demonstrates that nature is not rigid. Humanity (Francis) reached out to nature (the wolf), and the wolf responded. If we insist that wild nature be so rigid, we are denying one of the most important properties of nature—resilience. The unanswered question here is, Once the wolf comes to town, can he ever return to the wild? Life at a dog bowl in Gubbio may be easier than life that relies on the fang and the occasional berry. If the wolf is unable to return, then that particular wolf is a fallen creature. Would it matter that he was made that way initially by the fallen ecological context of humanity's making? Wolves and coons, unable to return to their original context because they have gained unwittingly accessibility to the world, may be little different from the New Guinea tribesmen or the native Americans. Stegner's phrase, "things that once possessed could not be done without," can be applied beyond people. Grizzlies in the garbage at Yellowstone and elephants in African dump heaps come to mind as modern expressions of the same problem. A wolf, or any other creature, unable to return is a fallen animal dependent on fallen humanity. And so another ethical question comes on the agenda: What right do we have to create a fallen world for other species when we know that life at the dog food bowl is second best? Following that line of thinking, our crops and livestock represent fallen species that accommodate fallen humanity.

Interpenetration of the Domestic and the Wild

The stories about the wolf in Gubbio and the coon on the porch illustrate the problem of trying to use nature as measure, for in those examples the interpenetration of the domestic and the wild is total. During the last five hundred years or so, the ratio of the domestic to the wild has increased so much, especially in the Western Hemisphere, that wilderness is becoming an artifact of civilization. Civilization is all that can save wilderness now. The wild that produced us, that we were dependent upon, is now dependent on us. We pay homage to wildness in the United States by regarding pristine wilderness as a kind of a saint. But that presents some problems, too.

In Christianity the tradition of sainthood calls upon the faithful to stand or kneel before an image of a saint, light a candle, meditate, think, and perhaps whisper some words before departure. Often these faithful go in peace, perhaps thinking, "Well, that's covered," and they carry on more or less as before. This isolation of virtue can also be found in countless wilderness advocates who clamor to have wilderness set aside as pristine. They will stand in forest wilderness, soak up its silence, walk out, and send money to defend it. They may say little in protest, however, about the spread of lethal farm chemicals over more than half a million square miles of the best agricultural land in the world, and soil erosion may be no concern of theirs. I do not object to either saints or wilderness, but to keep the holy isolated from the rest, to treat our wilderness as a saint and to treat Kansas or East Saint Louis otherwise, is a form of schizophrenia. Either all the earth is holy, or it is not. Either every square foot deserves our respect, or none of it does.

Would Earth First! activists or Deep Ecologists be as interested in cleaning up East Saint Louis, for example, as they are in defending wilderness? Would Earth First! activists be as fervent about defending a farmer's soil conservation effort or chemical-free crop rotation as they are about spiking a tree or putting sugar in the fuel tank of a bulldozer?

It is possible to love a small acreage in Kansas as much as John Muir loved the entire Sierra Nevada. That is fortunate, for the wilderness of the Sierra will disappear unless little pieces of nonwilderness become intensely loved by lots of people. In other words, Harlem and East Saint Louis and Iowa and Kansas and the rest of the world where wilderness has been destroyed will have to be loved by enough of us, or wilderness is doomed. Suddenly we see we are dealing with a range of issues. For that reason Saint Francis's entire life becomes an important example. People who struggle for social justice by working with the poor in cities and people out to prevent soil erosion and save the family farm are suddenly on the same side as the wilderness advocate. All have joined the same fight.

Nature as Measure in Agricultural Research

Rather than deal with problems *in* agriculture here and now, we at the Land Institute address the problem *of* agriculture, which began when agriculture began some eight to ten thousand years ago. We have seen that nature is an elusive standard. Nevertheless, it seems to us at the Land Institute less elusive than any other standard when sustainability is our primary objective. The nature we look to at the Land Institute is the never-plowed native prairie.

We have around one hundred acres of such land at the institute, and when we compare prairie with the ordinary field of corn or wheat, important differences become apparent. From our typical agricultural fields, valuable nutrients run toward the sea, where for all practical purposes most of them are gone for good. The prairie, on the other hand, by drawing nutrients from parent rock material or subsoil, all the while returning chemicals produced by life, actually builds soil. The prairie, like nearly all of nature, runs mostly on contemporary sunlight, whereas our modern agricultural fields benefit from the stored sunlight of extinct ancient floras. Diversity does not necessarily yield stability overall; nevertheless, the chemical diversity inherent in the diverse plant species of the prairie confronts insects and pathogens, making epidemics, so common to agricultural monocultures, rare on the prairie. Because no creature has an all-consuming enzyme system, diversity yields some protection. The prairie therefore does not require the introduction of chemicals with which species have had no evolutionary experience.

So what are the basic differences between a prairie and an agricultural field? A casual examination of the ordinary differences will help us to see that the prairie features perennials in a polyculture, whereas modern agriculture features annuals in a monoculture. Our work at the Land Institute is devoted primarily to exploring the feasibility of an agriculture that features herbaceous perennials grown in a mixture for seed production—that is, domestic prairies—as substitutes for annual monocultures grown in rows on ground that can erode.

We address four basic questions in our experiments at the institute. First, can herbaceous perenniality and high seed yield go together? Because perennial plants must divert some photosynthate to belowground storage for overwintering, it may be difficult to breed perennials to produce as much seed as annual crops that die after reproducing. Perennial species differ greatly in both relative and absolute amounts of energy devoted to seed production, however, so theoretically there seems to be no reason why a fast-growing, well-adapted species could not yield adequate seed while retaining the ability to overwinter.

Before we begin to breed for stable high seed yields in an herbaceous perennial, we determine its genetic potential. Whether we start with a wild introduced species or a wild native, the development of perennial seed-producing polycultures will require that we select for varieties that perform well in polyculture. The potential improvement, therefore, depends on the range of existing genetic variability in the wild. To assess this variation requires an adequate sample drawn from the geographic range of the species and then an evaluation of the collection within a common garden.

Now our second question: Can a polyculture of perennial seed producers outyield the same species grown in monoculture? Overyielding occurs when interspecific competition in a plant community is less intense than intraspecific competition. Thus, we believe that through differences in resource use and timing of demand, multispecies fields typically yield more per unit area than do monospecific stands.

Our third question is, Can a perennial polyculture provide much of its own fertility? Specifically, can such internal factors as nitrogen fixation and weathering of primary minerals compensate for nutrients removed in harvested seed? To answer this question, we must document nutrient cycling in the soil, nutrient content of seed, and capacity of crop plants to enrich the soil.

As our fourth and final question we ask, Can a perennial mixture successfully contend with phytophagous insects, pathogens, and weeds? If we are to protect a crop, a combination of breeding for resistant lines and studies on the effects of species diversity must converge. Insect pests can be managed through a combination of attracting predators and preventing insects from locating host plants. A mixture of species, and of genotypes within species, may reduce the incidence and spread of disease. Weeds may be controlled either allelopathically or via continuous shading of the soil surface by the perennials.

Though we keep all four of these questions in mind, the most pressing biological question at the Land Institute is whether perennials and high seed yield can go together. To answer this question, we started a plant inventory that had the following steps: (1) we reviewed the literature of seed yield in winter-hardy herbaceous perennials; (2) we collected seed and plants in nature and developed an herbary of approximately three hundred species, each grown in five-meter-long rows; and (3) we planted more than forty-three hundred accessions of more than one hundred species representing seven grass genera. Our inventory continues even though we are currently focusing on five species plus a hybrid of our making.

The relationship between perennials and high yield also involves the issue of sustained production. Prairies, after all, feature perennials, but they do not feature high seed yield. Ultimately, we have to explore the optimum balance between sustainability and yield.

In addition to the inventory of potentially high-yielding species, other sorts of inventories, such as an inventory of the vegetative structure, are necessary for long-term considerations. Because perennial roots are a major feature of our work, an inventory of the soil relationships in the prairie and in our plots is also essential. The ecological inventory includes more than analysis of the phytomass ratios; it also includes an ongoing inventory of the insects and pathogens in our herbary and in our experimental plots. We always compare the results with those from our prairie, the system that represents the least departure from what was here before white settlement.

The inventory phase will probably never end. The ecological inventory is particularly long-lasting because of the countless number of interactions over time. Even research on the question of perennials and high yield will require several years, for it amounts to an investigation of long-term demographic patterns in perennial seed production, a field that is largely unexplored. Studies thus far at the Land Institute have shown increases, decreases, and oscillations in seed yield over time. But we always come back to these questions: What was here? What will nature permit us to do here? And what will nature help us to do here? Wendell Berry once wrote in a letter, "When we cut the forest and plowed our prairies we never knew what we were doing because we never knew what we were undoing." It is now a matter of practical necessity to learn what we were undoing.

In a 1986 preliminary investigation, Jon Piper, the institute's ecologist, asked, How much aboveground plant life is supported each year by the prairie, and what are the proportions of grasses, legumes, and composites? Those plant families comprise most of our temperate agricultural species. Net production of the plants at Piper's grassland sites (five hundred to seven hundred grams per square meter) was similar to that of many midwestern crops. At their peaks, grasses composed 67 to 94 percent of plant matter, and legumes and composites represented 16 and 11 percent of vegetation, respectively. Piper concluded from these encouraging results that "a sustainable agricultural system for central Kansas is feasible if perennial grasses were featured followed by nearly equal proportions of legumes and composites."

In 1985 we began to examine insects and plant pathogens qualitatively in nine experimental plots at the Land Institute. Every week from May through August, and every other week from September through October, insects were collected with a sweep net or from individual plants. All diseased plants were sent to the Disease Diagnosis Laboratory at Kansas State University for pathogen identification. All sampled plots showed a diversity of both beneficial and harmful insects. Several foliar diseases were present, but few were serious. We continued that inventory in 1986 but with important modifications. The prairie was sampled using sweep nets every third week. Over the years, we have sampled the prairie, the herbary, and the experimental plots for insects and pathogens and have made numerous comparisons.

A final example of this soft approach to sustainable-agriculture research is the design of the large polyculture experiment we intend to establish in 1991. For that experiment, we think about the species components we intend to introduce, the planting density of each species, the ratios of species to one another, and so forth.

Three Final Questions

We have three final questions to consider. First, is perennial polyculture or ecosystem agriculture inherently more complicated and therefore less likely to succeed than monoculture agriculture, be it of the annual or the perennial variety?

My answer is, not necessarily. The disciplines of science are divided to explore the various levels in the hierarchy of structure from atoms to molecules, cells, tissues, organs, organ systems, and organisms. At each level of aggregation, it is the emergent qualities more than the contents that define the discipline. A physicist may have learned about the structure and workings of an atom in great detail. Though some understanding of atoms is necessary for a chemist, the chemist does not need to know the atom with the same intricacy of detail as the physicist. A chemist mostly studies reactions. On up the hierarchy, we see that chemistry is important to a cell biologist but does not define cell biology, and a good cell biologist does not need to have a chemist's detailed knowledge. Cell biology as a field is not more complicated than chemistry or physics, though cells are more complex than molecules or atoms. Likewise, ecosystem agriculture will be more complex than monoculture agriculture, but the management of agro-ecosystems may not be more complicated. Ecosystem agriculturalists will take advantage of the natural integrities of ecosystems worked out over the millennia.

When we deal with nature's designs, a great deal of ignorance on our part is tolerable. Much error is forgiven. Ignorance is tolerable until we begin to impose our own designs on nature's landscape. Even then certain kinds of ignorance and large amounts of forgetfulness will be tolerated. (Not knowing is a kind of ignorance preferred over knowing things that just are not so. At least one does not have to unlearn what is not known.) When we impose our own designs on nature's landscape, we do so with the presumption that we know what we are doing, and we have to assume responsibility for our mistakes. By imitating nature's patterns, we should be able to reduce error by taking advantage of nature's complexity, thus minimizing complications for ourselves. Farmers and scientists alike may not know why certain associations of plants and animals grant sustainability, just that they do. And though there is little wrong with finding out why certain associations work, from the point of view of a farmer interested in running a sustainable farm, knowing why is not always necessary.

Our second question is, How crucial is species diversity, and if it is necessary, how much and what kind are optimum? As mentioned earlier, diversity does not necessarily lead to stability. Numerous diverse ecosystems are less stable than simpler ones. We can raise a question about the inherent value of diversity by considering two extremes. At one extreme, we could assemble a diverse hodgepodge of species, plants that have never grown together in an ecosystem. At the other extreme, we could assemble plant species that have histories of growing together—on the prairie, let us say. In the latter case, natural integrities have evolved to the point that large numbers of genetic ensembles interact in a species mix. This area warrants much research.

Another important consideration is associated with the diversity question. As species are selected for future experimentation, we may need to determine to what extent the genetic profile is tuned to interspecific versus intraspecific complementarity. In all of our important domestic grains, the genetic assembly of an individual plant resonates against members of its own kind (intraspecific complementarity). On a prairie, that is not the case. Prairie plants are more tuned to interact with different species (interspecific complementarity).

The third question we ask is this: Is it true that, for any biotic system, internal control uses material and energy resources more efficiently than external control? In a hierarchy of structure—beginning with an individual plant, then the field (an ecosystem), then the farm (a larger ecosystem), and then the farm community (an even larger ecosystem)—it will be necessary to think about the efficient use of material and energy resources.

This philosophical consideration is of great practical importance. Consider a plant's resistance to an insect. If a plant uses its genetic code to make a chemical that is distasteful to an insect, thereby granting itself protection, we would call that internal control. If we, perhaps unknowingly, remove that ability through breeding, the plant is susceptible and we apply an insecticide on the plant's surface to grant it protection. That is external control. Yield increases, but the resource cost for protection is paid from the outside, and seemingly the total cost would be greater.

Another example is nitrogen fertility. If the feedstock for commercial nitrogen fertilizer is natural gas, the total energy cost would be higher than if the plant fixed its own nitrogen. In the first case, we are using what we might call vertical energy, or time-compressed energy; in the second case, we are using horizontal, or contemporary, energy from the sun. As our supplies of vertical energy run out and we are forced to use horizontal energy, then the answer to our major question becomes crucial, for at that point the energy source becomes a land-use problem.

A third example is weed control. If the roots of a plant produce an herbicide to keep back most weeds, then weed protection comes from within the plant (allelopathy). The plant's production of such an herbicide will come at a cost in yield. But let us say that a plant lacks the ability to produce the herbicide and that mechanical weeding is necessary. If we pay the cost on the farm the way we used to—that is, harvest biomass from a pasture or field to feed horses supplying the power for mechanical weed removal—then it seems obvious that the overall cost will be higher.

We are faced with extremely difficult choices and, I believe, extremely difficult times. Our goal must be a harmony between the human economy and nature's economy that will preserve both. In the greenhouse dedication speech mentioned earlier, Wendell Berry pointed out that such a goal is traditional: "The world is now divided between those who adhere to this ancient purpose and those who by intention do not, and this division is of far more portent for the future of the world than any of the presently recognized national or political or economic divisions."

Recalling his outline of the literary and scientific traditions, Berry concluded, "The remarkable thing about this division is its relative newness. The idea that we should obey nature's laws and live harmoniously with her as good husbanders and stewards of her gifts is old. . . . And I believe that until fairly recently our destructions of nature were more or less unwitting—the by-products, so to speak, of our ignorance or weakness or depravity. It is our present principled and elaborately rationalized rape and plunder of the natural world that is a new thing under the sun."

5 THE DIMENSIONS OF THE PESTICIDE QUESTION

Fewer than 1 percent of all 500,000 estimated species of plants, animals, and microbes in the United States are known pests. Most of the remaining 99 percent of the natural biota benefit agriculture and other sectors of the economy. Yet seldom if ever do we hear about the benefits provided by invertebrates, plants, microbes, and other natural biota. Some of the essential functions that these biota perform include degrading organic wastes; removing pollutants from water and soil; recycling vital chemicals within the ecosystem; buffering air pollutants; moderating climatic change; conserving soil and water; providing medicines, pigments, and spices; preserving genetic diversity; and supplying food via the harvest of fish and other wildlife (Pimentel et al., 1980b). These benefits are estimated to be worth much more than $1 trillion annually to the U.S. economy.

There is no question, however, that the pest component of the natural biota is costly to the U.S. economy. Yearly losses from pests are estimated at about $64 billion (Pimentel, 1986). Insects, plant pathogens, and weeds destroy about 37 percent of the country's potential agricultural production.

Approximately 500 million kilograms of pesticides are applied annually in an effort to control pests in the United States, at a cost of about $4 billion (Pimentel and Levitan, 1986; Pimentel et al., 1991). That $4 billion, however, does

David Pimentel

not include the indirect costs related to the destruction of natural biota, the disturbance of ecological systems, and human poisonings and illness. Such indirect costs are estimated to be at least $1 billion and could be twice that amount (Pimentel et al., 1980a).

The dilemma that society faces is how to protect the nation's food resources from pests while protecting the environment and public health. The objective of this chapter is to examine the ecology, economics, and ethics of pesticide use in U.S. agriculture and the implications for the natural ecosystems on which we all depend.

The Extent of Pesticide Use

In general the quantity of pesticides used has varied with changes in agricultural practices and with the availability of new pesticides. Of the estimated 500 million kilograms of all pesticides now used in the United States, 60 percent are herbicides, 24 percent are insecticides, and 16 percent are fungicides (Pimentel and Levitan, 1986). About 320 million kilograms of agricultural pesticides are applied to about 113 million hectares, or 61 percent of U.S. cropland. Thus, a significant portion of our cropland (39 percent) is not treated with pesticides.

The application of agricultural pesticides is not evenly distributed among all crops. For example, 93 percent of all land carrying row crops, including corn, cotton, soybeans, sorghum, and tobacco, is treated with some type of pesticide (Pimentel and Levitan, 1986). In contrast, less than 10 percent of forage crops are treated. Currently, herbicides are being used on more than 100 million hectares of cropland in the United States. Nearly three-quarters of these herbicides are applied to just two crops: corn and soybeans. Field corn alone accounts for 52 percent of agricultural herbicide use. About 74 million kilograms of insecticides are applied to 34 million hectares (18 percent) of U.S. cropland. Nearly 40 percent of these insecticides are used on cotton, and another 20 percent are applied to corn. Fungicides and soil fumigants are used primarily on fruit and vegetable crops, which account for a relatively small percentage of agricultural land. These fungicides and soil fumigants, however, are important residues in the human diet.

Changes in Agricultural Technologies

Of the estimated 37 percent of U.S. crops that are lost annually to pests, 13 percent are lost to insects, 12 percent to plant pathogens, and 12

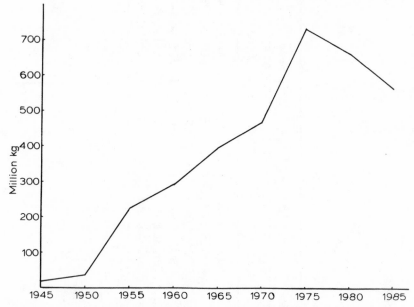

Figure 5.1. The amounts of synthetic pesticides (insecticides, herbicides, and fungicides) produced in the United States (Arrington, 1956; U.S. Bureau of the Census, 1971, 1988). About 90 percent are sold in the United States. The decline in total amount produced is in large part due to the tenfold-to-hundredfold increase in the toxicity and effectiveness of the newer pesticides.

percent to weeds (Pimentel, 1986). These losses occur despite the use of pesticides and nonchemical controls. Since 1945 the use of synthetic pesticides in the United States has grown more than thirtyfold (fig. 5.1). At the same time, the toxicity and the biological effectiveness of insecticides, fungicides, and herbicides have increased at least tenfold. In 1945, for example, the amount of DDT applied was about 2 kilograms per hectare; similar effective insect control is now achieved with the more powerful parathion and aldicarb applied at 0.2 and 0.05 kilograms per hectare, respectively.

According to survey data collected from 1942 to the present (table 5.1), crop losses due to plant pathogens (including nematodes) increased slightly, despite a dramatic rise in the use of synthetic fungicides during the past forty years (fig. 5.1). The increase in crop losses was due to changes in agricultural technology, especially a reduction of crop rotations, a reduction in sanitation, more stringent cosmetic standards, and changes in the amount of land planted with major field crops. Over that same period, crop losses attributed to weeds fluctuated but declined only

Table 5.1. Annual crop losses to pests in the United States.

| Period | Percentage of crops lost to pests | | | | | Crop value | |
	Insects	Diseases	Weeds	Total	Source	Billions of $	Source
1904	9.8	—	—	—	Marlatt, 1904	NA	Marlatt, 1904
1910–1935	10.5	—	—	—	Hyslop, 1938	6	USDA, 1936
1942–1951	7.1	10.5	13.8	31.4	USDA, 1954	27	USDA, 1954
1951–1960	12.9	12.2	8.5	33.6	USDA, 1965	30	USDA, 1961
1974	13.0	12.0	8.0	33.0	Pimentel, 1976	77	USDA, 1975
1986	13.0	12.0	12.0	37.0	Pimentel, 1986	150	USDA, 1986

Note: A dash indicates that information is not available.

slightly overall, despite a more-than-thousandfold increase in herbicide use. The increased herbicide use lowered the costs of weed control, however, especially the manpower and tractor input needed for mechanical cultivation (Pimentel et al., 1978).

In contrast to the moderate changes in crop losses due to plant pathogens and weeds, the percentage of crop losses due to insects nearly doubled from the 1940s to the present, despite a more-than-tenfold increase in the use of synthetic insecticides. The rise in crop losses can be attributed to direct and indirect changes in agricultural technology, such as the cultivation of some crop varieties that are more susceptible to insect pests; the destruction of natural enemies of pests, which increases the need for additional pesticide treatments (in cotton crops, for example—see van den Bosch and Messenger, 1973); an increase in pesticide-resistant insects (Roush and McKenzie, 1987); a reduction in crop rotations (in corn cultivation, for example—see Pimentel et al., 1977a); an increase in monocultures and a reduction in crop diversity (Pimentel, 1961); an increase in cosmetic standards that processors and retailers demand for fruits and vegetables (Pimentel et al., 1977b); a reduction in field sanitation; a reduction in tillage, resulting in more crop residues left on the land surface (in corn cultivation, for example); the cultivation of crops in climatic regions where they are more susceptible to insect attack (potatoes and broccoli, for example); and the use of pesticides that alter the physiology of crop plants, making them more susceptible to insect attack (as with corn, for example—see Oka and Pimentel, 1976). The impact of the increased crop losses to insects has been effectively offset by the use of higher-yielding crop varieties and the increased use of fertilizers and other inputs (Pimentel and Wen, 1990).

Reducing U.S. Pesticide Use by Half

Several studies have suggested that it is technologically feasible to reduce pesticide use in the United States by 35 to 50 percent without reducing crop yields (President's Science Advisory Committee, 1965; Office of Technology Assessment, 1979). Recent events in two European countries support this idea. In 1985 Denmark passed legislation to reduce the use of pesticides in agriculture 25 percent by 1990. In 1988 Sweden passed legislation to reduce pesticide use and risk by 50 percent by 1993 (National Board of Agriculture, 1988).

Strategies

The above discussion of changes in agricultural practices suggests strategies for reducing U.S. pesticide use by 50 percent while maintaining current high crop yields. Some of the possibilities are described below.

Insecticides Corn and cotton account for about 60 percent of the total insecticide use in agriculture. Thus, substituting nonchemical alternatives for the control of their major insect pests could contribute in a major way to a decrease in overall insecticide use.

During the early 1940s, little or no insecticide was applied to corn, and crop losses to insects were only 3.5 percent (U.S. Department of Agriculture, 1954). Since then insecticide use on corn has grown more than a thousandfold, and losses due to insects have increased to 12 percent (Ridgway, 1980). The major reason for these changes is the abandonment of crop rotations (Pimentel et al., 1977b). At present about 40 percent of U.S. corn is grown as a continuous crop, with the aid of fifteen million kilograms of insecticides applied. By growing all corn in rotation with soybeans and other nonhost crops, the use of most insecticides on corn could be avoided and insect losses would decrease (Lockeretz et al., 1981). Although rotating corn with crops other than soybeans might add a small amount to the cost of corn production, the increased cost could be offset by several benefits from rotations, including the reduction of soil erosion, of problems associated with rapid water runoff, and of crop losses to weeds and plant pathogens (Helmers et al., 1986; Cramer, 1988; Pimentel et al., 1991).

The potential for reducing pesticide use is also well illustrated in cotton production. Since 1966, insecticide use in Texas cotton production has been reduced nearly 90 percent (Office of Technology Assessment, 1979; R. Frisbie, pers. com., 1988). The following technologies accomplished this reduction: scouting (that is, monitoring populations of pests and their natural enemies to determine the best time to apply insecticides); biological controls; increased host-plant resistance; improved field sanitation, tillage practices, and management of water, fertilizer, and planting dates; crop rotations; and the use of clean seed (Office of Technology Assessment, 1979).

Currently, twenty-nine million kilograms of insecticide are applied annually to cotton in the United States. Readily available technologies could reduce that amount significantly. The effective application of a treat-when-necessary, or scouting, program could easily reduce insecticide use by 20 percent. An additional 10 percent reduction could be achieved by replacing the price support program with a free-land market for cotton production, making it possible to grow cotton in regions with fewer insect pests that need to be controlled (Pimentel and Shoemaker, 1974; National Academy of Sciences, 1989).

Growing varieties that are resistant to some major insect pests and altering planting dates in most growing regions could reduce insecticide use on cotton by another 3 percent (Frans, 1985; Frisbie, 1985). Giving greater care to the type of application equipment employed, especially reducing the use of ultra-low-volume-application equipment by aircraft, would increase the amount of insecticide reaching the target area from 25 percent to as much as 50 to 75 percent (Ware et al., 1970; Akesson and Yates, 1974, 1984; Mazariegos, 1985; Pimentel and Levitan, 1986). Covering the spray boom with plastic should further reduce drift by 85 percent (Ford, 1986). These improvements in pesticide application could well reduce insecticide use another 3 percent or more and would significantly decrease the spread of insecticides throughout the environment.

Depending on the particular conditions and the combination of alternative controls employed, insecticide use on cotton might be reduced much more than suggested above. Shaunak et al. (1982), for example, reported that insecticide use in the Lower Rio Grande Valley of Texas could be reduced 97 percent by growing short-season cotton under dryland conditions and that net profits could be twice those achieved with conventional insecticide practices.

The overall estimate is that insecticide use on cotton might be reduced by 45 percent through combinations of nonchemical pest controls. These alternative controls should pay for themselves by lowering the amount spent on insecticides and their application (Pimentel et al., 1991).

Fungicides Apples and potatoes are good examples for considering the reduced use of fungicides, because these two crops account for 26 percent of all the fungicides used in agriculture. About 90 percent of all fungicides are applied to apples, peaches, citrus, and other fruit crops (Pimentel and Levitan, 1986). Integrated pest management data on New York apples suggest that fungicide use on apples could be reduced about 10 percent, depending on the weather during the growing season (Kovach and Tette, 1988). Furthermore, a recent design improvement in spray nozzle equipment and application equipment demonstrated that the amount of fungicide applied to control apple scab could be reduced by 50 percent (Pimentel et al., 1991). Thus, a combination of techniques, including scouting, better weather forecasting, and improved application technologies, could reduce fungicide use on apples by 20 percent (Pimentel et al., 1991).

About 70 percent of potato cropland is treated with fungicides. Shields et al. (1984) reported that growing short-season potatoes in Wisconsin reduced the number of fungicide applications by one-third. Forecasting, scouting, or a combination of these techniques might also reduce fungicide use on potatoes about one-third, with an added cost of only $5 per hectare (Pimentel et al., 1980a).

Herbicides Corn and soybeans illustrate the potential of decreasing herbicide use, because they receive 74 percent of the herbicides applied in agriculture (Pimentel and Levitan, 1986). Fifty-three percent of the herbicides used on croplands are applied to corn. This means that slightly more than three kilograms of herbicide are applied per hectare of corn, and more than 90 percent of all corn is treated. In addition, about 80 percent of the corn crop is also cultivated to control weeds. Herbicide use on corn might be reduced two-thirds by increasing mechanical cultivation and crop rotations (Forcella and Lindstrom, 1988). Although I estimate that the costs of weed control in corn might then increase by about 30 percent, the effective use of rotations could significantly reduce those costs (Office of Technology Assessment, 1979).

Not only is about 80 percent of soybean cropland treated for weed control, but soybeans are also the second largest receiver of herbicides (Pimentel and Levitan, 1986). Using the rope-wick applicator rather than conventional application treatments can reduce herbicide use on soybeans by more than half and increase soybean yields by 51 percent (Dale, 1980). Also, a new model of recirculating sprayer saves 70 to 90 percent of the emitted spray that is not trapped by weeds (Matthews, 1985). Herbicide use on soybeans can also be reduced by available alternative cultivation techniques, including regular tillage, ridge tillage, mechanical cultivation, row spacing, planting-date management, crop rotations, and the use of weed-tolerant varieties (Wax and Pendleton, 1968; Walker and Buchanan, 1982; King, 1983; Helmers et al., 1986; Wilson et al., 1986; Jordan et al., 1987; Cramer, 1988; Forcella and Lindstrom, 1988). Tew et al. (1982), for example, reported that a rotation sequence of soybeans, wheat, and spinach in Georgia, along with effective management practices, reduced pesticide costs thirty-six-fold and increased net profits four and a half times. By combining several alternative techniques, herbicide use on soybeans could very well be reduced by as much as two-thirds. In addition, corn and soybean rotations can provide substantially higher returns than either crop grown separately and continuously (Helmers et al., 1986; Cramer, 1988).

Costs and Benefits

Although no efforts are being made to substantially reduce pesticide use in the United States, it is worthwhile to examine the potential economic and environmental benefits and costs if U.S. pesticide use were reduced by 50 percent. To obtain an estimate of these benefits and costs, the following factors have been considered: current patterns of pesticide use with forty major U.S. crops; current losses in these crops due to pests; estimates of the agricultural benefits and costs of reduced pesticide use; benefits and costs of substituting currently available biological, cultural, and environmental pest controls for some current pesticide controls; and public health and environmental benefits associated with reduced pesticide use (Pimentel et al., 1991).

It has been demonstrated that substituting nonchemical alternatives for some pesticide use on forty major crops could reduce total pesticide use in U.S. agriculture by 50 percent (Pimentel et al., 1991). The added costs for implementing these alternatives are estimated to be about $1 billion, which would increase total pest control costs by about 25 percent and increase total food costs at the farm by 0.6 percent. Actual retail food costs would increase about 0.2 percent, however, because farm prices make up only one-quarter of total retail food prices. If pesticide use were restricted and reduced yields resulted, then farmers would gain 9 percent in their income; the increase in cost to consumers would be about 1 percent of their disposable income (Kania and Johnson, 1981).

In the United States the economic benefits of pesticide use are estimated to be about $16 billion per year in increased crop yields. Balanced against these benefits is the cost of pesticide control measures, about $4 billion (Pimentel et al., 1991). Indirect costs are not included in these figures.

The most serious social and environmental cost attributed to pesticides is human poisonings. Yearly about forty-five thousand of such poisonings occur in the United States, with three thousand being serious enough to call for hospitalization of the victim and fifty resulting in accidental death (Pimentel et al., 1980a). Pesticides are also implicated in

Table 5.2. Estimated environmental and social costs of U.S. pesticide use

	Cost (millions of $)
Human poisonings	250
Animal poisonings and contaminated livestock products	15
Reduced natural enemies	150
Pesticide resistance	150
Honeybee poisonings and reduced pollination	150
Losses of crops and trees	75
Fishery and wildlife losses	15
Government regulations concerning pesticide pollution	150
Total	955

Source: Modified from Pimentel et al. (1980a).

numerous human diseases, including cancer and sterility. The number of U.S. citizens who develop pesticide-caused cancer is estimated to be six thousand each year (National Academy of Sciences, 1987).

Pesticide use has additional costly environmental effects (table 5.2). A large number of domestic animals are poisoned each year by pesticides, and significant amounts of contaminated meat and milk are destroyed. When pesticides are applied to crops, natural enemies that are important in controlling some pests are frequently destroyed; the resulting pest outbreaks must then be controlled with further pesticide applications. The development of pesticide resistance in pest populations requires farmers to use more pesticides and more expensive controls. Because large numbers of honeybees and wild bees are poisoned by pesticides, crop pollination is often reduced. Some pesticides, especially when applied by aircraft, drift into adjacent agricultural lands and destroy crops and trees. Drift and runoff of pesticides also cause substantial fishery and wildlife losses.

The costs associated with environmental and health damage are estimated to be $1 billion (Pimentel et al., 1980a). Obviously, this assessment is oversimplified and incomplete. In fact, there is no satisfactory way to estimate the environmental health and social costs associated with pesticide use. It is impossible, for example, to place an acceptable monetary value on human fatalities, diseases, and disabilities resulting from pesticide use. It is also impossible to place a monetary value on environmental losses. If we accept $1 billion as a minimum estimate of environmental costs, and we assume that reducing pesticide use by half might also reduce the environmental and public health risks from pesticides, then the added costs for the nonchemical alternatives (about $1 billion) would be somewhat offset by reduced environmental and public health risks.

Clearly, pesticides provide benefits but also cause serious public health problems and considerable damage to agricultural and natural ecosystems. Choosing a pest management program involves economics, ecology, and ethics. As a first step in mending the broken circle, I propose that current U.S. pesticide use be reduced by 50 percent. Such a step is economically feasible, would have little effect on food productivity, would cause but a slight rise in food prices, and would move us toward the ethically desirable goals of reducing environmental damage and undesirable health effects.

ENVIRONMENTAL VALUES   III

6 ENVIRONMENTAL ETHICS: VALUES IN AND DUTIES TO THE NATURAL WORLD

Environmental ethics stretches classical ethics to the breaking point. All ethics seeks an appropriate respect for life. But we do not need just a humanistic ethic applied to the environment as we have needed one for business, law, medicine, technology, international development, or nuclear disarmament. Respect for life does demand an ethic concerned about human welfare, an ethic like the others and now applied to the environment. But environmental ethics in a deeper sense stands on a frontier, as radically theoretical as it is applied. It alone asks whether there can be nonhuman objects of duty.

Neither theory nor practice elsewhere needs values outside of human subjects, but environmental ethics must be more biologically objective—nonanthropocentric. It challenges the separation of science and ethics, trying to reform a science that finds nature value-free and an ethics that assumes that only humans count morally. Environmental ethics seeks to escape relativism in ethics, to discover a way past culturally based ethics. However much our worldviews, ethics included, are embedded in our cultural heritages, and thereby theory-laden and value-laden, all of us know that a natural world exists apart from human cultures. Humans interact with nature. Environmental ethics is the only ethics that breaks out of culture. It

Holmes Rolston III

has to evaluate nature, both wild nature and the nature that mixes with culture, and to judge duty thereby. After accepting environmental ethics, you will no longer be the humanist you once were.

Environmental ethics requires risk. It explores poorly charted terrain, where one can easily get lost. One must hazard the kind of insight that first looks like foolishness. Some people approach environmental ethics with a smile—expecting chicken liberation and rights for rocks, misplaced concern for chipmunks and daisies. Elsewhere, they think, ethicists deal with sober concerns: medical ethics, business ethics, justice in public affairs, questions of life and death and of peace and war. But the questions here are no less serious: The degradation of the environment poses as great a threat to life as nuclear war, and a more probable tragedy.

Higher Animals

Logically and psychologically, the best and easiest breakthrough past the traditional boundaries of interhuman ethics is made when confronting higher animals. Animals defend their lives; they have a good of their own and suffer pains and pleasures like ourselves. Human moral concern should at least cross over into the domain of animal experience. This boundary crossing is also dangerous because if made only psychologically and not biologically, the would-be environmental ethicist may be too disoriented to travel further. The promised environmental ethics will degenerate into a mammalian ethics. We certainly need an ethic for animals, but that is only one level of concern in a comprehensive environmental ethics.

One might expect classical ethics to have sifted well an ethics for animals. Our ancestors did not think about endangered species, ecosystems, acid rain, or the ozone layer, but they lived in closer association with wild and domestic animals than we do. Hunters track wounded deer; ranchers who let their horses starve are prosecuted. Still, until recently, the scientific, humanistic centuries since the so-called Enlightenment have not been sensitive ones for animals, owing to the Cartesian legacy. Animals were mindless, living matter; biology has been mechanistic. Even psychology, rather than defending animal experience, has been behaviorist. Philosophy has protested little, concerned instead with locating values in human experiences at the same time that it disspirited and devalued nature. Across several centuries of hard science and humanistic ethics there has been little compassion for animals.

The progress of science itself smeared the human-nonhuman boundary line. Animal anatomy, biochemistry, cognition, perception, experience, behavior, and evolutionary history are kin to our own. Animals have no immortal souls, but then persons may not either, or beings with souls may not be the only kind that count morally. Ethical progress further smeared the boundary. Sensual pleasures are a good thing; ethics should be egalitarian, nonarbitrary, nondiscriminatory. There are ample scientific grounds that animals enjoy pleasures and suffer pains; and ethically there are no grounds to value these sensations in humans and not in animals. So there has been a vigorous reassessment of human duties to sentient life. The world cheered in the fall of 1988 when humans rescued two whales from winter ice.

"Respect their right to life": A sign in Rocky Mountain National Park enjoins humans not to harass bighorn sheep. "The question is not, Can they reason, nor Can they talk? but, Can they suffer?" wrote Jeremy Bentham (1948 [1789]), insisting that animal welfare counts too. The Park Service sign and Bentham's question increase sensitivity by extending rights and hedonist goods to animals. The gain is a vital breakthrough past humans, and the first lesson in environmental ethics has been learned. But the risk is a moral extension that expands rights as far as mammals and not much further, a psychologically based ethic that counts only felt experience. We respect life in our nonhuman but near-human animal cousins, a semianthropic and still quite subjective ethics. Justice remains a concern for just-us subjects. There has, in fact, not been much of a theoretical breakthrough, no paradigm shift.

Lacking that, we are left with anomaly and conceptual strain. When we try to use culturally extended rights and psychologically based utilities to protect the flora or even the insentient fauna, to protect endangered species or ecosystems, we can only stammer. Indeed, we get lost trying to protect bighorns, because, in the wild, cougars are not respecting the rights or utilities of the sheep they slay, and, in culture, humans slay sheep and eat them regularly, while humans have every right not to be eaten by either humans or cougars. There are no rights in the wild, and nature is indifferent to the welfare of particular animals. A bison fell through the ice into a river in Yellowstone Park; the environmental ethic there, letting nature take its course, forbade would-be rescuers from either saving or killing the suffering animal to put it out of its misery. A drowning human would have been saved at once. Perhaps it was a mistake to save those whales.

The ethics by extension now seems too nondiscriminating; we are unable to separate an ethics for humans from an ethics for wildlife. To treat wild animals with compassion learned in culture does not appreciate their wildness. Man, said Socrates, is the political animal; humans maximally are what they are in culture, where the natural selection pressures (impressively productive in ecosystems) are relaxed without detriment to the species *Homo sapiens*, and indeed with great benefit to its member persons. Wild animals cannot enter culture; they do not have that capacity. They cannot acquire language at sufficient levels to take part in culture; they cannot make their clothing or build fires, much less read books or receive an education. Animals can, by human adoption, receive some of the protections of culture, which happens when we domesticate them, but neither pets nor food animals enter the culture that shelters them.

Worse, such cultural protection can work to their detriment; their wildness is made over into a human artifact as food or pet animal. A cow does not have the integrity of a deer, or a poodle that of a wolf. Culture is a good thing for humans but often a bad thing for animals. Their biology and ecology—neither justice nor charity, nor rights nor welfare—provide the benchmark for an ethics.

Culture does make a relevant ethical difference, and environmental ethics has different criteria from interhuman ethics. Can they talk? and, Can they reason?—indicating cultural capacities—are relevant questions; not just, Can they suffer? *Equality* is a positive word in ethics, *discriminatory* a pejorative one. On the other hand, simplistic reduction is a failing in the philosophy of science and epistemology; to be "discriminating" is desirable in logic and value theory. Something about treating humans as equals with bighorns and cougars seems to "reduce" humans to merely animal levels of value, a "no more than" counterpart in ethics of the "nothing but" fallacy often met in science. Humans are "nothing but" naked apes. Something about treating sheep and cougars as the equals of humans seems to elevate them unnaturally and not to value them for what they are. There is something insufficiently discriminating in such judgments; they are species-blind in a bad sense, blind to the real differences between species, valuational differences that do count morally. To the contrary, a discriminating ethicist will insist on preserving the differing richness of valuational complexity, wherever found. Compassionate respect for life in its suffering is only part of the analysis.

Two tests of discrimination are pains and diet. It might be thought that pain is a bad thing, whether in nature or culture. Perhaps when dealing with humans in culture, additional levels of value and utility must be protected by conferring rights that do not exist in the wild, but meanwhile we should at least minimize animal suffering. That is indeed a worthy imperative in culture where animals are removed from nature and bred, but it may be misguided where animals remain in ecosystems. When the bighorn sheep of Yellowstone caught pinkeye, they were blinded, injured, and starving as a result, and three hundred of them, more than half the herd, perished. Wildlife veterinarians wanted to treat the disease, as they would have in any domestic herd, and as they did with Colorado bighorns infected with an introduced lungworm, but the Yellowstone ethicists left the animals to suffer, seemingly not respecting their life.

Had those ethicists no mercy? They knew rather that, although intrinsic pain is a bad thing whether in humans or in sheep, pain in ecosystems is instrumental pain, through which the sheep are naturally selected for a more satisfactory adaptive fit. Pain in a medically skilled culture is pointless, once the alarm to health is sounded, but pain operates functionally in bighorns in their niche, even after it becomes no longer in the interests of the pained individual. To have interfered in the interests of the blinded sheep would have weakened the species. Even the question, Can they suffer? is not as simple as Bentham thought. What we ought to do depends on what is. The *is* of nature differs significantly from the *is* of culture, even when similar suffering is present in both.

At this point some ethicists will insist that at least in culture we can minimize animal pain, and that will constrain our diet. There is predation in nature; humans evolved as omnivores. But humans, the only moral animals, should refuse to participate in the meat-eating phase of their ecology, just as they refuse to play the game merely by the rules of natural selection. Humans do not look to the behavior of wild animals as an ethical guide in other matters (marriage, truth telling, promise keeping, justice, charity). Why should they justify their dietary habits by watching what animals do?

But the difference is that these other matters are affairs of culture; these are person-to-person events, not events at all in spontaneous nature. By contrast, eating is omnipresent in wild nature; humans eat because they are in nature, not because they are in culture. Eating animals is not an event between persons but a human-to-animal event; and the rules for this act come from the ecosystems in which humans evolved and have no duty to remake. Humans, then, can model their dietary habits from their ecosystems, though they cannot and should not so model their interpersonal justice or charity. When eating, they ought to minimize animal suffering, but they have no duty to revise trophic pyramids whether in nature or culture. The boundary between animals and humans has not been rubbed out after all; only what was a boundary line has been smeared into a boundary zone. We have discovered that animals count morally, though we have not yet solved the challenge of how to count them.

Animals enjoy psychological lives, subjective experiences, the satisfaction of felt interests—intrinsic values that count morally when humans encounter them. But the pains, pleasures, interests, and welfare of individual animals are only one of the considerations in a more complex environmental ethics that cannot be reached by conferring rights on them or by a hedonist calculus, however far extended. We have to travel further into a more biologically based ethics.

Organisms

If we are to respect all life, we have still another boundary to cross, from zoology to botany, from sentient to insentient life. In Yosemite National Park for almost a century humans entertained themselves by driving through a tunnel cut in a giant sequoia. Two decades ago the Wawona tree, weakened by the cut, blew down in a storm. People said, "Cut us another drive-through sequoia." The Yosemite environmental ethic, deepening over the years, answered, "No. You ought not to mutilate majestic sequoias for amusement. Respect their life." Indeed, some ethicists count the value of redwoods so highly that they will spike redwoods, lest they be cut. In the Rawah Wilderness in alpine Colorado, old signs read, "Please leave the flowers for others to enjoy." When the signs rotted out, new signs urged a less humanist ethic: "Let the flowers live!"

But trees and flowers cannot care, so why should we? We are not considering animals that are close kin, nor can they suffer or experience anything. Plants are not valuers with preferences that can be satisfied or frustrated. It seems odd to assert that plants need our sympathy, odd to ask that we should consider their point of view. They have no subjective life, only objective life.

Perhaps the questions are wrong, because they are coming out of the old paradigm. We are at a critical divide. That is why I earlier warned that environmental ethicists who seek only to extend a humanistic ethic to mammalian cousins will get lost. Seeing no moral landmarks, those ethicists may turn back to more familiar terrain. Afraid of the naturalistic fallacy, they will say that people should enjoy letting flowers live or that it is silly to cut drive-through sequoias, that it is aesthetically more excellent for humans to appreciate both for what they are. But these ethically conservative reasons really do not understand what biological conservation is in the deepest sense.

It takes ethical courage to go on, to move past a hedonistic, humanistic logic to a bio-logic. Pains, pleasures, and psychological experience will no further be useful categories, but—lest some think that from here on I as a philosopher become illogical and lose all ethical sense—let us orient ourselves by extending logical, propositional, cognitive, and normative categories into biology. Nothing matters to a tree, but much is vital to it.

An organism is a spontaneous, self-maintaining system, sustaining and reproducing itself, executing its program, making a way through the world, checking against performance by means of responsive capacities with which to measure success. It can reckon with vicissitudes, opportunities, and adversities that the world presents. Something more than physical causes, even when less than sentience, is operating within every organism. There is information superintending the causes; without it, the organism would collapse into a sand heap. This information is a modern equivalent of what Aristotle called formal and final causes; it gives the organism a telos, or end, a kind of (nonfelt) goal. Organisms have ends, although not always ends in view.

All this cargo is carried by the DNA, essentially a linguistic molecule. By a serial reading of the DNA, a polypeptide chain is synthesized, such that its sequential structure determines the bioform into which it will fold. Ever-lengthening chains are organized into genes, as ever-longer sentences are organized into paragraphs and chapters. Diverse proteins, lipids, carbohydrates, enzymes—all the life structures—are written into the genetic library. The DNA is thus a logical set, not less than a biological set, and is informed as well as formed. Organisms use a sort of symbolic logic, using these molecular shapes as symbols of life. The novel resourcefulness lies in the epistemic content conserved, developed, and thrown forward to make biological resources out of the physicochemical sources. This executive steering core is cybernetic—partly a special kind of cause-and-effect system and partly something more. It is partly a historical information system discovering and evaluating ends so as to map and make a way through the world, and partly a system of significances attached to operations, pursuits, and resources. In this sense, the genome is a set of conservation molecules.

The genetic set is really a propositional set—to choose a provocative term—recalling that the Latin *propositum* is an assertion, a set task, a theme, a plan, a proposal, a project, as well as a cognitive statement. From this, it is also a motivational set, unlike human books, because these life motifs are set to drive the movement from genotypic potential to phenotypic expression. Given a chance, these molecules seek organic self-expression. They thus proclaim a lifeway; and with this an organism, unlike an inert rock, claims the environment as source and sink, from which to abstract energy and materials and into which to excrete them. It takes advantage of its environment. Life thus arises out of earthen sources (as do rocks), but life (unlike rocks) turns back on its sources to make resources out of them. An acorn becomes an oak; the oak stands on its own.

So far we have only description. We begin to pass to value when we recognize that the genetic set is a normative set; it distinguishes between what is and what ought to be. This does not mean that the organism is a moral system, for there are no moral agents in nature; but the organism is an axiological, evaluative system. So the oak grows, reproduces, repairs its wounds, and resists death. The physical state that the organism seeks, idealized in its programmatic form, is a valued state. Value is present in this achievement. *Vital* seems a better word here than *biological*. We are dealing not simply with another individual defending its solitary life but with an individual having situated fitness in an ecosystem. Still, we want to affirm that the living individual, taken as a point-experience in the web of interconnected life, is per se an intrinsic value.

A life is defended for what it is in itself, without necessary further contributory reference, although, given the structure of all ecosystems, such lives necessarily do have further contributory reference. The organism has something it is conserving, something for which it is standing: its life. Though organisms must fit into their niche, they have their own standards. They promote their own realization, at the same time that they track an environment. They have a technique, a know-how. Every organism has a good of its kind; it defends its own kind as a good kind. In that sense, as soon as one knows what a giant sequoia tree is, one knows the biological identity that is sought and conserved.

There seems no reason why such own-standing normative organisms are not morally significant. A moral agent deciding his or her behavior ought to take account of the consequences for other evaluative systems. Within the community of moral agents, one has not merely to ask whether x is a normative system but also, because the norms are at personal option, to judge the norm. But within the biotic community, organisms are amoral normative systems, and there are no cases in which an organism seeks a good of its own that is morally reprehensible. The distinction between having a good of its kind and being a good kind vanishes, so far as any faulting of the organism is concerned. To this extent, everything with a good of its kind is a good kind and thereby has intrinsic value.

One might say that an organism is a bad organism if, during the course of pressing its normative expression, it upsets the ecosystem or causes widespread disease. Remember, though, that an organism cannot be a good kind without situated environmental fitness. By natural selection the kind of goods to which it is genetically programmed must mesh with its ecosystemic role. In spite of the ecosystem as a perpetual contest of goods in dialectic and exchange, it is difficult to say that any organism is a bad kind in this instrumental sense either. The misfits are extinct, or soon will be. In spontaneous nature any species that preys upon, parasitizes, competes with, or crowds another will be a bad kind from the narrow perspective of its victim or competitor.

But if we enlarge that perspective, we typically have difficulty in saying that any species is a bad kind overall in the ecosystem. An "enemy" may even be good for the "victimized" species, though harmful to individual members of it, as when predation keeps the deer herd healthy. Beyond this, the "bad kinds" typically play useful roles in population control, in symbiotic relationships, or in providing opportunities for other species. The *Chlamydia* microbe is a bad kind from the perspective of the bighorns, but when one thing dies, something else lives. After the pinkeye outbreak among the bighorns, the golden eagle population in Yellowstone flourished, preying on the bighorn carcasses. For the eagles, *Chlamydia* is a good kind instrumentally.

Some biologist-philosophers will say that even though an organism evolves to have a situated environmental fitness, not all such situations are good arrangements; some can be clumsy or bad. True, the vicissitudes of historical evolution do sometimes result in ecological webs that are suboptimal solutions, within the biologically limited possibilities and powers of interacting organisms. Still, such systems have been selected over millennia for functional stability, and at least the burden of proof is on a human evaluator to say why any natural kind is a bad kind and ought not to call forth admiring respect. Something may be a good kind intrinsically but a bad kind instrumentally in the system; such cases will be anomalous however, with selection pressures against them. These assertions about good kinds do not say that things are perfect kinds or that there can be no better ones, only that natural kinds are good kinds until proven otherwise.

In fact, what is almost invariably meant by a bad kind is an organism that is instrumentally bad when judged from the viewpoint of human interests, often with the further complication that human interests have disrupted natural systems. *Bad* as so used is an anthropocentric word; there is nothing at all biological or ecological about it, and so it has no force in evaluating objective nature, however much humanistic force it may sometimes have.

A vital ethic respects all life, not just animal pains and pleasures, much less just human preferences. The old signs in the Rawah Wilderness—"Please leave the flowers for others to enjoy"—were application signs using an old, ethically conservative, humanistic ethic. The new ones invite a change of reference frame—a wilder ethic that is more logical because it is more biological, a radical ethic that goes down to the roots of life, that really is conservative because it understands biological conservation at depths. What the injunction "Let the flowers live!" means is this: "Daisies, marsh marigolds, geraniums, and larkspurs are evaluative systems that conserve goods of their kind and, in the absence of evidence to the contrary, are good kinds. There are trails here by which you may enjoy these flowers. Is there any reason why your human interests should not also conserve these good kinds?" A drive-through sequoia causes no suffering; it is not cruel. But it is callous and insensitive to the wonder of life.

Species

Sensitivity to the wonder of life, however, can sometimes make an environmental ethicist seem callous. On San Clemente Island, the U.S. Fish and Wildlife Service and the Natural Resource Office of the U.S. Navy planned to shoot two thousand feral goats to save three endangered plant species (*Malacothamnus clementinus*, *Castilleja grisea*, and *Delphinium kinkiense*), of which the surviving individuals numbered only a few dozen. After a protest, some goats were trapped and relocated. But trapping all of them was impossible, and many thousands were killed. In this instance, the survival of plant species was counted more than the lives of individual mammals; a few plants counted more than many thousands of goats.

Those who wish to restore rare species of big cats to the wild have asked about killing genetically inbred, inferior cats presently held in zoos, in order to make space available for the cats needed to reconstruct and maintain a population that is genetically more likely to survive upon release. All the Siberian tigers in zoos in North America are descendants of seven animals; if these tigers were replaced by others nearer to the wild type and with more genetic variability, the species might be saved in the wild. When we move to the level of species, sometimes we decide to kill individuals for the good of their kind.

Or we might now refuse to let nature take its course. The Yellowstone ethicists let the bison drown, in spite of its suffering; they let the blinded bighorns die. But in the spring of 1984 a sow grizzly and her three cubs walked across the ice of Yellowstone Lake to Frank Island, two miles from shore. They stayed several days to feast on two elk carcasses, and the ice bridge melted. Soon afterward, they were starving on an island too small to support them. This time the Yellowstone ethicists promptly rescued the grizzlies and released them on the mainland, in order to protect an endangered species. They were not rescuing individual bears so much as saving the species.

Coloradans have declined to build the Two Forks Dam to supply urban Denver with water. Building the dam would require destroying a canyon and altering the Platte River flow, with many negative environmental consequences, including further endangering the whooping crane and endangering a butterfly, the Pawnee montane skipper. Elsewhere in the state, water development threatens several fish species, including the humpback chub, which requires the turbulent spring run-off stopped by dams. Environmental ethics doubts whether the good of humans who wish more water for development, both for industry and for bluegrass lawns, warrants endangering species of cranes, butterflies, and fish.

A species exists; a species ought to exist. An environmental ethics must make these assertions and move from biology to ethics with care. Species exist only instantiated in individuals, yet they are as real as individual plants or animals. The assertion that there are specific forms of life historically maintained in their environments over time seems as certain as anything else we believe about the empirical world. At times biologists revise the theories and taxa with which they map these forms, but species are not so much like lines of latitude and longitude as like mountains and rivers, phenomena objectively there to be mapped. The edges of these natural kinds will sometimes be fuzzy, to some extent discretionary. One species will slide into another over evolutionary time. But it does not follow from the fact that speciation is sometimes in progress that species are merely made up and not found as evolutionary lines with identity in time as well as space.

A consideration of species is revealing and challenging because it offers a biologically based counterexample to the focus on individuals—typically sentient and usually persons—so characteristic in classical ethics. In an evolutionary ecosystem, it is not mere individuality that counts; the species is also significant because it is a dynamic life-form maintained over time. The individual represents (re-presents) a species in each new generation. It is a token of a type, and the type is more important than the token.

A species lacks moral agency, reflective self-awareness, sentience, or organic individuality. The older, conservative ethic will be tempted to say that specific-level processes cannot count morally. Duties must attach to singular lives, most evidently those with a self, or some analogue to self. In an individual organism, the organs report to a center; the good of a whole is defended. The members of a species report to no center. A species has no self. It is not a bounded singular. There is no analogue to the nervous hookups or circulatory flows that characterize the organism.

But singularity, centeredness, selfhood, and individuality are not the only processes to which duty attaches. A more radically conservative ethic knows that having a biological identity reasserted genetically over time is as true of the species as of the individual. Identity need not attach solely to the centered organism; it can persist as a discrete pattern over time. From this way of thinking, it follows that the life the individual has is something passing through the individual as much as something it intrinsically possesses. The individual is subordinate to the species, not the other way around. The genetic set, in which is coded the telos, is as evidently the property of the species as of the individual through which it passes. A consideration of species strains any ethic fixed on individual organisms, much less on sentience or persons. But the result can be biologically sounder, though it revises what was formerly thought logically permissible or ethically binding. When ethics is informed by this kind of biology, it is appropriate to attach duty dynamically to the specific form of life.

The species line is the vital living system, the whole, of which individual organisms are the essential parts. The species too has its integrity, its individuality, its right to life (if we must use the rhetoric of rights); and it is more important to protect this vitality than to protect individual integrity. The right to life, biologically speaking, is an adaptive fit that is right for life, that survives over millennia. This idea generates at least a presumption that species in a niche are good right where they are, and therefore that it is right for humans to let them be, to let them evolve.

Processes of value that we earlier found in an organic individual reappear at the specific level: defending a particular form of life, pursuing a pathway through the world, resisting death (extinction), regenerating, maintaining a normative identity over time, expressing creative resilience by discovering survival skills. It is as logical to say that the individual is the species' way of propagating itself as to say that the embryo or egg is the individual's way of propagating itself. The dignity resides in the dynamic form; the individual inherits this form, exemplifies it, and passes it on. If, at the specific level, these processes are just as evident, or even more so, what prevents duties from arising at that level? The appropriate survival unit is the appropriate level of moral concern.

A shutdown of the life stream is the most destructive event possible. The wrong that humans are doing, or allowing to happen through carelessness, is stopping the historical vitality of life, the flow of natural kinds. Every extinction is an incremental decay in this stopping of life, no small thing. Every extinction is a kind of superkilling. It kills forms (species) beyond individuals. It kills essences beyond existences, the soul as well as the body. It kills collectively, not just distributively. It kills birth as well as death. Afterward nothing of that kind either lives or dies.

Ought species x to exist? is a distributive increment in the collective question, ought life on Earth to exist? Life on Earth cannot exist without its individuals, but a lost individual is always reproducible; a lost species is never reproducible. The answer to the species question is not always the same as the answer to the collective question, but because life on Earth is an aggregate of many species, the two are sufficiently related that the burden of proof lies with those who wish deliberately to extinguish a species and simultaneously to care for life on Earth.

One form of life has never endangered so many others. Never before has this level of question—superkilling by a superkiller—been deliberately faced. Humans have more understanding than ever of the natural world they inhabit and of the speciating processes, more predictive power to foresee the intended and unintended results of their actions, and more power to reverse the undesirable consequences. The duties that such power and vision generate no longer attach simply to individuals or persons but are emerging duties to specific forms of life. What is ethically callous is the maelstrom of killing and insensitivity to forms of life and the sources producing them. What is required is principled responsibility to the biospheric Earth.

Human activities seem misfit in the system. Although humans are maximizing their own species interests, and in this respect behaving as does each of the other species, they do not have any adaptive fitness. They are not really fitting into the evolutionary processes of ongoing biological conservation and elaboration. Their cultures are not really dynamically stable in their ecosystems. Such behavior is therefore not right. Yet humanistic ethical systems limp when they try to prescribe right conduct here. They seem misfits in the roles most recently demanded of them.

If, in this world of uncertain moral convictions, it makes any sense to assert that one ought not to kill individuals without justification, it makes more sense to assert that one ought not to superkill the species without superjustification. Several billion years' worth of creative toil, several million species of teeming life, have been handed over to the care of this late-coming species in which mind has flowered and morals have emerged. Ought not this sole moral species do something less self-interested than count all the produce of an evolutionary ecosystem as nothing but human resources? Such an attitude hardly seems biologically informed, much less ethically adequate. It is too provincial for intelligent humanity. Life on Earth is a many-splendored thing; extinction dims its luster. An ethics of respect for life is urgent at the level of species.

Ecosystems

A species is what it is where it is. No environmental ethics has found its way on Earth until it finds an ethic for the biotic communities in which all destinies are entwined. "A thing is right," urged Aldo Leopold (1968 [1949]), "when it tends to preserve the integrity, stability, and beauty of the biotic community. It is wrong when it tends otherwise." Again, we have two parts to the ethic: first, that ecosystems exist, both in the wild and in support of culture; second, that ecosystems ought to exist, both for what they are in themselves and as modified by culture. Again, we must move with care from the biological assertions to the ethical assertions.

Giant forest fires raged over Yellowstone National Park in the summer of 1988, consuming nearly a million acres despite the efforts of a thousand fire fighters. By far the largest ever known in the park, the fires seemed a disaster. But the Yellowstone land ethic enjoined: "Let nature take its course; let it burn." So the fires were not fought at first, but in midsummer, national authorities overrode that policy and ordered the fires put out. Even then, weeks later, fires continued to burn, partly because they were too big to control but partly too because Yellowstone personnel did not really want the fires put out. Despite the evident destruction of trees, shrubs, and wildlife, they believe that fires are a good thing—even when the elk and bison leave the park in search of food and are shot by hunters. Fires reset succession, release nutrients, recycle materials, and renew the biotic community. (Nearby, in the Teton wilderness, a storm blew down fifteen thousand acres of trees, and some people proposed that the area be declassified from wilderness to allow commercial salvage of the timber. But a similar environmental ethic said, "No, let it rot.")

Aspen are important in the Yellowstone ecosystem. Although some aspen stands are climax and self-renewing, many are seral and give way to conifers. Aspen groves support many birds and much wildlife, especially beavers, whose activities maintain the riparian zones. Aspen are rejuvenated after fires, and the Yellowstone land ethic wants the aspen for their critical role in the biotic community. Elk browse the young aspen stems. To a degree this is a good thing, because it provides the elk with critical nitrogen, but in excess it is a bad thing. The elk have no predators, because the wolves are gone, and as a result the elk overpopulate. Excess elk also destroy the willows, and that destruction in turn destroys the beavers. So, in addition to letting fires burn, rejuvenating the aspen might require park managers to cull hundreds of elk—all for the sake of a healthy ecosystem.

The Yellowstone ethic wishes to restore wolves to the greater Yellowstone ecosystem. At the level of species, this change is desired because of what the wolf is in itself, but it is also desired because the greater Yellowstone ecosystem does not have its full integrity, stability, and beauty without this majestic animal at the top of the trophic pyramid. Restoring the wolf as a top predator would mean suffering and death for many elk, but that would be a good thing for the aspen and willows, the beavers, and the riparian habitat and would have mixed benefits for the bighorns and mule deer (the overpopulating elk consume their food, but the sheep and deer would also be consumed by the wolves). Restoration of wolves would be done over the protests of ranchers who worry about wolves eating their cattle; many of them also believe that the wolf is a bloodthirsty killer, a bad kind. Nevertheless, the Yellowstone ethic demands wolves, as it does fires, in appropriate respect for life in its ecosystem.

Letting nature take its ecosystemic course is why the Yellowstone ethic forbade rescuing the drowning bison but required rescuing the sow grizzly and her cubs, the latter case to insure that the big predators remain. After the bison drowned, coyotes, foxes, magpies, and ravens fed on the carcass. Later, even a grizzly bear fed on it. All this is a good thing because the system cycles on. On that account, rescuing the whales trapped in the winter ice seems less of a good thing, when we note that rescuers had to drive away polar bears that attempted to eat the dying whales.

Classical, humanistic ethics finds ecosystems to be unfamiliar territory. It is difficult to get the biology right and, superimposed on the biology, to get the ethics right. Fortunately, it is often evident that human welfare depends on ecosystemic support, and in this sense all our legislation about clean air, clean water, soil conservation, national and state forest policies, pollution controls, renewable resources, and so forth is concerned about ecosystem-level processes. Furthermore, humans find much of value in preserving wild ecosystems, and our wilderness and park system is impressive.

Still, a comprehensive environmental ethics needs the best, naturalistic reasons, as well as the good, humanistic ones, for respecting ecosystems. Ecosystems generate and support life, keep selection pressures high, enrich situated fitness, and allow congruent kinds to evolve in their places with sufficient containment. The ecologist finds that ecosystems are objectively satisfactory communities in the sense that organismic needs are sufficiently met for species to survive and flourish, and the critical ethicist finds (in a subjective judgment matching the objective process) that such ecosystems are satisfactory communities to which to attach duty. Our concern must be for the fundamental unit of survival.

An ecosystem, the conservative ethicist will say, is too low a level of organization to be respected intrinsically. Ecosystems can seem little more than random, statistical processes. A forest can seem a loose collection of externally related parts, the collection of fauna and flora a jumble, hardly a community. The plants and animals within an ecosystem have needs, but their interplay can seem simply a matter of distribution and abundance, birth rates and death rates, population densities, parasitism and predation, dispersion, checks and balances, and stochastic process. Much is not organic at all (rain, groundwater, rocks, soil particles, air), and some organic material is dead and decaying debris (fallen trees, scat, humus). These things have no organized needs. There is only catch-as-catch-can scrimmage for nutrients and energy, not really enough of an integrated process to call the whole a community.

Unlike higher animals, ecosystems have no experiences; they do not and cannot care. Unlike plants, an ecosystem has no organized center, no genome. It does not defend itself against injury or death. Unlike a species, there is no ongoing telos, no biological identity reinstantiated over time. The organismic parts are more complex than the community whole. More troublesome still, an ecosystem can seem a jungle where the fittest survive, a place of contest and conflict, beside which the organism is a model of cooperation. In animals the heart, liver, muscles, and brain are tightly integrated, as are the leaves, cambium, and roots in plants. But the so-called ecosystem community is pushing and shoving between rivals, each aggrandizing itself, or else seems to be all indifference and haphazard juxtaposition—nothing to call forth our admiration.

Environmental ethics must break through the boundary posted by disoriented ontological conservatives, who hold that only organisms are real, actually existing as entities, whereas ecosystems are nominal—just interacting individuals. Oak trees are real, but forests are nothing but collections of trees. But any level is real if it shapes behavior on the level below it. Thus the cell is real because that pattern shapes the behavior of amino acids; the organism, because that pattern coordinates the behavior of hearts and lungs. The biotic community is real because the niche shapes the morphology of the oak trees within it. Being real at the level of community requires only an organization that shapes the behavior of its members.

The challenge is to find a clear model of community and to discover an ethics for it: better biology for better ethics. Even before the rise of ecology, biologists began to conclude that the combative survival of the fittest distorts the truth. The more perceptive model is coaction in adapted fit. Predator and prey, parasite and host, grazer and grazed, are contending forces in dynamic process in which the well-being of each is bound up with the other—coordinated as much as heart and liver are coordinated organically. The ecosystem supplies the coordinates through which each organism moves, outside which the species cannot really be located.

The community connections are looser than the organism's internal interconnections but are not less significant. Admiring organic unity in organisms and stumbling over environmental looseness is like valuing mountains and despising valleys. The matrix that the organism requires to survive is the open, pluralistic ecological system. Internal complexity—heart, liver, muscles, brain—arises as a way of dealing with a complex, tricky environment. The skin-out processes are not just the support; they are the subtle source of the skin-in processes. In the complete picture, the outside is as vital as the inside. Had there been either simplicity or lockstep concentrated unity in the environment, no organismic unity could have evolved. Nor would it remain. There would be less elegance in life.

To look at one level for what is appropriate at another makes a mistake in categories. One should not look for a single center or program in ecosystems, much less for subjective experiences. Instead, one should look for a matrix, for interconnections between centers (individual plants and animals, dynamic lines of speciation), for creative stimulus and open-ended potential. Everything will be connected to many other things, sometimes by obligate associations but more often by partial and pliable dependencies, and, among other things, there will be no significant interactions. There will be functions in a communal sense: shunts and crisscrossing pathways, cybernetic subsystems and feedback loops. An order arises spontaneously and systematically when many self-concerned units jostle and seek to fulfill their own programs, each doing its own thing and forced into informed interaction.

An ecosystem is a productive, projective system. Organisms defend only their selves, with individuals defending their continuing survival and with species increasing the numbers of kinds. But the evolutionary ecosystem spins a bigger story, limiting each kind, locking it into the welfare of others, promoting new arrivals, increasing kinds and the integration of kinds. Species increase their kind, but ecosystems increase kinds, superposing the latter increase onto the former. Ecosystems are selective systems, as surely as organisms are selective systems. The natural selection comes out of the system and is imposed on the individual. The individual is programmed to make more of its kind, but more is going on systemically than that; the system is making more kinds.

Communal processes—the competition between organisms, statistically probable interactions, plant and animal successions, speciation over historical time—generate an ever-richer community. Hence the evolutionary toil, elaborating and diversifying the biota, that once began with no species and results today in five million species, increasing over time the quality of lives in the upper rungs of the trophic pyramids. One-celled organisms evolved into many-celled, highly integrated organisms. Photosynthesis evolved and came to support locomotion— swimming, walking, running, flight. Stimulus-response mechanisms became complex instinctive acts. Warm-blooded animals followed cold-blooded ones. Complex nervous systems, conditioned behavior, and learning emerged. Sentience appeared—sight, hearing, smell, taste, pleasure, pain. Brains coupled with hands. Consciousness and self-consciousness arose. Culture was superposed on nature.

These developments do not take place in all ecosystems or at every level. Microbes, plants, and lower animals remain, good of their kinds and, serving continuing roles, good for other kinds. The understories remain occupied. As a result, the quantity of life and its diverse qualities continue—from protozoans to primates to people. There is a push-up, lock-up ratchet effect that conserves the upstrokes and the outreaches. The later we go in time, the more accelerated are the forms at the top of the trophic pyramids, the more elaborated are the multiple trophic pyramids of Earth. There are upward arrows over evolutionary time.

The system is a game with loaded dice, but the loading is a pro-life tendency, not mere stochastic process. Though there is no Nature in the singular, the system has a nature, a loading that pluralizes, putting natures into diverse kinds: $nature_1$, $nature_2$, $nature_3$ . . . $nature_n$. It does so using random elements (in both organisms and communities), but this is a secret of its fertility, producing steadily intensified interdependencies and options. An ecosystem has no head, but it heads toward species diversification, support, and richness. Though not a superorganism, it is a kind of vital field.

Instrumental value uses something as a means to an end; intrinsic value is worthwhile in itself. No warbler eats insects to become food for a falcon; the warbler defends its own life as an end in itself and makes more warblers as it can. A life is defended intrinsically, without further contributory reference. But neither of these traditional terms is satisfactory at the level of the ecosystem. Though it has value *in* itself, the system does not have any value *for* itself. Though it is a value producer, it is not a value owner. We are no longer confronting instrumental value, as though the system were of value instrumentally as a fountain of life. Nor is the question one of intrinsic value, as though the system defended some unified form of life for itself. We have reached something for which we need a third term: systemic value. Duties arise in encounters with the system that projects and protects these member components in biotic community.

Ethical conservatives, in the humanistic sense, will say that ecosystems are of value only because they contribute to human experiences. But that mistakes the last chapter for the whole story, one fruit for the whole plant. Humans count enough to have the right to flourish in ecosystems, but not so much that they have the right to degrade or shut down ecosystems, not at least without a burden of proof that there is an overriding cultural gain. Those who have traveled partway into environmental ethics will say that ecosystems are of value because they contribute to animal experiences or to organismic life. But the really conservative, radical view sees that the stability, integrity, and beauty of biotic communities are what are most fundamentally to be conserved. In a comprehensive ethics of respect for life, we ought to set ethics at the level of ecosystems alongside classical, humanistic ethics.

Value Theory

In practice the ultimate challenge of environmental ethics is the conservation of life on Earth. In principle the ultimate challenge is a value theory profound enough to support that ethics. In nature there is negentropic construction in dialectic with entropic teardown, a process for which we hardly yet have an adequate scientific theory, much less a valuational theory. Yet this is nature's most striking feature, one that ultimately must be valued and of value. In one sense, nature is indifferent to mountains, rivers, fauna, flora, forests, and grasslands. But in another sense, nature has bent toward making and remaking these projects, millions of kinds, for several billion years.

These performances are worth noticing, are remarkable and memorable—and not just because of their tendencies to produce something else; certainly not merely because of their tendency to produce this noticing in certain recent subjects, our human selves. These events are loci of value as products of systemic nature in its formative processes. The splendors of Earth do not simply lie in their roles as human resources, supports of culture, or stimulators of experience. The most plausible account will find some programmatic evolution toward value, and not because it ignores Darwin but because it heeds his principle of natural selection and deploys it into a selection exploring new niches and elaborating kinds, even a selection upslope toward higher values, at least along some trends within some ecosystems. How do we humans come to be charged up with values, if there was and is nothing in nature charging us up so? A systematic environmental ethics does not wish to believe in the special creation of values or in their dumbfounding epigenesis. Let them evolve. Let nature carry value.

The notion that nature is a value carrier is ambiguous. Much depends on a thing's being more or less structurally congenial for the carriage. We value a thing and discover that we are under the sway of its valence, inducing our behavior. It has among its strengths (Latin: *valeo*, "be strong") this capacity to carry value. This potential cannot always be of the empty sort that a glass has for carrying water. It is often pregnant fullness. Some of the values that nature carries are up to us, our assignment. But fundamentally there are powers in nature that move to us and through us.

No value exists without an evaluator. So runs a well-entrenched dogma. Humans clearly evaluate their world; sentient animals may also. But plants cannot evaluate their environment; they have no options and make no choices. A fortiori, species and ecosystems, Earth and Nature, cannot be bona fide evaluators. One can always hang on to the assertion that value, like a tickle or remorse, must be felt to be there. Its *esse* is *percipi*. To be, it must be perceived. Nonsensed value is nonsense. There are no thoughts without a thinker, no percepts without a perceiver, no deeds without a doer, no targets without an aimer.

Such resolute subjectivists cannot be defeated by argument, although they can be driven toward analyticity. That theirs is a retreat to definition is difficult to expose, because they seem to cling so closely to inner experience. They are reporting, on this hand, how values always excite us. They are giving, on that hand, a stipulative definition. That is how they choose to use the word *value*.

If value arrives only with consciousness, experiences in which humans find value have to be dealt with as appearances of various sorts. The value has to be relocated in the valuing subject's creativity as a person meets a valueless world, or even a valuable one—one able to be valued but one that before the human bringing of valuableness contains only possibility and not any actual value. Value can only be extrinsic to nature, never intrinsic to it.

But the valuing subject in an otherwise valueless world is an insufficient premise for the experienced conclusions of those who respect all life. Conversion to a biological view seems truer to world experience and more logically compelling. Something from a world beyond the human mind, beyond human experience, is received into our mind, our experience, and the value of that something does not always arise with our evaluation of it. Here the order of knowing reverses, and also enhances, the order of being. This too is a perspective but is ecologically better-informed. Science has been steadily showing how the consequents (life, mind) are built on their precedents (energy, matter), however much they overleap them. Life and mind appear where they did not before exist, and with them levels of value emerge that did not before exist. But that gives no reason to say that all value is an irreducible emergent at the human (or upper-animal) level. A comprehensive environmental ethics reallocates value across the whole continuum. Value increases in the emergent climax but is continuously present in the composing precedents. The system is value-able, able to produce value. Human evaluators are among its products.

Some value depends on subjectivity, yet all value is generated within the geosystemic and ecosystemic pyramid. Systemically, value fades from subjective to objective value but also fans out from the individual to its role and matrix. Things do not have their separate natures merely in and for themselves, but they face outward and co-fit into broader natures. Value-in-itself is smeared out to become value-in-togetherness. Value seeps out into the system, and we lose our capacity to identify the individual as the sole locus of value.

Intrinsic value, the value of an individual for what it is in itself, becomes problematic in a holistic web. True, the system produces such values more and more with its evolution of individuality and freedom. Yet to decouple this value from the biotic, communal system is to make value too internal and elementary; this decoupling forgets relatedness and externality. Every intrinsic value has leading and trailing *and*'s.

Such value is coupled with value from which it comes and toward which it moves. Adapted fitness makes individualistic value too system-independent. Intrinsic value is a part in a whole and is not to be fragmented by valuing it in isolation.

Everything is good in a role, in a whole, although we can speak of objective intrinsic goodness wherever a point-event—a trillium, for example—defends a good (its life) in itself. We can speak of subjective intrinsic goodness when such an event registers as a point-experience, at which point humans pronounce both their experience and what it is to be good without need to enlarge their focus. Neither the trilliums nor the human judges of it require for their respective valuings any further contributory reference.

When eaten by foragers or in death resorbed into humus, the trillium has its value destroyed, transformed into instrumentality. The system is a value transformer where form and being, process and reality, fact and value, are inseparably joined. Intrinsic and instrumental values shuttle back and forth, parts-in-wholes and wholes-in-parts, local details of value embedded in global structures, gems in their settings, and their setting-situation a corporation where value cannot stand alone. Every good is in community.

In environmental ethics one's beliefs about nature, which are based upon but exceed science, have everything to do with beliefs about duty. The way the world is informs the way it ought to be. We always shape our values in significant measure in accord with our notion of the kind of universe that we live in, and this process drives our sense of duty. Our model of reality implies a model of conduct. Differing models sometimes imply similar conduct, but often they do not. A model in which nature has no value apart from human preferences will imply different conduct from one in which nature projects fundamental values, some objective and others that further require human subjectivity superimposed on objective nature.

This evaluation is not scientific description; hence it is not ecology per se but metaecology. No amount of research can verify that, environmentally, the right is the optimum biotic community. Yet ecological description generates this valuing of nature, endorsing the systemic rightness. The transition from *is* to *good* and thence to *ought* occurs here; we leave science to enter the domain of evaluation, from which an ethics follows.

What is ethically puzzling and exciting is that an *ought* is not so much derived from an *is* as discovered simultaneously with it. As we progress from descriptions of fauna and flora, of cycles and pyramids, of autotrophs coordinated with heterotrophs, of stability and dynamism, on to intricacy, planetary opulence and interdependence, unity and harmony with oppositions in counterpoint and synthesis, organisms evolved within and satisfactorily fitting their communities, and we arrive at length at beauty and goodness, we find that it is difficult to say where the natural facts leave off and where the natural values appear. For some people at least, the sharp *is-ought* dichotomy is gone; the values seem to be there as soon as the facts are fully in, and both values and facts seem to be alike properties of the system.

There is something overspecialized about an ethic, held by the dominant class of *Homo sapiens*, that regards the welfare of only one of several million species as an object and beneficiary of duty. If the remedy requires a paradigm change about the sorts of things to which duty can attach, so much the worse for those humanistic ethics no longer functioning in, or suited to, their changing environment. The anthropocentrism associated with them was fiction anyway. There is something Newtonian, not yet Einsteinian, besides something morally naive, about living in a reference frame in which one species takes itself as absolute and values everything else relative to its utility. If true to its specific epithet, which means wise, ought not *Homo sapiens* value this host of life as something that lays on us a claim to care for life in its own right?

Only the human species contains moral agents, but perhaps conscience on such an Earth ought not to be used to exempt every other form of life from consideration, with the resulting paradox that the sole moral species acts only in its collective self-interest toward all the rest. Is not the ultimate philosophical task the discovery of a whole great ethic that knows the human place under the sun?

POLLUTION AND WASTE   IV

7 THE DISPOSABLE SOCIETY

When some people look into a trash bag, they see things like plastic, paper, metal, and food waste. I see our whole world being thrown away.

Paul H. Connett

It is an astonishing and disturbing fact that since World War II, we have consumed more of the world's finite energy resources than had been consumed by the whole of human history up to World War II (Hubert, 1971). Some people would blame this increase on the growing world population, but when we note that the average U.S. citizen consumes 50 times more steel, 56 times more energy, 170 times more newsprint, 250 times more motor fuel, and 300 times more plastic than the average Indian citizen (Miller, 1988), it is clear that we are looking at overconsumption, as well as overpopulation. Although overpopulation will certainly exacerbate the problem, one could argue that a preoccupation with overpopulation is a convenient way of shifting the ethical issue overseas.

Taken as a whole, the United States, with 4.8 percent of the world's population, consumes about 33 percent of the world's processed energy and mineral resources (Miller, 1988). If we include other industrial powers, 24 percent of the world's population consumes about 80 percent of those resources. Other people have raised the ethical issue of this inequitable use of resources across our globe, but

99

here I would like to raise the ethical issue of the inequitable use of resources across time. A few generations are using up resources that should be spread thin across centuries, if not millennia. It is almost as if we are colonizing the future. Although we can be moved to tears by plays written more than two thousand years ago and symphonies composed two hundred years ago, we hardly blink at depriving future generations of the resources they will need to survive.

Not only do we overconsume, but we also compound the crime by throwing much away. In America, each year we throw away 1.6 billion pens, 2 billion disposable razors, 16 billion diapers, 22 billion plastic grocery bags, and enough office paper to build a twelve-foot-high wall from New York City to Los Angeles (Environmental Defense Fund, 1988; Lichiello and Snyder, 1988; Environmental Protection Agency, 1989). But that's not all we are throwing away to serve our insatiable thirst for consumption. Thousands of animal and plant species are being lost as the rain forests are cut and converted to pasture. Our topsoil is being thrown away through unsound tillage and overreliance on synthetic fertilizers and pesticides. Our small farmers are being thrown away as our chemical manufacturers take over American farming. Our sense of community has been lost to the isolationism of hours and hours in front of the television screen, and our sense of reality is being thrown away to the advertising industry as it sells us a set of dreams and fantasies attached to an endless stream of objects we do not need.

Fortunately, planet earth functions via feedback mechanisms: We can push things only so far before it complains. The complaints ensuing from overconsumption of our resources are coming to us at both the global level and the local level. At the global level the complaints, or warning signals, are taking the form of global warming; damage to the ozone layer; and the buildup of man-made toxic residues in the biota, in our food chains, in our fatty tissues, and in mothers' breast milk. Right now in Germany breast-fed children get one hundred times their so-called allowable daily intake of dioxins and furans (Fürst et al., 1989, and references within; Bailey and Connett, 1990). We can only hope that the safety margins for these standards are sufficiently large for there to be no subtle damage to a child's immune system or other developing tissues.

At the local level, the warning signal is the trash crisis. We are running out of places to dispose of the disposables of our disposable society.

At both the global level and the local level, these warning signals are delivering the same message: We can't run a throwaway society on a finite planet. We were foolish ever to believe that we could. The ethical imperative is clear. We have to stop living as if future generations had another planet to go to. With this ethical imperative in mind, I will discuss the trash crisis that is currently affecting many communities in North America. I will be discussing waste management as if the future mattered.

Making Waste

If the future really mattered to us, we wouldn't be talking about waste management. We would be talking about resource management. Nature makes no waste. We make waste; nature makes soil. One creature's waste is another creature's nutrients. Nature recycles everything, or rather it did until we started to put our synthetic materials into the environment.

We make waste in several ways. Our manufacturers make waste by overusing some materials and misusing others. We, as consumers, make waste by mixing all our discarded materials together. When we mix the smelly with the nonsmelly, everything becomes smelly. When we mix the toxic with the nontoxic, we have to treat the whole mixture as if it were all toxic. And if we mix the useless with the useful, the whole lot becomes practically useless. Moreover, this act of mixing all our discarded materials together creates something else: a very negative attitude toward the mixture, an attitude that is betrayed by the words we use to describe it—*waste, trash, refuse, garbage, rubbish*. This negative attitude predisposes us to want this material out of our lives as quickly as possible, and as far away from us as possible. But as environmentalists have pointed out, there is no "away." The "away" we are using for most of our trash in the United States is landfills. About 80 percent of our household trash is currently going to landfills (Environmental Protection Agency, 1989). But these landfills are causing many problems.

Landfills

Five main types of problems are associated with the disposal of raw waste in landfills. First, we are running out of space to site new landfills, especially near major urban centers. Second, toxic chemicals from households and from industry are leaking out of landfills and getting into surface water and groundwater. Third, many problems are created by putting organic matter such as food and yard waste and other biodegradable materials into landfills. Undesirable animals like rats and gulls feed on this material and multiply. The organic materials are broken down by anaerobic microorganisms into a variety of substances, including the gas methane, some very smelly compounds, and a mixture of organic acids. It is these organic acids that help to leach out the toxics from the rest of the waste. Fourth, raw-waste disposal in landfills presents an ethical problem. Currently, many objects and materials that could be used again are thrown into landfills, thus depriving future generations of these resources. Finally, a political problem is created. People don't want to live near landfills. They don't like the smell, the rats, the dangers, or the traffic. Politicians know that siting new landfills in their district is tantamount to committing political suicide.

Because no strategy of waste management eliminates landfills completely, we must find ways to site new ones or expand old ones. The traditional approach to siting new landfills is to attempt to convince the public that a particular strategy will control what comes out of them. Promoters talk of plastic liners, clay liners, leachate collection and treatment, daily cover, final cover, and capping. The problem is that no one, including the Environmental Protection Agency (*Federal Register,* 1981, 1982), believes that a landfill can be made leakproof. A better approach is to control what goes into the landfill. The most controversial debate in waste management today is the form that such control should take.

Currently, a debate rages over two possible strategies for controlling what goes into a landfill. The high-tech approach is to burn unseparated trash in massive incinerators and bury only the ash residue and noncombustibles in a landfill. The low-tech approach is to separate the trash and bury only what remains after intensive efforts to remove toxics, reuse objects, recycle materials, and compost biodegradables.

Incineration

A complication in the decision-making process in the United States is that the building of trash incinerators has become the biggest boost to construction engineering since the building of nuclear power plants (fig. 7.1). Indeed, a number of major engineering companies that were building nuclear power plants are currently engaged in building trash incinerators.

Trash incineration is also embraced by municipal officials who are

Figure 7.1. Existing (•) and proposed (□) sites of trash incinerators in the northeastern United States. Data are from Environmental Protection Agency (1987) and Kidder and Peabody (1988).

daunted by the task of getting people to separate and recycle their trash. Building trash incinerators seems advantageous because it requires no change in the habits of citizens, waste haulers, or manufacturers. Therein lies the problem with incineration, from an ethical point of view. It represents business as usual, a prop for the disposable society.

Despite the formidable forces promoting incinerators, they have excited intense public opposition. From 1986 through 1990, more than a hundred incinerator projects have been either canceled or put on hold (Lipsett and Farrell, 1990). Citizens have opposed incinerators for many reasons, including concerns about huge financial costs and about the health and environmental impacts of air emissions (fig. 7.2). As the industry has moved to reduce air emissions by a combination of better devices to control combustion and air pollution, it has gotten itself into a

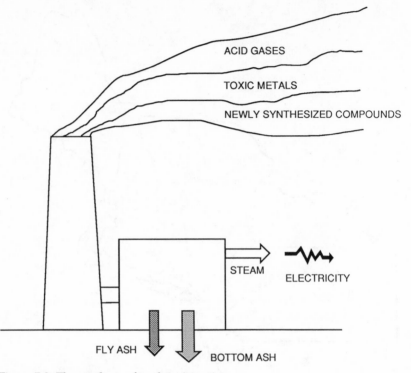

Figure 7.2. The products of trash incineration.

catch-22. The better the air pollution control devices, the more toxic the ash that is produced and the more difficult to site the ash landfill that must be developed along with the incinerator.

For every three tons of trash that is burned in an incinerator, one ton of ash is produced. Approximately 10 percent is fly ash and 90 percent bottom ash. Under the Resource Conservation and Recovery Act, large generators of solid waste are required to ascertain if the material is toxic before dispatching it to a landfill. The Environmental Protection Agency devised a test that attempts to simulate the leaching conditions of a regular landfill: the Extraction Procedure Toxicity Test, or EP Tox Test (Environmental Protection Agency, 1986). Material that fails this test must be sent to a designated hazardous waste facility; material that passes can be sent to a regular landfill. The Environmental Defense Fund (1987) compiled a list of EP Tox Test results for ash from U.S. incinerators. According to the report, 100 percent of all fly ash samples, 38 percent of all bottom ash samples, and 47 percent of all combined ash samples failed the test for lead, cadmium, or both. Those test results have brought cries of protest from the industry, its proponents in Washington, and various state regulatory agencies. As David Sussman, vice president of the major incinerator company Ogden Martin, stated, "It means *finito, morte*, the end, for the resource recovery industry if ash is treated as hazardous waste" (*Waste-to-Energy Report*, 1986). Anxious to avoid shutting down the industry, several states, including New York, have reclassified the ash as "special waste," even when it fails the toxicity test (*New York Times*, 1987).

More than any other factor, the ash presents us with concrete evidence that incineration is not the answer to the trash crisis. It doesn't make economic or environmental sense to convert three tons of trash into one ton of toxic ash. Ash landfills are proving as difficult to site as raw-waste landfills. People don't want the ash in their backyard any more than they wanted the trash. Nor will future generations thank us for these acres of toxic ash. We have to question the ethics of leaving future generations with the problems of containing, guarding, and monitoring our permanent toxics for eternity.

Source Separation

Household trash is made by mixing all our discarded materials together. Clearly, the key step to unmaking it is to separate it, or rather to keep it separate, because most of the materials are used separately.

The Components of Trash

The typical breakdown of materials in household trash in America is shown in figure 7.3. Our classification system for sorting trash will be influenced by what we want to do with the materials. The classification system described below has several important goals: reducing waste, conserving resources, conserving topsoil, removing toxics from the waste stream, minimizing our dependence on landfills, and changing the nature of what goes into landfills. Our trash can be divided into six categories: avoidables, reuseables, recyclables, compostables, toxics, and the rest.

Avoidables We have been persuaded that many of the items we use add to the convenience of our daily lives. Whether disposable razors, flash-

Corrugated cardboard	12.6
Newspaper	8.3
Books, magazines and paperboard	6.6
Office paper	3.3
Other paper	11.2
Yard wastes	16.1
Food wastes	7.3
Glass containers	8.6
Aluminum	1.1
Other metals	8.1
Plastic containers	1.6
Other plastics	4.9
Wood wastes	3.4
Rubber and leather	2.3
Textiles	1.9
Rest	2.7
	100.0

Figure 7.3. The typical breakdown (in percent) of discarded materials from the American household (Franklin Associates, 1986).

lights, lighters, cameras, pens, plastic bags, and many other disposable items really make our lives significantly more convenient is highly debatable. But whether they do or not, we have to question their continued use if they compound our waste and pollution problems and threaten to deprive future generations of a fair share of the planet's finite resources. At this point, we are talking about changing personal purchasing habits, but if the problems get more acute, then we may be talking about legislation or taxation to require manufacturers to share in the costs of disposal of the materials they use.

Reusables When someone throws out an object like a couch or a refrigerator, it probably means that the owner no longer wants the object in his or her living space. It probably does not mean that the object is entirely useless, fit only for the garbage heap or to be burned. Objects with a useful life left in them should not be compounding our trash problem or our resource problem. We already have many common mechanisms for handling such objects. We can give or sell them to a friend, we can have a yard sale, or we can give them to a thrift shop run by a voluntary organization such as the Salvation Army or Goodwill Industries. Such mechanisms are seldom comprehensive, however, and an important community task is to set up a comprehensive system, such as a community reuse-and-repair center. Such a center, in conjunction with voluntary organizations and voluntary help, can maximize the reclamation and reuse of useful objects, as well as stimulate job training opportunities and other positive community developments.

Recyclables If we cannot recover and reuse the object, then the next best thing is to recover the material from which it is made. Many materials in our waste stream can be recycled, although their marketability varies with location in the United States. Such materials include newspaper, office paper, mixed paper, corrugated cardboard, clear glass, colored glass, aluminum, other metals, and several plastics. Of these, the most problematic component is mixed paper, for which the market is very unstable.

Compostables Compostables are all the materials that will biodegrade in a landfill and are not otherwise recyclable, such as food waste, yard waste, tissues, food-contaminated paper, and kitty litter. In a landfill this biodegradable material causes a whole host of problems, but if composted (biodegraded by microorganisms that use oxygen), it can be converted into a more stable product that can be used for a variety of purposes, depending upon its final quality. These uses include landfill cover; landscaping material for parks, roadsides, and golf courses; topsoil for strip-mine reclamation and for forest management. For households with the requisite space, composting can be done in the backyard. For others, it can be done at a central facility. The simple act of keeping this smelly material out of the trash accomplishes two things: It makes the business of recycling and upgrading more palatable, more profitable, and far easier, and it makes the residue after recycling more benign in a landfill.

Toxics One German study indicates that about 1 percent by weight of the materials that we use in the household is toxic, and that about 50 percent of this toxic material is in household and car batteries (Koch et al., 1986). Other household toxics are contained in substances like paint, paint thinners, paint strippers, cleaners, solvents, and pesticides. Three conclusions become apparent if we wish to minimize the pollution caused by the toxics in our waste: We should look for ways to clean and protect our homes that do not involve toxics (Greenpeace, 1988); we should try to use up those toxics that we do use, rather than throw them away; and we should keep the remaining unavoidable toxics separate from the rest of the trash and put them aside for special handling.

The Rest After we have removed the above items from our trash, the remainder is what we might call the new trash: the stuff that we couldn't reuse, recycle, or compost and that isn't toxic. A lot of this material will be junk mail; packaging that blends two or more materials such as plastic paper and foil (small fruit juice containers, for example), and plastics that can't be readily recycled (expanded polystyrene containers, for example). In the short term we should try to avoid purchasing such materials. In the long term we should try to legislate or tax them out of existence. One of the valuable results of source separation is that it educates people to the massive waste of resources this sixth category of trash represents, and it thereby leads to growing political pressure on the manufacturing industry to use less packaging and more recyclable materials in its products. Put simply, when you burn three tons of trash, you convert it into one ton of ash that no one wants, but when you separate three tons of trash, you can convert it into one ton of recyclables, one ton of compostables, and one ton of education. Ultimately, the education reduces to one irresistible message to manufacturers: If you can't recycle it, don't make it.

Many communities in the United States either have passed or are considering legislation to ban expanded polystyrene and other disposable plastic containers (Nancy Skinner, pers. com., 1989). These efforts have been so successful that a recent memorandum from the Society of the Plastics Industry complained, "The image of plastics among consumers is deteriorating at an alarmingly fast pace. Opinion research experts tell us that it has plummeted so far and so fast, that we are approaching a point of no return." The Society estimated that the effort to combat the decline would cost more than $50 million a year for the next three years (Thomas, 1989).

Household Handling of Separated Materials
Figure 7.4 is a rough schematic of a simple and convenient system combining household separation of trash with community collection and handling. In this system all the compostables are put into one container, all the recyclables into another, and the rest (minus the toxics, reusables, and avoidables) into a third. These three categories, which represent the

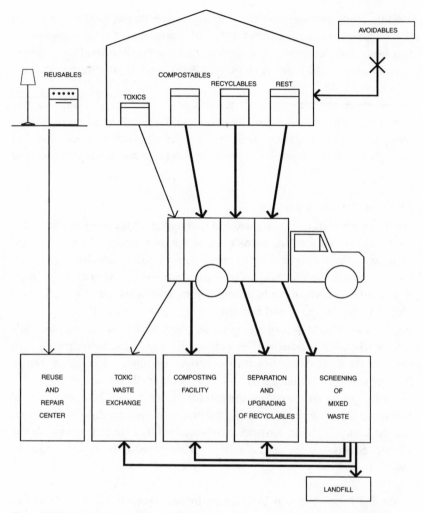

Figure 7.4. Source separation, collection, and handling of household discards.

bulk of the discards, are collected on the regular trash day, using a variety of modified garbage trucks, and are taken to a recycling and composting facility. The reusables are either collected by a voluntary organization or delivered by the householder to the reuse-and-repair center. The toxics are either collected intermittently or delivered by the householder to the toxic waste exchange (which could be part of the reuse-and-repair center), where materials like paints and paint thinners and strippers can be used by other members of the community. Special plastic containers can also be given to householders for the collection of such items as waste oil and household batteries. This approach is currently operating successfully in Hamburg, New York (Kroll, 1985), and Neunkirchen, Austria (Work on Waste, 1988).

The three-container system for compostables, recyclables, and the rest is currently operating in Heidelberg and a number of other communities in Germany (Bailey and Connett, 1986). Pilot projects are also operating in the United States with considerable success (Commoner et al., 1989).

Materials Recovery Facilities

The modules that could be included in a materials recovery facility are a reuse-and-repair section; a waste exchange for household toxics; a composting section; a section for separating, upgrading, and marketing the mixed recyclables; a section for screening mixed residue before putting it in a landfill; a section for handling commercial waste; and a section for handling landscaping and building debris. The more ambitious centers might also include sections to process some of the recovered materials into marketable products. The Belgian ET-1 system, for example, can convert comingled plastics into a variety of objects like fence posts, lumber sections, traffic signs, and park benches (Brewer, 1987).

Although no single community in the United States has yet to put all these modules together, working examples of each module, and several combinations of them, are operating successfully in both Europe and the United States (Bailey and Connett, 1986, 1987a, b, c, d, 1988a, b, 1989a, b).

Reuse and Repair Several U.S. communities have excellent examples of reuse-and-repair centers, including Wellesley, Massachusetts; Berkeley, California; Portage, Michigan; and Wilton, New Hampshire. The Wellesley center is affectionately called the dump, but it is a dump that no one wants to get rid of. It is built around an old defunct incinerator in attractive parklike surroundings. The usual drop-off containers for separated recyclables are conveniently placed adjacent to adequate parking arrangements. Next to the drop-off containers is a trailer owned by Goodwill Industries, which accepts used clothing and small appliances. In the basement of the old incinerator is an area set aside for waste oil, car batteries, and tires. At the rear of the building is an area where residents can drop off leaves and lawn clippings and can help themselves to compost. There is also a "take it or leave it" section where residents can drop off their old appliances and help themselves to other people's bric-a-brac. Finally, residents can leave books on a large bookshelf, help themselves to other books, and even order books. In Wellesley, parents keep their kids in line by threatening not to take them to the dump, and politicians, looking for votes during a campaign, know where to find people on a Saturday morning (Pat Berdau, pers. com., 1988; Bailey and Connett, 1989b).

In Berkeley several voluntary organizations and small businesses operate several materials recovery modules in conjunction with the city's transfer station. These modules include a curbside collection program, a drop-off center, a buy-back center, and a large reuse section. The reuse section, which is run by a small business called Urban Ore, looks like a huge flea market. It grosses seventeen thousand dollars a month and provides a number of good jobs. Urban Ore grosses another twenty-five thousand dollars by selling reusable building items like doors, windows, and bathtubs. The company lives up to the motto of its owner, Dan Knapp, who is a former sociology professor: It's not waste until it is wasted (Knapp, pers. com., 1988; Bailey and Connett, 1989b).

An excellent example of a recycling center that does extensive repair work is the one run by Jay Eaton in Portage, Michigan (Eaton, pers. com., 1988; Bailey and Connett, 1989b). Eaton says that if you stay in his recycling center long enough, anything you want will come through the door. It is an inspiration to see the quantity and variety of objects that Eaton is able to get back into useful service. He has a particular affection for handtools, and after replacing the handles and removing the rust, he puts the finishing touch on with discarded paint.

Many of the features discussed above are also incorporated in a small rural recycling center in Wilton, New Hampshire. This facility was set up by five towns in August 1979. According to the operators, the people who use the facility have willingly cooperated with the extensive separation demanded. In addition to recycling more materials than any other comparable recycling facility in New Hampshire, the center offers many reuse opportunities. In addition to selling reclaimed clothing, it offers reclaimed books, bric-a-brac, and furniture for a small fee to people who can afford it and at no charge to those who cannot (Pat Johannesen, pers. com., 1991).

At its best, a reuse-and-repair center could become the nucleus of an

COMMUNITY RESOURCE PARK

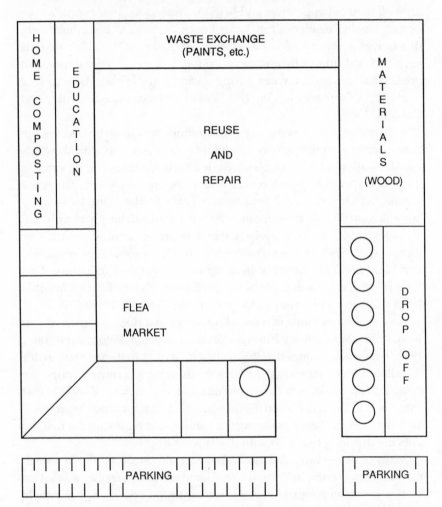

Figure 7.5. A community resource park can be the center of a variety of voluntary activities, job-training possibilities, and community development.

exciting community resource park (fig. 7.5). Were an enlightened munic-
ipality to provide the buildings and area needed to set up such a facility,
it could generate enormous dividends in the form of community education, motivation, and development; involvement of senior-citizen and
youth groups; job training; exchange and reuse of toxic wastes, such as

paints; and the demonstration of backyard composting. Such a facility could become self-supporting, and once the creativity and enthusiasm of the local community had been unleashed, many kinds of positive and exciting components could be incorporated, such as a trash museum; a competition for the most valuable object recovered or the most creative use found for junk; a natural history museum tied to the composting section and featuring recycling in nature; and a community garden that uses some of the compost. I can think of no better way to take us away from the negative image of disposing of trash and toward the positive notion of conserving both human and material resources.

Separation of Mixed Recyclables

Many facilities—ranging from the modest shed built by volunteer labor in the village of Rodman, New York, to Joe Garbarino's three-acre, $10 million building in San Rafael, California—separate, upgrade, and market recyclable materials (Bailey and Connett, 1987a, 1988a, 1989b; Garbarino, pers. com., 1987; Charles Valentine, pers. com., 1988). Such facilities are labor-intensive, and they use fairly modest equipment: conveyor belts, glass crushers, magnetic separators, balers, and shredders, and a variety of forklift trucks. Some of the most elegant aids to separation have been developed by the Bezner Corporation in Germany and are being imported into the United States by New England Container Recycling, Inc., a company that recently built a materials recovery facility in Johnston, Rhode Island (Bailey and Connett, 1986, 1989b; Richard Kattar, pers. com., 1989).

As communities begin to rely on large private companies to streamline the separation of mixed recyclables, it's important that we don't eliminate the small operations and voluntary organizations that have traditionally earned money by collecting separated recyclables like aluminum cans and corrugated cardboard. They can be protected by making sure that the separation facility offers a buy-back option for already separated materials.

Separation of Commercial Waste People have been so preoccupied with the waste produced by households that they sometimes forget to consider commercial waste in waste management scenarios, even though commercial waste can be a significant contributor to the landfill problem. Fortunately, from the point of view of materials recovery, commercial waste is much easier to handle than household waste because it is more

homogeneous, being dominated by corrugated cardboard and office paper. Commercial waste is also easier to separate because it is less contaminated with smelly material.

An excellent example of a facility that handles a large quantity of commercial waste is in Burbank, California (Bailey and Connett, 1989b). The facility, which processes nine hundred tons of waste per day, separates out the usual bottles, cans, newspaper, office paper, and corrugated cardboard. It has also taken the innovative step of bringing in equipment from the paper industry to convert the mixed-paper fraction to a gray paper pulp, because the pulp is much easier to sell to the paper industry on a regular basis than mixed paper, which is so vulnerable to market conditions.

Composting The weakest module in the United States is the composting section. Composting is underused by many communities and is oversold by companies asserting that the entire waste stream can be composted. That argument doesn't make biological or economic sense, because microbes cannot destroy heavy metals or many of the synthetic organic materials in the waste stream. If communities wish to use or sell the compost, it is critical that they carefully select clean, organic material. On the other hand, communities are far too timid when they compost only yard waste such as leaves and lawn clippings.

A variety of equipment and strategies, from the low-tech windrow approach and the intermediate indoor-trough method to high-tech in-vessel systems, can successfully compost a wide range of organic material (BioCycle, 1989). The windrow system simply involves putting the material out in long rows that are regularly turned by a front loader or by a specially designed windrow turner that can turn a whole row in one sweep (Bailey and Connett, 1989a, b). The drawbacks to this system are that it needs a lot of space, is vulnerable to the weather, and takes longer to produce finished compost than the other systems.

The trough method is like an internal windrow system. A good example of this method is currently operating in Lebanon, Connecticut, by a company called International Processing Systems (Bailey and Connett, 1989b). It handles a variety of organic waste, including animal manures, sawdust from a gun factory, apple pumice, mycelium waste from a pharmaceutical company, mushroom waste, sewage sludge, and wood chips. The waste is placed in concrete troughs that are 6 feet wide, 6 feet high, and 180 feet long. Rails along the top of the troughs carry a machine that mixes the material and shifts it 10 feet each day, so that after eighteen days it has moved the length of the trough and is ready for curing. The troughs are situated in sheds, four troughs to a shed. Air is blown through the material from vents underneath the troughs and is removed from the system by suction vans in the roof. This air can be cleaned by pushing it through soil filters, or Boden filters (Bailey and Connett, 1986, 1989b). This elegant system can process different materials in separate troughs to produce various grades of compost.

In-vessel systems come in two major types: horizontal cylinders that are rotated, and vertical cylinders containing paddles that rotate inside the system (Bailey and Connett, 1986, 1989b). Such systems allow the operating parameters to be tightly controlled. Of particular concern is the control of air and temperature. An adequate supply of air is necessary to keep the system aerobic, because anaerobic organisms take over the biodegradation in the absence of air (as in landfills) and produce smelly compounds. Temperature is important because, left to itself, the compost pile will overheat, destroying many of the microorganisms that do the work and rendering the process inefficient and anaerobic (Feinstein et al., 1987).

I recommend that communities use composting for two distinct purposes: to produce a salable product (topsoil) and to keep biodegradable organic material out of landfills. To achieve the first purpose, good source separation is essential, so that contamination from household toxics is kept to a minimum. The better this control, the better the overall economics of the operation becomes. After obtaining a high-grade compost in this fashion, a second composting operation can be used as part of the screening process at the landfill.

Screening Materials at the Landfill In a comprehensive materials recovery program, no unscreened waste would be allowed into the landfill. In fact, no waste truck would be allowed direct access to the landfill. Instead, the residue from the source separation program, and any other mixed waste, would be dumped on conveyor belts where well-paid and well-protected workers would remove any toxics or recyclables missed in source separation programs, as well as other nonrecyclable and non-biodegradable materials, such as certain plastics, synthetic textiles, and rubberized materials. These latter materials would be baled to conserve space and buried in the landfill. Their nature would also be carefully studied, because a more resource-conscious future will demand either that ways be found for these materials to be recycled or that their manufacture be curtailed. In a well-organized screening facility, the material left on the conveyor belts would be essentially nontoxic, nonrecyclable, and biodegradable. Consisting largely of mixed-paper products, food waste, and other organic materials, it would be shredded and composted, perhaps with sewage sludge, to produce a low-grade compost suitable for landfill cover and possibly other nonagricultural purposes, such as road shoulders, strip-mine reclamation, and reforestation. The uses will hinge upon careful analysis for heavy-metal content. The closest I have seen to such a screening-composting operation is in Fillmore County, Minnesota (Bailey and Connett, 1989a).

Not only does such a screening facility offer a community the maximum diversion of material from a landfill, but it also offers the decision makers their most likely strategy for successfully siting a landfill. The siting process could be further facilitated if the community is given the opportunity to define precisely what material is acceptable in the landfill and is given a contract in which community representatives are allowed inspection rights to both the screening facility and the landfill, and the right to close the landfill if unlawful material is found entering it.

It is important to remember that although reuse and recycling can reduce the quantity of material going into landfills, composting and the removal of toxics are what dramatically change a landfill's character. Moreover, community inspection rights and the landfill screening facility are more likely to win a community's acceptance than leachate control devices and governmental monitoring.

Practical Considerations

How Much Will Materials Recovery Cost? Although some of the objects and materials recovered using source separation will provide a net income (after collection, upgrading, and transport to market), it would be a mistake to see the whole program as a profit-making venture. Just as we do not expect landfills to make a profit for a community, we should not expect recycling scenarios to make a net profit. We should see recycling as providing a service to both the local community and the environment as a whole. The economics of the system will be driven by avoided disposal costs—the money saved by not putting the materials into an expensive landfill. In this respect, we should welcome the increased costs of landfills, because those costs will put taxpayers and environmentalists on the same side.

Three recent major studies—conducted for Buffalo, New York (Commoner et al., 1988); North Hempstead, New York (Latham et al., 1988); and Seattle, Washington (Seattle Solid Waste Utility, 1988)—indicated that source separation, coupled with intensive materials recovery, is cheaper than incineration. Although avoided disposal costs will be the key economic driving force behind our proposed scenario at the local level, further stimulus could be provided at the state and federal level. Both state and federal authorities could stimulate markets for the reclaimed materials, especially with government procurement policies. The federal government could further reward communities with what could be called conserved-resource credits for each ton of material recycled or composted. Such a reward system would recognize the improvement to the national economy by conserving energy and finite resources, as well as the reduction in global pollution that will ensue. Such federal recognition would be a critical step in the paradigm shift from waste management to resource management.

Can Materials Recovery Make a Big Difference? As far as extending the life of landfills is concerned, the volume reduction achieved by a waste-handling strategy is of key importance. Unfortunately, recycling results are usually recorded by weight because recyclable materials are sold by weight. Many items that are currently recycled are light in weight, such as corrugated cardboard and plastics, or they contain a lot of air, such as bottles and cans. A rudimentary recycling program often achieves a far more impressive volume reduction than weight reduction. After two years of a mandatory recycling program in North Stonington, Connecticut, for example, consulting engineers recorded a 65 percent reduction in landfill space requirements (Bailey and Connett, 1987c). After four months of a mandatory recycling program, Rodman, New York, a small rural community with a population of 850, recorded a 71 percent volume reduction in the material sent to the landfill (Bailey and Connett, 1988a; Charles Valentine, pers. com., 1988).

The town of Neunkirchen, Austria, achieved 65 percent and 67 percent reductions (by weight) in 1986 and 1987, respectively, via a combination of source separation, recycling, and composting (Work on Waste, 1988). A pilot study conducted by the Center for the Biology of Natural

Systems for the town of East Hampton, Long Island, showed that one hundred households using a four-container system (two for recyclables, one for compostables, and one for the rest) achieved a massive 84 percent reduction by weight (Commoner et al., 1989). Critics have pointed out that this project used committed volunteers and cannot be considered indicative of potential achievements in other communities. But if an 84 percent reduction can be achieved when the necessary commitment is available, shouldn't we be putting our efforts into getting that kind of commitment from the average citizen?

Will People Participate? Several factors can maximize citizen participation. First, source separation needs to be as convenient as possible, and no program is more convenient than having recyclables picked up on the same day as the regular trash. The actual separation need not take more than a few minutes a day, because what we are talking about is only a new set of habits. Second, the urgency and value of such an effort, for the community and for the environment, need to be conveyed. With the growing awareness of global environmental problems, that should not be difficult. Third, there is no point in stressing the urgency of a situation and then allowing people to take part on a voluntary basis. With few exceptions, mandatory programs achieve far greater participation than voluntary ones.

The enforcement need not be extremely punitive to be effective. The curbside separation program in Hamburg, New York, achieves a 98 percent participation rate by not picking up unseparated waste (Kroll, 1985). Nor need the program be grim. In Rockford, Illinois, a humorous note is added by having a colorful "trashman," in a gaudy outfit and a polka-dotted truck, inspect the trash of one household each week. If he finds no recyclables in the trash, the householder wins a thousand dollars. If the householder doesn't win, someone the following week could win two thousand dollars, and so on—a garbage lottery. Since the program started, the participation rate has increased fourfold (Bailey and Connett, 1987b, 1989b).

In High Bridge, New Jersey, another financial incentive has proved successful. Citizens are required to purchase trash coupons. Each time a garbage bag is put out, a coupon must be used, but material put out for recycling and composting requires no coupon. Large objects are also assessed. For example, a couch requires six trash coupons for municipal disposal. As a result, people are becoming more imaginative about getting reusable objects to places where some extra life can be extracted from them. Officials estimate that the waste stream has been reduced by 25 percent with this approach (*New York Times*, 1988).

According to the Institute for Local Self Reliance, at least ten U.S. communities now achieve a recycling and composting rate greater than 40 percent (Platt et al., 1990). A 40 percent rate was considered impossible by many analysts in the early 1980s.

Do Markets Exist for Recyclables? Trash separation alone does not make recycling successful. To be truly recycled, materials have to be reused. That means someone has to want the materials enough to pay for them. The three factors for maximizing the recyclability of materials are quality, quantity, and regularity.

Will the Markets Be Flooded? As recycling gets more and more popular across North America, some people fear that markets for certain materials, particularly the lower grades of paper, will become flooded. Most analysts believe, however, that this phenomenon will be only temporary, as industries adjust to a large and dependable supply of cheap material. Indeed, in February 1990, Red Cavaney, the president of the American Paper Institute, announced that the paper industry was increasing its recycling goal from 25 percent to 40 percent of its total production (*Kalamazoo Gazette*, 1990). The plastics industry is also expected to increase its recycling commitment dramatically, in part because of the efforts of many communities to ban a number of disposable plastic products. Meanwhile, state and federal agencies could sustain this momentum by adjusting their own procurement policies to stimulate the markets for secondary materials and look for other incentives to encourage their use. In the long run, the national economy, the global environment, and future generations will benefit as we decrease our dependence on the extraction of virgin resources. The economic, ecological, and ethical imperatives are clear: We must make recycling work.

Do Markets for Compost Exist? The better the control on the organic inputs to compost, the more likely the product can be used and sold. The most important market for compost is probably landscaping. One only has to check the price of topsoil in the local horticulture supply store to verify this point. Lower-grade composts can be used for landfill cover and the reclamation of strip mines and deforested areas. Such areas could use every ounce of compost the United States could produce. From the most pessimistic view, even if the compost ends up in a landfill, the community is still much better off because composting produces a significant volume reduction and the landfill will be far more benign.

Will Incineration Still Be Necessary? I believe that if the strategy outlined is pursued, an incinerator will be unnecessary. But one does not have to accept this position to recognize the wisdom of postponing the decision to build an incinerator until the community has seen what it can do with a more beneficial strategy of source separation and materials recovery. From an economic point of view, it is important to note that the only materials that can be burned and that cannot be composted are synthetic materials like plastic. Not only is composting technology much cheaper (in terms of initial capital and the costs of maintenance and replacement) and safer than incineration, but the remaining unrecycled plastics can also be far more safely and cheaply placed in a landfill than the residual ash from an incinerator can.

Over the last year or so the catchphrase of incinerator promoters has been *integrated waste management*. What that term means in practice is a combined program of recycling and incineration. This seemingly even-handed approach, however, is actually the promotion of incineration by other means, a fact that can be confirmed by comparing the funds budgeted for the two components. Moreover, one has to know only that 80 percent of the waste stream is both recyclable and combustible to realize the difficulty of marrying these incompatible components in one program. Our best shot at an integrated program is to integrate expensive landfills (with the major expense going to the screening facility at the landfill) with source separation and materials recovery. In short, if an expensive trash incinerator is built, its use must be maximized to pay back the bonds that are issued to cover its enormous cost. If, on the other hand, an expensive landfill is established, the minimization of its use is in everyone's interest.

Is Materials Recovery Realistic? Fortunately, we have an interesting and recent historical example in the energy crisis in the 1970s. The high-tech approach was labeled as the practical, realistic solution and the low-tech approach was labeled as pie in the sky. Some people said that massive nuclear power stations must be built, but others suggested that the more practical solution was to conserve energy via the use of more-efficient appliances, home insulation, and smaller cars. The response was deafening: The American people would never drive smaller cars. History has shown, however, that since 1973 the United States has saved more energy through conservation measures than it has generated in new power plants (Flavin and Durning, 1988). I believe that as more evidence comes in, it will become clear that in both the short term and the long term, the simpler strategy of source separation and materials recovery is the more *practical* way of reducing our dependence on unacceptable landfills.

A Commitment to the Future

The landfill crisis has been a blessing in disguise. It is a timely reminder at the local level that a throwaway society cannot succeed on a finite planet. It is a clear indicator that we have broken the circle that binds the ecology, economics, and ethics of wise resource management.

The modern state-of-the-art waste-to-energy trash incinerator is a sophisticated answer to the wrong question. Our task is not to find a new place to put trash but to find ways to unmake trash. Incineration merely burns the embarrassing evidence of the throwaway ethic. We have to challenge the ethic. Instead of spending millions of dollars perfecting the art of destruction of throwaway objects, we must stop making objects we have to throw away.

The trash crisis will not be solved with magic machines and costly consultants but by mobilizing our citizens' common sense, creativity, and need for community. Although some materials can be recycled and composted for a net profit, the main economic driving force for the materials recovery approach will be the avoided costs of expensive landfills and modern trash incinerators. Most local officials will recognize this benefit, but they might not fully consider the larger benefits for future generations and the national economy that can be gained by reducing our demand for raw materials.

Some people have seen the solving of the trash crisis as a rather grim and boring task. Others have seen it as an exciting and challenging opportunity. Of all the environmental problems with which we are confronted, this is the one with which every citizen is intimately involved. Every day that we make trash exacerbates the problem. When we learn to source separate and recycle we can be part of the solution. Moreover, many communities have also shown that when they go about maximizing material recovery, it can also be a source of considerable community pride and community development.

No one can pretend that any solution to the trash crisis is going to be simple or cheap. What is important is that we choose a solution that takes us in the right direction. Any problems with source separation and materials recovery are worth overcoming because this strategy is the only one that offers a genuine long-term solution on a finite planet. More than any other single demand, the strategy of source separation and materials recovery requires that local decision makers put their faith back in the people rather than in magic machines.

In wartime, societies recycle. Our task is to convince our people and our leaders that the way we are currently handling our raw materials and our waste is a war on the future. The economic, ecological, and ethical imperatives are clear: We must make recycling work. It is not a question of *if* but *how*, not a question of *when* but *now*. We must start handling our discarded materials as if the future mattered.

8 GROUNDWATER: THE BURIED LIFE

The purpose of this book is to explore the interactions among ecology, economics, and ethics. Sometimes a fourth element, aesthetics, can provide a frame of reference for responding to a challenge of this magnitude. Although it is an exaggeration to describe a poet as an unacknowledged legislator, a great poet can see things steadily and see them whole, stimulating new insights into problems outside the realm of aesthetics.

Matthew Arnold, the late-Victorian English poet, essayist, and school inspector, was preoccupied by the tension between alienation and estrangement on the one hand, and integration and reconciliation on the other. The "unplumbed, salt, estranging sea" is Arnold's most powerful symbol of human separateness, whereas subsurface water (groundwater) is his hydrologic countersymbol of oneness. Arnold evokes groundwater most successfully in the poem entitled "The Buried Life," published in 1852.

In the poem, Arnold realized that we devote much of our time and energy to hiding our real selves—our common human nature:

I knew the mass of men conceal'd
Their thoughts, for fear that if reveal'd
They would by other men be met
With blank indifference, or with blame reproved;

William Goldfarb

I knew they lived and moved
Trick'd in disguises, alien to the rest
Of men, and alien to themselves—and yet
The same heart beats in every human breast!

We seem destined to repress our deepest congruities, but the buried lifestream within us will not be ignored:

Fate, which foresaw
How frivolous a baby man would be—
By what distractions he would be possess'd,
How he would pour himself in every strife,
And well-nigh change his own identity—
That it might keep from his capricious play
His genuine self, and force him to obey
Even in his own despite his being's law,
Bade through the deep recesses of our breast
The unregarded river of our life
Pursue with indiscernible flow its way;
And that we should not see
The buried stream, and seem to be
Eddying at large in blind uncertainty,
Though driving on with it eternally.

But often, in the world's most crowded streets,
But often, in the din of strife,
There rises an unspeakable desire
After the knowledge of our buried life;
A thirst to spend our fire and restless force
In tracking out our true, original course;
A longing to inquire
Into the mystery of this heart which beats
So wild, so deep in us—to know
Whence our lives come and where they go.

In these moments of recognition we are capable of making contact with ourselves and others:

A bolt is shot back somewhere in our breast,
And a lost pulse of feeling stirs again.
The eye sinks inward, and the heart lies plain,

And what we mean, we say, and what we would, we know.
A man becomes aware of his life's flow,
And hears its winding murmur; and he sees
The meadows where it glides, the sun, the breeze.

And there arrives a lull in the hot race
Wherein he doth for ever chase
That flying and elusive shadow, rest.
An air of coolness plays upon his face,
And an unwonted calm pervades his breast.
And then he thinks he knows
The hills where his life rose,
And the sea where it goes.

At the end of the poem, the buried life has been disinterred, the sea and groundwater are no longer discrete, contrasting symbols but interrelated stages of a single hydrologic cycle, as all animate and inanimate denizens of planet earth participate in the concatenation of cycles that we call environment.

The Abuse of Groundwater

For Arnold, recognition of the buried life is a prerequisite for understanding ourselves, other individuals, and other nations. It enables us to surmount the ostensible alienation of the human condition and realize that "the same heart beats in every human breast!"

Similarly, our comparatively recent perception of the vulnerability of groundwater symbolizes environmentalism's first premise, that all of nature is interrelated. Life depends upon usable water. Groundwater and surface water are inextricably connected. Aquifers transcend national, state, and substate boundaries. Recharge areas may lie great distances from potable water wells. Overpumping of groundwater creates a cone of depression that not only reduces hydraulic pressure in neighboring wells but also facilitates the intrusion of saline or other contaminated water into the aquifer. If we continue to overheat our atmosphere, sea levels will rise and significant saline intrusion will occur. Whatever wastes we discharge into the air will ultimately reach groundwater through precipitation. Whatever wastes we discharge onto or into land will ultimately leach into groundwater, no matter how secure our mode of containment is thought to be. Whenever we over-pump an aquifer, we risk subsidence of the overlying land and increased infiltration of needed surface water. The wetlands that protect us from flooding and pollution, while providing irreplaceable wildlife habitat, presuppose a stable and relatively uncontaminated source of ground-water. In these and other ways the buried life pervades our being.

We have been slow to appreciate the vulnerability of groundwater to pollution and depletion for a number of reasons. First, groundwater abuse exemplifies the adage, Out of sight, out of mind. We cannot often see, smell, or taste the consequences of groundwater contamination as we can with surface water pollution. Because groundwater moves quite slowly (only several feet per year), pollution is frequently undetectable by ambient monitoring. Water tables undergo natural fluctuations, and it is simpler to attribute apparent declines to temporary natural factors and deepen one's well than it is to suspect that an aquifer is being systemati-cally pumped in excess of its safe yield. Ironically, in spite of the impor-tance of groundwater as a source of potable water, the public feels less affinity with it than with surface water because groundwater lacks direct aesthetic and recreational value. Once again, the peculiar logic of "It's a necessity; thus it's invulnerable" prevails.

Heavy groundwater use is a relatively recent phenomenon in the United States. In many areas of the country, surface water supplies are abundant, and where they are not naturally present, we have created them through public subsidies. Historically, it has been cheaper and easier to divert flows from bodies of surface water than to pump water out of the ground. But this is no longer true: In many areas, surface water supplies cannot meet increased demands for water; most of the available dam sites have already been developed; environmental concerns militate against large impoundments; and subsidies for public water develop-ment have been precluded by budget deficits and a heightened sen-sitivity to the inequities of most public water subsidies. Scarcity of sur-face water, in turn, has led to improvements in pump technology. These days, water users commonly prefer groundwater to surface water be-cause groundwater is comparatively clean and inexpensive to store, produce, and deliver.

Moreover, groundwater pollution has also increased in recent years. As we prohibited or strictly regulated discharges of wastes into the air and surface waters, land disposal and deep-well injection became the dumping methods of choice. The unwelcome results of this toxic shell game are Superfund sites, abandoned wells, illnesses, deformities, and premature deaths. With increasing population and affluence, ground-water pollution from nonpoint sources has increased dramatically. Construction of commercial complexes and new homes causes groundwater pollution by infiltration of construction site runoff and uncontrolled storm-water runoff containing household, commercial, and lawn chemicals and by overconcentration and poor maintenance of septic systems. New road construction leads to contamination of groundwater by automobile-related pollutants (such as benzene, toluene, xylene, and lead) and road deicing agents. More intensive agriculture causes runoff and infiltration of nitrates from fertilizers and of organic chemicals from pesticides and fertilizers. Furthermore, increased land development exacerbates groundwater pollution by decreasing groundwater levels as recharge areas are paved over and water purveyors draw on groundwater and discharge municipal wastewater to surface water bodies.

Because of groundwater's late appearance on the regulatory scene, the science and law of groundwater are primitive compared with the science and law of surface water. Until the 1950s, common-law courts would routinely refuse to impose liability upon a polluter of groundwater because "courses of subterranean waters are indefinite and obscure," and thus it would be unjust to subject a landowner to liability unless the plaintiff could prove that the defendant landowner should have foreseen the consequences of her or his actions. The supposed inscrutability of groundwater also led many states to adopt the absolute ownership rule: All landowners have the right to pump groundwater from under their land at whatever rate and for whatever purpose they wish, without bearing any responsibility to neighboring landowners except for "spite pumping." The absolute ownership rule enshrined the counterproductive view of groundwater as a commons. Moreover, a number of states based their groundwater allocation systems on the premise that groundwater, like surface water, flows in distinct streams. (Matthew Arnold also drew this false but forgivable analogy.) With the rapid development of groundwater hydrogeology, many of these legal doctrines have been abolished, but groundwater law still lags far behind surface water law. Texas, for example, has retained the absolute ownership rule for determining groundwater rights while moving toward the more modern prior appropriation rule for surface water diversions.

The federal Clean Water Act also illustrates the immaturity of groundwater law. In 1972 Congress enacted a sweeping revision of the nation's water pollution control laws entitled the Federal Water Pollution Control

Act of 1972, now called the Clean Water Act. This statute prohibits a discharge to "waters of the United States" without a discharge permit incorporating minimum federally stipulated effluent limitations based on the best available technology economically achievable. The phrase "waters of the United States" is much broader than the term "navigable waters," which limited the scope of prior federal water pollution control law. However, in defining "waters of the United States," Congress did not explicitly include groundwater. In spite of ample legislative history to the effect that groundwater should be included within the ambit of the act, in spite of several favorable court decisions, and in spite of the obvious policy drawbacks of regulating surface water and groundwater pollution under different legal regimes, the federal Environmental Protection Agency (EPA) concluded that the Clean Water Act does not cover groundwater. Unfortunately, the EPA's cramped definition of "waters of the United States" has not been overturned by Congress or the courts. Thus, groundwater pollution is addressed haphazardly by approximately a dozen federal statutes, leading to confusion, loopholes, and regulatory inefficiencies.

The EPA's reluctance to manage water pollution control in a comprehensive manner has been, at least in part, political. States jealously guard their traditional dominance in the area of water allocation and realize that water pollution control and water allocation overlap, especially with reference to groundwater pollution, which moves so slowly and is so difficult to clean up. States fear that a federal groundwater pollution control juggernaut will usurp their precious water allocation powers. To allay these fears, each federal administration—Democratic and Republican alike—reiterates the tired argument that water allocation is primarily a state bailiwick where the federal government will tread lightly if at all.

In one sense, this entire issue is a red herring. Federal pollution control law rests on the principle of the federal-state partnership. Federal agencies set minimum standards and delegate program administration to the states. Although the federal government makes program grants to states, offers technical assistance, and retains backup monitoring and enforcement powers, modern pollution control programs are essentially state programs. In this climate of federal fiscal austerity, there is no reason to believe that the federal government can afford to increase its decision-making capabilities in the area of water allocation, an area that historically has been left to the states. If the Clean Water Act were amended to include groundwater, states would continue to make water allocation decisions under the federal-state partnership.

In another sense, the states have good reason to beware of an enhanced federal presence in groundwater allocation. The federal government was established to manage interstate spillovers, the kinds of impacts that are increasingly evident in water resources management. Interstate aquifers, like the Ogallala aquifer, are being swiftly depleted by their overlying states, which are treating them as commons. When these regional aquifers have been exhausted, the overlying water-short states will clamor for massive interbasin transfers of water from other states and even other nations. Furthermore, aquifers located entirely within the boundaries of a single state may have national economic and ecological significance. The federal government should indeed reassess its hands-off policy with regard to water allocation.

This bifurcated attitude on the part of governmental officials toward water pollution control and water allocation is reflected in a split within the field of water law. Most water lawyers—practitioners and academics alike—perceive themselves as dealing with water allocation. In the evolution of water law, the field has become virtually coterminous with the law of water rights. Some water lawyers, particularly in the western United States, envision two distinct fields: water law and water quality law. This invidious distinction is breaking down as water shortages compel the realization that wastewater from sewage treatment plants is valuable and that a first-priority right to divert contaminated water may be valueless. But the old two-gun water resources law still roams the western plains, although it is now riding a lame horse.

To a great extent, the form and content of a statutory system dictate the structure and functions of those agencies that administer the statutes involved. Because state legislatures have typically treated water allocation and water pollution control in different statutes, administrative responsibilities for these functions have been placed in different administrative agencies or in different divisions, bureaus, or elements of a single agency. This fragmentation of water resources management results in bad policy and bad administration. We must reevaluate the ways in which we organize our water resources agencies. For example, instead of perpetuating separate bureaus of groundwater and surface water, or water allocation and water pollution control, why not create integrated divisions of planning, standard setting, permitting, monitoring and enforcement, and funding and technical assistance?

Groundwater management in the United States will not achieve its potential until (1) the same legal regime is applied to groundwater and surface water, (2) water allocation and water pollution control are seen as interrelated and equally important aspects of water law and comprehensive water resources management, and (3) the federal government assumes regulatory responsibility for interstate and nationally significant aquifers.

Groundwater Management

Managing groundwater entails complex and contentious questions of ecology, economics, and ethics. The following are examples: Do we have a moral right to allow any degradation of groundwater at all? What are our ethical responsibilities to our descendants and the rest of our planet? Can we anticipate the development of new mitigative technology? How expensive will it be to attain or maintain natural or background levels of quality? How do we compare economic costs and environmental benefits? Over what periods and to whom should these costs and benefits be determined?

Do we know enough about the behavior of groundwater systems and the environmental effects of contaminants to set minimum standards? Is nondegradation necessary as a hedge against uncertainty? What are the costs of information and misinformation?

If we decide to allow some degradation of groundwater, how should minimum standards be set? Should they be set at potable water quality, regardless of whether the groundwater is now used, or capable of being used, for drinking? at levels capable of being achieved by the best available technology economically achievable? at the limits of detectability? at different levels for different contaminants or different geographical areas? Should criteria be based on uses other than potable water, such as ecological, industrial, or agricultural uses?

Should increased treatment costs be paid by those who contaminate groundwater? by those who benefit from a relatively uncontaminated supply? by the general public? by some combination of these? At what point should we forgo cleaning up contaminated groundwater because it is simply too expensive when contrasted with more dangerous threats such as atmospheric warming or indoor air pollution?

Finally, how should trade-offs be made between groundwater and surface water use, and between groundwater quantity and quality?

Unfortunately, no absolute principles exist for applying ecology, economics, and ethics to groundwater management. Each decision regarding protection, restoration, and allocation of groundwater is hydrologically and politically unique; each decision must be made operationally in the context of a particular situation. The key to improving groundwater management decisions is the design and implementation of a process that is capable of bringing ecology, economics, and ethics, as well as other approaches, to bear on specific problems involving the groundwater resource.

Environmental management, to a greater extent than any other management area, must be multidisciplinary and interdisciplinary. Optimal groundwater management decisions should be made, or strongly influenced, by multidisciplinary teams. For a major policy decision, such a team might include persons educated in communications, ecology, economics, engineering, ethics, geology, hydrology, information systems, law, planning, politics, public administration, public health, public participation, and sociology and social psychology. Each of these participants should be familiar with the language and fundamental concepts of the other disciplines represented, able to communicate his or her insights to nonspecialists, and experienced in multidisciplinary decision making. The team leader should be a capable environmental generalist as well as a trained and experienced facilitator. Support for this team should be provided by a multidisciplinary staff qualified to produce information that is suitable in form and content for the multidisciplinary team.

In spite of its obvious advantages for environmental decision making, groundwater management by multidisciplinary teams is the exception, whereas management by isolated specialists is the rule. As I stated in the preface to the first edition of *Water Law* (1984):

> The most formidable obstacle to rational water resources management is the failure of communication among water resources professionals and among students in the water resources field. Narrow specialization generates esoteric jargon that impairs effective cooperation in pursuit of desirable social goals. When scientists, engineers, lawyers, planners, social scientists, and management specialists speak intelligibly only to their disciplinary colleagues and students, the results are misunderstandings, chauvinism, and frustration. All too frequently, disciplinary separations are institu-

tionalized in water resources management and study organizations. However, optimum water resources policy outcomes can be realized only if all aspects of water resources management, i.e., physical, social-scientific, and legal-institutional, are integrated into comprehensive analysis and decision-making.

Compartmentalized decision making regarding groundwater survives because it has a political life of its own. This mode of decision making is popular, first, with politicians. Their goal is a short-term one: reelection. Consequently, they seek quick outcomes achieved at a minimum expense of political capital. Dealing with a few like-minded administrators in a particular agency is considerably better, to a politician's way of thinking, than having to muster support among a variety of administrators located in several agencies. Moreover, decisions made in this fragmented way will probably be low-visibility ones, from which other administrators, other politicians, and the general public will be excluded because of their presumed lack of expertise in the one area that matters.

For these reasons, groups favoring groundwater extraction and development resist widening the contexts of decisions that affect their financial interests. To them, decisions regarding applications to divert groundwater are purely hydrological and technological decisions to be made by state engineers on the basis of available quantities of water. Finally, many administrators feel comfortable with specialized decision making regarding groundwater, not only because they desire bureaucratic insularity but also because narrow horizons enable them to make suboptimal, low-visibility decisions that might be helpful to friendly lobbyists and politicians.

Comprehensive water resources management, on the other hand, entails a broad, long-term view of the resources that is based on multidisciplinary analysis and genuine public participation. To some extent, statutes dictating study, consultation, and disclosure, such as the National Environmental Policy Act, have encouraged comprehensive water resources management. But these statutes are too limited and too deeply flawed to slay the hydra of excessive specialization. What is needed is a thorough reorientation of public perceptions, a reorientation that can be achieved only by means of a fifth element (along with ecology, economics, ethics, and aesthetics): education.

Matthew Arnold would have realized that education is the primary factor in generating a multidisciplinary environmental management process. He himself was an inspector of schools, and his father, Thomas Arnold of Rugby School, was one of the foremost educators of nineteenth-century England. Throughout his works, Matthew Arnold preached, as a weapon against the "ignorant armies [that] clash by night," a new Hellenism—the sweetness and light that accompany a knowledge of the best that has been thought and said in the world. In his poem "The Buried Life," apprehension of the "unregarded river of our life" is, in Richard Poirier's words, a "work of knowing": We are overcome by "an unspeakable desire / After the knowledge of our buried life"; we long to "inquire / Into the mystery of this heart which beats / So wild, so deep in us—to know / Whence our lives come and where they go." Finally, "a man becomes aware of his life's flow,"

> And then he thinks he knows
> The hills where his life rose,
> And the sea where it goes.

The characteristic note of self-doubt in this conclusion reemphasizes Arnold's dedication to the tentative, self-correcting, and continual nature of the educational process.

Environmental higher education can be improved in a number of ways. For the most part, environmental education at American universities does not prepare students for multidisciplinary teams and interdisciplinary interactions. At the undergraduate level, students are introduced to environmental awareness through necessary but inevitably superficial courses about issues and then are expected to choose a disciplinary major that will exhaust between one-quarter and one-third of their undergraduate credits. Some majors, such as environmental studies or environmental management, attempt to be interdisciplinary by allotting elective credits to courses in various disciplines and encouraging their students to obtain broad environmental educations. But the choice of courses within these structures is desultory. Moreover, nowhere is an undergraduate environmental affairs major expected to participate in a multidisciplinary team. Senior-major seminars and team-taught courses are poor approximations of a genuinely interdisciplinary experience. At the graduate level, the disciplinary focus becomes even more pronounced, with the ultimate goal consisting of a substantial individual research project.

We have heard a good many diatribes lately against postmodernism and the disintegration of the university curriculum. In the context of environmental education, we should be decrying the overemphasis on disciplinary training and the virtual neglect of that distinguishing feature of successful environmental management, interdisciplinary decision making by multidisciplinary teams. Preparation for engaging in this process should be the common element of environmental higher education. Accurate information is, of course, a prerequisite for making intelligent decisions; but without a holistic context for applying that information, the result is ill-conceived, narrow, and illegitimate environmental policy.

How can environmental education be redesigned to combine the acquisition of specialized information with participation in an enlightened multidisciplinary decision-making process? Most important, undergraduate students of the environment should concentrate on an issue, expressed as a case study, rather than a discipline. Such a problem-centered curriculum would be initiated by the formation of teams during the sophomore year. Each fledgling team would meet with a multidisciplinary faculty advisory board to define the parameters of the issue and determine information acquisition priorities. Individual team members would then be delegated—based as far as possible on personal choice—to acquire the relevant information by enrolling in appropriate courses. The team would continue to meet during the junior and senior years, under the aegis of a faculty facilitator, to integrate new information and redirect the project if necessary. Each team member would be responsible for obtaining his or her assigned portion of the informational whole and communicating it, along with the fundamental concepts and language of the discipline from which it arises, to the rest of the team. Each participant would also serve a term as associate facilitator. During the senior year, the team would produce a written and oral report in the form of a symposium.

It would be more difficult to establish this model of environmental education on the graduate level because of the traditional orientation of graduate schools toward individual, disciplinary research. In addition, the academic publication system militates against multidisciplinary graduate work. Each graduate student in an environmentally related discipline, however, should be required to enroll in at least one multidisciplinary graduate seminar along the lines of the undergraduate education suggested above.

Until we reconcile our environmental management and educational systems, we cannot satisfactorily address the myriad and complex groundwater problems that beset us. Our task as students and educators is to understand and teach that the buried life flows through each of us and through our educational and political institutions as well as through the natural world.

TOXIC WINDS: 9 WHOSE RESPONSIBILITY?

Gene E. Likens I have worked with a number of colleagues at the Hubbard Brook Experimental Forest in New Hampshire since 1963 in a large multidisciplinary study of air-land-water interactions. Our goal has been to understand the ecology of natural ecosystems and the linkages between systems over time. To maintain research funding over a long period, ideas and results must be generated to convince peers that funding should be continued. We have received continuous funding for our research at Hubbard Brook from the National Science Foundation for more than twenty-five years, and recently we received another grant to carry us through 1992. This span of continuous funding is very unusual from this particular federal agency.

In part, we have been funded because our research results have been visible. Much of this visibility has occurred because we have published our results in peer-reviewed journals. Second, we have attempted from the beginning to bring all of our diverse results together and to

Financial support was provided by the National Science Foundation, the Andrew W. Mellon Foundation, and the Mary Flagler Cary Charitable Trust. This chapter is a contribution to the program of the Institute of Ecosystem Studies and to the Hubbard Brook Ecosystem Study. The Hubbard Brook Experimental Forest is operated and maintained by the USDA Forest Service, Radnor, Pennsylvania. I also thank Joseph S. Warner for many helpful comments and suggestions on the manuscript.

make some sense of them (a process called synthesis, in today's jargon). This synthesis was done primarily in three books (Likens et al., 1977; Bormann and Likens, 1979; Likens, 1985a). Because people like to read material that has been brought together into a "story," the books gave us a certain amount of visibility. Third, some of our findings contributed to controversies, and these controversies helped us maintain funding. (I do not know how to test the validity of that last statement, but I believe that it is true.)

The Hubbard Brook Experimental Forest is in a large, bowl-shaped valley in the White Mountains of New Hampshire. The Hubbard Brook Valley is a unit of the landscape, and its boundaries are clear. Individual watershed-ecosystem units within this valley were established to help us focus conceptually and quantitatively on large-scale and complex ecological problems, such as nutrient flux and cycling through a forested landscape. Once we obtained some background information, we developed a broad conceptual model (Bormann and Likens, 1967), began to ask questions, and then did experiments. Our experiments involved whole watershed-ecosystems (Likens, 1985b) because we wanted our results to be pertinent and realistic, that is, to be drawn from actual natural ecosystems, not just laboratory simulations. The results from these large-scale experiments were quantitative and exciting, but sometimes controversial. An early experiment tested an ostensibly simple question: What happens to the forest ecosystem when all of the live trees are removed? Not much was known quantitatively about such a perturbation before that experiment. We killed all of the trees on one of the watershed-ecosystems and prevented regrowth for three years. We did not want any vegetation on the system at all (fig. 9.1). As a result, the chemistry of the stream water changed dramatically, especially the concentrations of nitrate. Six months after the trees were killed, the concentrations of nitrate shot up to enormously high values and in the second year went even higher, exceeding the concentrations allowed for drinking water in public water supplies (Likens et al., 1970). This experiment began in 1965, in the midst of a major drought period (1964–1966) in the northeastern United States. During this time, it was necessary to ask for a glass of water at a restaurant in New York City, and some people made semi-serious proposals "to cut those trees in New England that are wasting water by evapotranspiration, to produce more liquid water for the thirsty megalopolis between Boston and New York City." The Hubbard Brook results, however, suggested that such water might not be fit

Figure 9.1. An experimentally deforested watershed at the Hubbard Brook Experimental Forest. This watershed-ecosystem was deforested in 1965 and maintained in that condition with herbicides for three years. Cut trees were left in place instead of being removed, as would be the case in a normal timber harvest. Photo by author.

to drink. Undesirable algal blooms in the stream from the experimentally deforested watershed-ecosystem also attested to the increased levels of nutrients and light in these drainage waters. The nutrients were coming from the soil, and some people thought that the soil was being impoverished of nutrients. In the mid-1970s, for example, I attended a lecture at Cornell University about chemical defoliation in Vietnam. The speaker said that defoliation in Vietnam caused results like those at Hubbard Brook, where "they cut down the trees, and all the nutrients washed out of the soil." I almost fell off my chair. Obviously, the Vietnam situation was much different from Hubbard Brook's in many ways, and that extrapolation was unfounded.

Also at this time, legislative bills were being considered in Congress to regulate the clear-cutting of forests, primarily in the western United States. Opponents of clear-cutting used data from Hubbard Brook to suggest that the soils in the West would become sterile. Although we had published our data actively and aggressively in scientific journals (Likens et al., 1970, for example), only once were we asked to comment to Congress about the clear-cutting issue.

At one point during this period, a Program Officer of the National Science Foundation (NSF), in reviewing our continuation proposal, told us that NSF would continue to fund us, essentially providing all the money we had asked for, but we would not be allowed to study forest cutting anymore. The reason given was that our results were embarrassing to another federal agency, apparently because clear-cutting was an accepted federal policy for harvesting timber, and our results indicated that there were potential environmental problems. We fought this issue all the way to the Director of the NSF and succeeded in convincing the foundation that we should be allowed to study the effects of clear-cutting if our proposals were judged scientifically worthy by peer review. In fact, we have continued these studies until the present time. Such sustained ecological research has contributed significantly to an understanding of natural ecosystems, but that aspect of the Hubbard Brook study has been discussed elsewhere (Likens et al., 1977; Bormann and Likens, 1979; Likens, 1983, 1985a, 1989a).

A second controversy emerged after we learned that the rain and snow at Hubbard Brook were quite acid, about pH 4.1. We thought this result was interesting but did not know how widespread this potential problem might be, because there were too few measurements in North America for comparison. It was not until I established monitoring stations in the Finger Lakes region of New York in 1970 that I discovered that the rain and snow there essentially had the same pH as we had found in the White Mountains of New Hampshire (Likens, 1989b).

We published the first paper on acid rain in North America in 1972 (fig. 9.2). A Swedish scientist, Svante Odèn (1968), already was writing about the acidity of rain in Scandinavia. In the title of our first paper (Likens et al., 1972), we used the term *acid rain* for its potential visibility and impact. We didn't know that it had been used more than one hundred years earlier by an Englishman (Smith, 1872). Our second paper on acid rain was published in *Science* (Likens and Bormann, 1974), and a week later, the results were described on the front page of the *New York Times* (June 13, 1974).

Some 70 percent of total sulfur emissions in the United States occur from the combustion of fossil fuels in the production of electricity, largely in the Tennessee and Ohio River valleys. As the air moves from west to east, it transports these sulfur pollutants to somewhere else where they

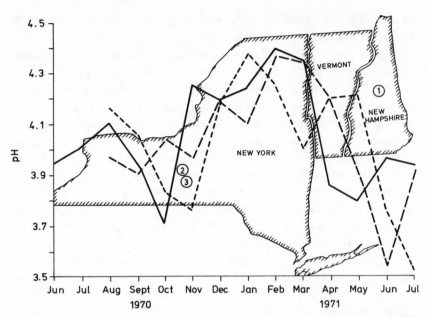

Figure 9.2. The volume-weighted pH of rain and snow at the Hubbard Brook Experimental Forest, New Hampshire (1; solid line); at Aurora, New York (2; line of smaller dashes); and at Ithaca, New York (3; line of larger dashes), during 1970–71. From Likens, 1989b.

are dumped on somebody else. This aspect of the phenomenon—that somebody is generating waste and dumping it on somebody else—has a large emotional impact. How can you protect yourself from polluters far away when you do not even know who they are? Large industries, huge investments, and thus many vested interests are involved in the problem.

Today probably more than ten thousand scientific articles, a dozen or so major federal reports, and a vast number of popular reports have been written about acid rain. It now is well accepted that winds can transport toxic materials of many kinds throughout the global atmosphere (for example, see Brown, 1987a).

The Premise

With so many strong, opposing interests in environmental issues, such as environmentalists on one side and industrialists on the other, should scientists, dressed in shiny armor, ride on white steeds between these two forces, fending off exaggerations from both sides? An example of the exaggerations and half-truths is seen in an article, by W. M. Brown (1986), published in *Fortune* magazine:

> Acid rain is only a minor contributor to the environmental damage. . . . So far as the lakes are concerned, the principal sources of damage are likely to be natural sources of acid. . . . The amount of acid generated by nature is now known to be far greater than that contributed by industrially generated acid rain. Take bird droppings, which are a relatively minor contributor to the problem. A calculation based on Audubon Society data showed that the droppings hit the U.S. at a rate of about one million per second, and the 150 million tons of droppings per year outweigh sulfur dioxide emissions by something like six to one.

Brown seemed unconcerned that sulfuric acid, not uric acid (in bird feces), is the dominant acid in recently acidified lakes, that bird droppings are not focused on lakes, that bird populations have not increased dramatically in the last fifty years but sulfur dioxide emissions have, and so forth. How does this naive or contrived confusion between apples (bird droppings) and oranges (anthropogenic sulfur dioxide emissions) help to resolve an important societal issue? It doesn't.

Out of frustration at the exaggerations and half-truths being generated about acid rain, largely in the nonscientific literature, two colleagues and I wrote an article, published in a peer-reviewed scientific journal, called "Red Herrings in Acid Rain Research" (Havas et al., 1984). We wondered why anybody would intentionally want to divert attention from scientific issues by introducing some irrelevant topic. We suggested that a number of red herrings in the acid rain issue had been generated by industrial groups, and we explained why they were red herrings.

The general pattern of response to environmental issues such as acid rain is remarkably similar, whether the issue is the ecological effects of pesticides, the disposal of toxic wastes, the destruction of stratospheric ozone, the ecological effects of nuclear war, or toxic winds (fig. 9.3). First, someone identifies a potential "problem." The problem simmers until for some reason it becomes highly visible, usually by getting into the popular press. Visibility for the issue of pesticides came with one book, *Silent Spring*, by Rachel Carson (1962), a powerful best-seller. As the problem becomes visible, public awareness increases dramatically, and people start pointing fingers. Who caused this problem? Then comes the reac-

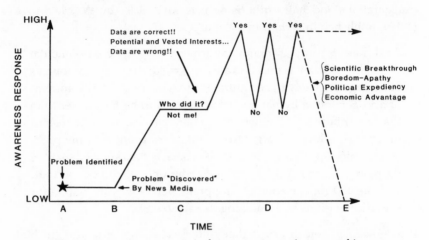

Figure 9.3. A pattern of awareness and response to environmental issues.

tion from the vested interests: "We didn't do it," "You must be wrong," or "The data must be wrong."

After this peak in awareness, reaction, and debate, the issue advances to one of several possible outcomes: (1) Everybody gets tired of it, and it fades away unresolved; (2) a scientific breakthrough makes clear to everyone what needs to be done; or (3) more likely it becomes politically expedient or economically advantageous to "solve" the problem, at least in terms of public awareness.

The role of chlorofluorocarbons (CFCs) in the destruction of stratospheric ozone provides a good example of this pattern (Brodeur, 1986; Rowland, 1989). The problem was identified clearly in the mid-1970s (Molina and Rowland, 1974; Rowland and Molina, 1975). Molina and Rowland's predictions about the serious destruction of ozone in the stratosphere by CFCs led to a ban on CFCs as aerosol propellants, effective in the United States in 1978. The urgency and severity of the problem was pooh-poohed by many scientists and particularly by industry. DuPont, for example, actively and aggressively opposed any restrictions on the production of CFCs because the ozone destruction theory had not been "proven." As a result, additional proposed regulations on CFCs in the United States were abandoned in 1981. The discovery of the Antarctic ozone hole in the early 1980s (Farman et al., 1985) sparked a new surge of public awareness and concern. That finding led rapidly to the signing of a United Nations Environment Program convention in 1985 and a multinational protocol in 1987 to restrict emissions of CFCs (see Rowland, 1989).

The financial stakes for industry are relatively low for CFC reduction or elimination. The production of CFCs represents a small part (about 2 percent) of the total revenues of DuPont, the major producer of CFCs, and few jobs are threatened. Any losses might be reduced ". . . by the windfall profits to be earned on the dwindling supply of the chemical" (Shea, 1988). Also, it appears that DuPont's opposition to controls on the production of CFCs may have eased at the same time the corporation was announcing a substitute for CFCs. In contrast, midwestern utilities have asserted that ratepayers and coal miners will be hurt seriously if emissions of sulfur dioxide are controlled. It should be pointed out, however, that there are other ways to deal with financial problems that may be caused by regulation of industrial activities besides threatening the elimination of jobs.

Radioactive radon gas is a particularly interesting environmental issue. It occurs naturally, so nobody is blamed or held responsible for cleanup or mitigation. Although scientists do not agree on the indoor concentrations at which radon should be regulated, there is no major group with a vested financial interest (although real estate agents are starting to appear in phase C–D of fig. 9.3) to argue that radon is safe or not proven harmful as has been the case for tobacco smoke, sulfur emissions, and CFCs.

With regard to stratospheric ozone, science apparently was important in resolving the issue. It is not clear, however, that science plays a decisive role in political decision making about environmental issues. In 1984 we held a conference at the Institute of Ecosystem Studies that brought together policymakers and scientists to debate the question, Does scientific information really matter in policy decisions? The scientists were pessimistic, but the policymakers were less so. At the end of the meeting, we focused on acid rain and asked the question, Is there a scientific consensus on acid rain? If there were a consensus, then it would be obvious that decisions could and should be made. Of course, other major factors affect decision making—in particular, political and economic considerations. We selected six major governmental reports on acid rain that had been prepared by scientists. We listed questions and then looked for the answers in these reports. We copied verbatim, the "answers" from the federal reports (Driscoll et al., 1985). We then distributed our report ("Is There Scientific Consensus on Acid Rain?") widely to politicians, colleagues, and the news media. In fact, the six federal reports, including one commissioned by the Reagan administration's Office of Science and Technology Policy (OSTP), all showed a great amount of consensus. Indeed, the President's Acid Rain Peer Review Panel of OSTP stated in 1984:

> Additional steps should be taken now which will result in meaningful reductions in the emissions of sulfur compounds into the atmosphere. . . . The overall scientific understanding of the various aspects of acidic precipitation is incomplete at the present time, and will continue to have major uncertainties well into the future. . . . For these reasons, any current scientifically-derived recommendations must be based on an imperfect, always increasing, body of pertinent data whose quality and completeness can be expected to improve for decades. Recommendations based on imperfect data run the risk of being in error; recommendations for inaction pending collection of all the desirable data entail even greater risk of damage.

The effort in 1985 to summarize the scientific understanding (Driscoll et al., 1985) seemed to have little impact on the policymakers dealing with the acid rain issue in the United States.

For eight years beginning in 1980, the Reagan administration opposed consistently any regulatory action to reduce acid rain, always citing a "need" for more information. For example, Kathleen M. Bennett, the Environmental Protection Agency's assistant administrator for air, noise, and radiation, testified in February 1982 at a hearing of the Senate Environment and Public Works Committee, "Within two or three years, we expect to have some very important findings that will help guide us. It is possible that those will suggest further activities that are necessary, and it is possible that they won't." In 1989, however, President George Bush, Secretary of State James Baker, and Environmental Protection Agency administrator William Reilly all identified acid rain as a high-priority issue needing resolution. Most noteworthy, however, was the replacement in 1989 of Senator Robert C. Byrd (West Virginia) by Senator George J. Mitchell (Maine) as Senate majority leader. Senator Byrd consistently had fought any acid rain legislation, whereas Mitchell had sponsored several legislative proposals on the subject.

A legitimate question to ask, then, is, what scientific finding caused this sudden turnaround in the political climate related to acid rain? Clearly, there was none, even though the National Academy of Sciences, another relatively conservative force regarding controls on acid rain from 1980 through 1988, produced a white paper in the autumn of 1988 for the Bush transition team; it called for action on acid rain. In my opinion, there have been no major scientific breakthroughs relative to acid rain research during the past several years that would call for these *sudden* political actions to resolve the problem. During the spring of 1990, both the House and Senate of the U.S. Congress overwhelmingly passed legislation to amend the Clean Air Act, including provisions to reduce acid rain.

Scientific Reporting

During the hot, dry, and polluted summer of 1988, numerous articles about the environment appeared in the news media. A major article in the *Boston Globe* on July 14 (Tye, 1988) described various environmental problems related to acid rain, particularly those in Canada. It is well known that if you want to attract people's attention, you need a picture. Although there was little in this article about lakes, the *Globe* used a picture of a scientist collecting water samples. The caption read, "Tony Blouin of Dalhousie University, Halifax, Nova Scotia, demonstrates the Van Dorn sampler, which collects lake algae that are later analyzed for levels of acidity." Of course, such measurements of acidity are not done, and the caption was incorrect. The picture was not very pertinent to the article anyway. Another article appeared ten days later on the front page of the *New York Times*. To capture attention, it featured a dramatic picture (fig. 9.4). All the dead trees in the picture look dreadful and provided a frightening illustration. The caption read: "Dead trees on Mount Mitchell in North Carolina, which was covered with red spruce five years ago." Unfortunately, the trees were not red spruce and they may not have been killed by air pollutants, which was the main topic of the article.

The question that I am raising is multifaceted and complex. These news reports were highly visible, but they contained serious mistakes. Such mistakes are common in the news media. Are these mistakes important? Is it permissible to tell little white lies to achieve a valuable result?

I would like to share some questions that may be at the crux of this problem in reporting scientific information. These questions relate to

Figure 9.4. Photo by Duane Hall, *The New York Times*, July 24, 1988.

ethical behavior, scientific research, and the formulation of public policy. First, do scientists have an ethical obligation to make their research results known to the public? My answer would be an immediate "Of course!" We get most of our research funds from taxpayers, and thus we have an obligation to report our results and to inform the public. We must publish, but must we publish only in peer-reviewed journals? I have stressed earlier the value of publishing in peer-reviewed scientific journals to establish scientific credibility. But is that where our ethical obligation ends? What is a peer-reviewed journal? Does this mean only that a peer must have seen the paper and commented on it? My favorite examples for the type of review comments that scientists sometimes receive are these: "Great article—publish it" and "Excellent proposal— wish I had time to read it." I have received reviews such as "I didn't like it"—nothing more. Were these peer *reviews?* If so, they were not helpful in improving the product. Fortunately, most scientific reviews are thorough and helpful. In my opinion, a proper peer review includes an opportunity to reject the article when it does not meet clearly stated standards. Unfortunately, however, that is often not the current definition of peer review, particularly in large federal "assessment" projects.

Next, should scientists talk to reporters? If scientists have an obligation to make their results known to the public, what better way is there than to talk to reporters?

Most scientists probably would agree that they have an obligation to inform the public about their research findings. Why then wait until these findings appear in technical language in a peer-reviewed journal and hope that an intelligent and curious reporter will choose to write about them? Why not go directly to the public via the news media? We might save a life, or we might save a forest. Why then are scientists reluctant or afraid to talk with reporters?

Scientists frequently are misquoted or misunderstood by reporters to the point that they are embarrassed by news accounts, and their peers respond with criticism: "Why did Likens say that? He ought to know better. Is he that stupid?" When a scientist's peers have such an impression, how do you think the scientist fares when it is time to be evaluated for promotion or for salary increase? Indeed, at such times, being quoted on the front page of the *New York Times* may not be an advantage to a scientist, particularly a young scientist. As a result, many scientists will not talk to reporters at all. During the autumn of 1987 the National Acid Precipitation Assessment Program (NAPAP) produced a controversial *Interim Assessment* (Kulp, 1987). I was called by a number of prominent science reporters, and each one of them complained bitterly to me that most other scientists would not talk with them about this highly charged report, for fear of losing their jobs or their research grants. Why do some scientific peers frown on colleagues for talking to reporters, and some university and governmental administrators attempt to control or even forbid their scientists from talking to reporters?

Scientists know how the standards of quality control are applied in scientific journals. Our best journals and the majority of our grant proposals are peer-reviewed fairly and intelligently, with an opportunity to reject. How is quality controlled by the news media? I could write a report indicating that I had discovered a new cure for AIDS, carry it to the editorial offices of the *New York Times,* and say, "Here. You should publish this tomorrow on the front page. This is important information." Obviously, the paper would not do it. Why then was the bird-droppings story, which was not peer-reviewed, printed in about every newspaper in the country—and on the front page of many of them?

How do we reach consensus in science? When a report claims to present a consensus, or when a report appears on the front page of the

New York Times, does that constitute a consensus? If an article were to appear in the *New England Journal of Medicine* and then be reported in the *New York Times,* one might think that the information represented a consensus. Sometimes the statement is made that "most scientists believe so-and-so." But what does anyone know about what most scientists believe?

And finally there is a major ethical question: Can any answer be purchased? Many people believe that scientific answers are for hire. If so, that shiny armor quickly becomes tarnished.

Recently I had a disquieting experience in this regard. I was invited to meet with representatives of one of the largest coal companies in the United States. During the course of the meeting, the coal company representatives admitted that their company had hired a "whole room full of Ph.D. scientists to obfuscate, confuse, and delay at every opportunity" the acid rain issue and its regulation. I was shocked and asked, "But who then cares about the human condition?" They responded, "We do, but we must maintain this activity if we are to sell our coal to the electrical utilities, who oppose any regulation."

Such aspects of the interface between scientists and the news media deserve serious consideration, discussion, and analysis if communication of scientific results to the public is to be improved.

Taking Responsibility

At the moment, the issue of global climate change has politicians and scientists throughout the whole world in turmoil. How are we going to make decisions about such difficult environmental issues? How can we inform the public about these issues? How do we make decisions about important environmental matters where vast sums of money are at stake? It is clear that major environmental problems lie ahead. How do we make accurate scientific information available to the public, including politicians, so that they will understand it, and the uncertainties associated with it, and thus develop wise policies and take intelligent action?

The acid rain issue and the explosion at the Chernobyl nuclear power plant have refocused attention on what has been recognized for a long time about the scientific, political, economic, and ethical considerations involved when a toxic substance is produced or used in one place and then released or discarded in another. The titles *The Toxic Cloud* (Brown,

1987a), "Toxic Winds" (Brown, 1987b), "What Goes Up . . ." (Fish, 1988), "Something in the Air" (Kahaner, 1988), and *Ill Winds* (Mackenzie and El-Ashry, 1988) all refer to hazardous materials transported in the atmosphere to new locations. Of the numerous examples of this phenomenon, several are very visible: organic pesticides (the accident in Bhopal, India), radioactive materials (Chernobyl), toxic metals such as lead, and acid rain.

Who has responsibility for dealing with the numerous complicated issues related to toxic winds, and what must they do?

- Reporters must get it right.
- Scientists must work with reporters to disseminate new findings and make them clear and understandable to the public. Scientists must be certain that uncertainties are understood.
- Corporate emitters and releasers of toxic materials must stop making irresponsible decisions that attempt only to maximize profits, and instead they must accept roles of social responsibility and leadership.
- Politicians must provide leadership and form partnerships with the public to make it easier for individuals to accept responsibility about environmental issues.
- Students must learn more about environmental issues and ethics in order to develop a "meaningful philosophy of life" (fig. 9.5).
- Teachers must provide meaningful examples to students. "Universities should be among the first to reaffirm the importance of basic values, such as honesty, promise-keeping, free expression and nonviolence, for these are not only principles essential to civilized society; they are values on which all learning and discovery ultimately depend" (Bok, 1988).
- Universities should increase course offerings about the relationship between ethics and environment, and they should require students to take them.
- Individuals must accept responsibility for their part in these problems. We must conserve, recycle, and be efficient, all of which will reduce waste.

Each of us in society has a role in resolving environmental problems. Each of us has an ethical obligation to be responsible and to do our part in protecting a healthy environment. Such shared ethical responsibilities

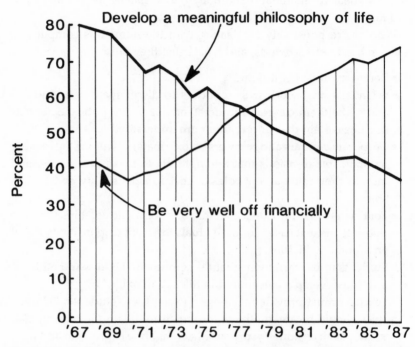

Figure 9.5. Goals of university freshmen. From Astin et al., 1987. Copyright © 1988 by The New York Times Company. Reprinted by permission.

were the central tenet for the original Earth Day in 1970. We must be willing to accept this responsibility again. The political and emotional climate was appropriate twenty years ago to embrace this responsibility, but is it today? Many people disconnect pollution control devices from automobiles and use leaded gasoline in vehicles designed for unleaded fuel. Corporations sell leaded gasoline and pesticides that are banned in the United States to developing countries with less environmental awareness and fewer regulations. Automobile manufacturers in the United States lobby Congress to push back the deadline for improved mileage. Powerful engines and higher speeds are gaining in popularity

Table 9.1. Spending on environmental versus military security

Environmental project	Cost (billions of $ per year)	Equivalent world military expenditure (days)
Develop action plan for tropical forests	1.3	0.5
Provide clean water in Third World	30	10
Halve emissions of SO_2 and NO_x to reduce acid rain		
In eastern United States	6	2
In European Economic Community	5–7	3

Source: Modified and expanded from Brundtland, 1987.
Note: The world spent more than $900 billion on military purposes in 1985, more than $2.5 billion per day.

and at the same time are increasing carbon dioxide and other emissions to the atmosphere.

The costs for environmental protection are quite large, but they are insignificant relative to the expenditures that nations of the world make for their military security (table 9.1). What are our priorities for spending? How are these priorities established? What can we afford in the future? I would argue that science, ethics, and an enlightened public are critical components for developing wise answers to such questions, which are critical to the survival of human societies.

It is tempting to close this chapter on a pessimistic note. Much of what sustained ecological research has revealed to us is a relentless degradation of the global environment. It is impossible to pick up a major daily newspaper without learning of some new environmental assault or additional evidence of slow deterioration. Much of this information is not news to ecologists, particularly to ecosystem ecologists. Our careers often involve taking the pulse of some part of the global ecosystem over long periods.

Although I have been critical of the quality of reporting on subjects that I know about, I am compelled to acknowledge that these subjects are at least being put before the American public. Acid rain, stratospheric ozone depletion, tropical deforestation, global climate change, toxic wastes, ocean dumping—who would have thought a few years ago that these topics would compete successfully for space on the front page of the *New York Times*? On the other hand, why have we permitted ourselves to be so destructive of our very life-support systems (natural aquatic and terrestrial ecosystems) so that our actions now make front-page news?

Philosophers embracing utilitarianism say that good actions are those that promote the greatest benefits for the greatest number of people. This concept seems particularly difficult for political leaders or corporate CEOs to take seriously unless they modify it slightly—the greatest good for the greatest number of voters in my district, or for the greatest number of stockholders in my company. If—and this is a big if—people in positions of power would shift gears to look beyond greedy, short-term profits or the next election, they might be forced to think about who is responsible for toxic winds. That thought process might prompt them to accept responsibility and to act for the benefit of those of us who live downstream. We all need a renewed sense of individual responsibility. Such a sense of responsibility is vital if we are to resolve these enormously complex and multifaceted environmental problems.

There are now in Washington an administration and a president eager to set high ethical standards for public service. As the speechwriters and political observers are fond of saying, "There's a new breeze blowing through our nation's capital." I for one will be looking with great interest at the rainwater samples from Hubbard Brook to see if the toxic burden carried by this new breeze is reduced.

MARKET MECHANISMS V

10 ECONOMICS, ECOLOGY, AND ETHICS: MENDING THE BROKEN CIRCLE FOR TROPICAL FORESTS

This chapter explores the prospects for reconnecting eco- **Malcolm** nomics, ecology, and ethics. Properly made, such a resto- **Gillis** ration could be valuable in coping with serious problems in the use of natural resources in general and of tropical forests in particular. The linkages have been severed, or at least obscured, in the modern practice of all three disciplines, perhaps because of the pursuit of greater specialization within disciplines.

I doubt that many modern economists are aware that their discipline has its roots in what was called moral philosophy hardly a century ago. Some economists who do know this would be loathe to admit it. Some, including Lionel Robbins in his influential 1935 treatise, have gone so far as to deny any association (other than mere juxtaposition) between economics and ethics (Robbins, 1935). Nonetheless, the venerable Adam Smith was well known as a moral philosopher long before he published the *Wealth of Nations* in 1776. In the United States the first courses labeled as economics were often taught by clergy, many of whom were trained in moral philosophy. Mason (1982) noted that the economics taught in U.S. colleges before 1890 was almost invariably considered an adjunct to moral

I thank my Duke colleagues Bob Coats, Neil deMarchi, and Bruce Payne for comments provided on earlier drafts of this chapter.

philosophy, and that an extraordinary number of instructors in economics departments that have risen to great distinction in the last fifty nomics departments, that have risen to great distinction in the last fifty years, preachers dominated the economics faculties until almost 1880.[1] And at Cambridge University, economics was taught until fairly recently as part of the moral science tripos (Sen, 1987). Furthermore, the modern discipline of economics grew up hand in hand with the utilitarian philosophy of Bentham, Mill, and others.

The moral and ethical content of economics instruction was in any case once much more explicit than now. It has not been absent in the mainstream economics of the past quarter century. Rather, it has been largely unacknowledged, as many modern economists contend that the prevailing paradigm in their field is or could be made to be value-free, just as Talcott Parsons believed that sociology should be value-neutral. No less a figure than A. K. Sen has argued that modern economics has been substantially impoverished by the distance that has grown between economics and ethics (Sen, 1987). Economics, as practiced by an overwhelming majority of economists, is in fact fundamentally based on the value judgment that individual preferences should count in the allocation of society's scarce resources. Many economists who do recognize that this moral judgment lies at the heart of their discipline are, like the author, quite comfortable in having it there. But to ignore the ethical foundations of economists' normative prescriptions is to increase the serious risk that economic rhetoric will be used in debates over questions that by itself economics cannot resolve. Consider, for example, the economist's marginal productivity theory of income distribution, which holds that in equilibrium all factors of production are paid according to their marginal return. This is, under certain precisely specified conditions, a condition for efficiency, not for justice, but it is not always recognized as such.

At the same time, the discipline of economics cannot by itself be expected to provide answers to ethical dilemmas. A central ethical issue in controversies over natural resource use and the environment is, of course, the issue of intergenerational equity: To what extent should current decisions affecting exhaustible resources and the environment

---

1. See Mason (1982). Indeed, the first professor of political economy at Harvard was the moral philosopher Francis Bowen. The Reverend John McVickar occupied the first chair in political economy in the United States, at Columbia in 1817.

reflect the interests of generations to follow? Indeed, how can those interests be identified or even defined? An answer to these questions can be provided not by economics but perhaps by some ethical system. Even given an ethical system, the question is not easily resolved. An egalitarian set of ethical criteria such as the max-min principle proposed by philosopher John Rawls (1971), for example, may indicate that the current generation should consume either more or less resources than the next, depending upon future rates of technical progress, population change, and the current stock of exhaustible resources.[2] Alternatively, an elitist set of ethical criteria, wherein the welfare of society is measured by the well-being of the best-off individual, would call for no use of natural resources by the current generation, if we expect future generations to be wealthier than the current one (Kneese et al., 1983). In any case, economists can no more identify an optimal rate of deforestation across generations than they can specify an optimal rate of savings. Economic analysis, however, may be useful in sensibly framing the questions to be asked in problems involving the interests of several generations.

The ethical foundations and the limitations of economic analysis are not at all difficult to demonstrate. But what of the nexus between the older word *economics* and the word *ecology*, the latter being a modern word that first appeared in the 1870s? Indeed the *Oxford English Dictionary* defines *ecology* as the science of the economy of animals and plants. The etymology of the two words also suggests that they were once more tightly bound than at present. The first two syllables of each is, according to the *Oxford English Dictionary*, formed on the Greek *oiko(s)*, meaning "house."[3] But does the concatenation between economics and ecology extend beyond etymology? It is argued here that this is decidedly so, that good economics not only is good ecology but indeed is required for good ecology. The dichotomy that many perceive to have arisen between

2. For a thorough and rigorous expression of these points, see Arrow's (1973) application to the problem of "just savings," Solow (1974), and Hartwick (1977, 1978).

3. The *Random House Unabridged Dictionary* also suggests that the word *ecology* was modeled on or formed after the word *economy*. That dictionary's German notation suggests that the Germans did this first and that the English scientists followed their lead. It is also worth noting that the last two syllables in *economics* derive from the root *nomos*, the word for "law" and, earlier, for "custom." The last two syllables of *ecology* go back to the Greek *logos*: a word, saying, speech, discourse, or thought. I am grateful to my colleague Bruce Payne for calling this to my attention.

economics and ecology is false and has persisted primarily because of bad economics.

Moreover, the economist's approach to problems in the distribution of income between rich and poor, a matter that can be decided only by resort to ethical norms, turns out to be helpful in dealing with questions at the intersection of ecology and economics. We will cite examples showing that major ecological disasters have been almost always economic disasters, even though the reverse is not generally true. Instances abound in which ecological calamities have had catastrophic implications for income distribution, and the reverse is often true: Maldistribution of income has often been a prime cause of ecological calamity.

The interactions between economic, ecological, and distributional (ethical) factors have been nowhere more apparent than in the widespread destruction and degradation of the world's tropical forests, particularly over the past quarter century. But examples abound also in the United States and the Soviet Union. In both nations, misguided economic policies, in which the role of prices in conservation has been ignored, have led to ecological and economic catastrophes that may or may not be reversible soon, with consequences for income distribution that are yet to be measured. In the American West, overgrazing left a lasting imprint on the arid rangelands, particularly before the Taylor Grazing Act of 1934 began to limit grazing privileges. But even well into the seventies and eighties, only 19 percent of public lands showed "improving" conditions, while 16 percent were in "declining" conditions (Dregne, 1983). As late as 1986, grazing fees charged for cattle on government-owned lands were, according to the U.S. General Accounting Office (1986), set at one-fourth to one-fifth of the fair market value of grazing on public rangelands in the West. Artificially low grazing fees naturally led to overgrazing, contributing first to "cowburnt" pastures and then to accelerated desertification in the West (Dregne, 1983).

In the Soviet Union, near-zero prices charged for irrigation water taken from the Aral Sea, and consequently the massive wastage of this resource, have reduced the area of this freshwater body, once larger than West Virginia, by fully 40 percent in the past three decades (Sumarkova and Degtyarev, 1985; Vol'futsen, 1986; Micklin, 1988). The immediate economic costs of the resultant steep loss of biological productivity of the sea have included the disappearance of the commercial fish catch and sixty thousand jobs in the area (Micklin, 1988). Environmental consequences have included powerful dust storms arising from overdried areas of land surface, as well as distinct alterations in temperature and moisture conditions over a wide area adjacent to the sea. In the future the sea could dry to a residual brine lake (Micklin, 1988), and recession of the sea threatens further climatic changes and desertification, stemming from dust and from sharp increases in reflected radiation in the territory occupied previously by the sea (Kondrat'ev et al., 1985). Sadly, virtually none of the schemes discussed by Western and Soviet scientists to preserve the Aral mention the role that higher prices for irrigation water might play in water conservation.

These examples suggest that before we begin searching for a different economics to deal with ecological questions in their ethical settings, we had better be sure that we are properly using the economics we already have. In the case of publicly owned U.S. rangelands and in that of the Aral Sea, higher prices for grazing fees and water, respectively, could have forestalled much of the environmental damage that has already occurred.

The remainder of this chapter contends that the circle between economics, ecology, and ethics need not remain broken, at least where tropical forests are concerned. Mending the circle, however, calls first for substitution of good economics for the not-so-good economics that have formed the basis for many of the policies that have encouraged forest destruction.

The Problem in Tropical Forests

Deforestation and forest degradation in the tropics are and have long been occurring primarily on lands owned not by private citizens but by governments, primarily central governments.[4] In developing nations generally, more than 80 percent of closed forest area is public land (Lanley, 1982; Repetto, 1988).[5] Moreover, in many nations with large

---

4. *Deforestation* here refers to a change in forest land use from forestry to other purposes, such that it no longer functions as a forest ecosystem. *Degradation* involves the depletion and/or damage of forest vegetation such that the forest area becomes suitable only for uses economically inferior to those in its undamaged state.

5. Closed forests are those that have not been recently cleared for shifting cultivation or heavily exploited. In closed forest formations, tree crowns, underlayer, and undergrowth combine to close off most of the ground from light, so that continuous grass cover cannot develop. Open forest formations, by contrast, are marked by a continuous grass cover on the ground.

tropical forest endowments, nearly 100 percent of all natural forest is government-owned, as defined by national constitutions in some countries (Indonesia, the Philippines, Papua New Guinea) or by other legal institutions (Malaysia, Ghana, Thailand). Governments, then, affect tropical forest use in two ways: as owners of property rights to these natural resources and as sovereign authorities in taxation and regulation.

Recent rates of deforestation and forest degradation in the tropics have been high enough in many countries to call into question governmental performance in defending the public interest in public lands. This phenomenon has been amply documented in dozens of publications (Eckholm, 1976; Spears, 1979; Myers, 1980, 1984, 1985; Lanley, 1982; Brown et al., 1985; and Repetto and Gillis, 1988) and therefore need not be treated in much detail here. The problem is not uniformly severe across all tropical nations, however. Rates of deforestation remained low through 1985 in such important timber provinces as Zaire and Gabon. But this news may be of little comfort: Forests in these two countries have been relatively undisturbed only because of the inaccessibility of much of the forest estate, a condition that is changing, particularly in Gabon with the recent completion of the Trans-Gabon railway.

Overall, the annual rate of deforestation for all tropical nations does not appear, at first glance, to have been particularly high: Of the world's tropical forests, 0.6 percent were deforested each year from 1980 through 1985, resulting in total annual deforestation of about 7.5 million hectares. In addition, each year another 4 million hectares of virgin tropical forest are converted into "secondary" forests by logging (Repetto, 1988), which damages or destroys between a third and a fifth of the residual stands (Gillis, 1988a). But in a number of nations, including Costa Rica, El Salvador, the Philippines, the Ivory Coast, and Nigeria, the natural forest could, at present rates of deforestation, disappear completely within thirty years. And in the countries with the largest remaining tropical forest estates, including Brazil, Indonesia, and Zaire, rates of deforestation have accelerated sharply since the early 1950s. In those three countries alone, the total area deforested in the five years after 1980 exceeded 11 million hectares, an area three times the size of Belgium. Elsewhere, in Central America and in Africa, the area of forest and woodland declined by 38 percent and 24 percent, respectively, between 1950 and 1983 (Repetto, 1988). Finally, deforestation rates are low in some countries only because so little forest remains. Since 1945, natural forest cover in the Philippines has shrunk from two-thirds of the total land area to only 22 percent (Myers, 1988). In Ghana, natural forests covered one-third of the nation's total land area in 1900. By 1980, natural closed forest covered only one-tenth of the land area, and by 1985, formerly forested areas under shifting cultivation and logging exceeded 11.3 million hectares, an area 4.6 times greater than the total area of closed forest in 1980 (Gillis, 1988d). The forest in once-verdant Haiti had retreated to a mere 48,000 hectares by 1985, an area much smaller than the typical single Indonesian timber concession in the seventies (Gillis, 1988a; Repetto, 1988).

The Consequences

Except in a few very low-income and not already heavily deforested nations, present and future generations face no shortage of wood. But continuation of present rates of degradation and deforestation means that present and future generations confront a critical shortage of tropical forests. This shortage will almost certainly lead to needless destruction of important tangible economic values, as well as equity values. Moreover, all indications are that continued recession of the world's tropical forest estate involves sizable risks of destruction of other important social, biological, and intangible economic values ranging from loss of productive habitat—for traditional human forest dwellers and for forest creatures—to climatic changes, loss of biodiversity, and extinction of species.

Destruction of Tangible Economic Values
Popular discussions of the world tropical forest dilemma often focus upon a supposed clash between economic and broader social values in tropical forest use. Positing the problem in this way is appropriate in only one limited sense. Some types of economic returns from forest use not only are tangible and easily measured but also are readily appropriable by loggers and agriculturalists large and small. Many of the real costs of generating these returns, however, are neither easily assignable to the activity nor clearly apparent. Other types of returns from leaving tropical forest assets intact are not easily appropriable and are much more intangible. Many of such returns are in fact social benefits of the type identified below, but many others are manifestly economic in nature and stem from both the productive and the protective functions of the forest. They include those returns flowing from commercial use of nonwood forest products, provision of food for hunting-gathering forest peoples, and

material benefits arising from protective services of the forest, such as soil retention and regulation of water runoff.

Besides involving a clash between more tangible and measurable economic values and broader, less tangible social values, present patterns of use of natural forests involve a conflict of economic values. On the one hand is the economic value of wood and land clearing for crops and cattle, and on the other is the economic value of nonwood forest products and of the important but not readily measurable soil and watershed protection furnished by intact forests. In virtually all countries with tropical forest endowments, this conflict consistently has been resolved in favor of the former set of economic values.

Examples abound. In dozens of nations from Southeast Asia to Latin America and Africa, the owner of property rights to the natural forest has placed far heavier value on the productive resources provided by the forest than on the protective resources. Moreover, the natural tropical forest has been exploited as if only two of its productive resources were of any economic value: the timber stands and the poor-quality agricultural land lying beneath the canopy. A third economic resource has been consistently overlooked: the forest's capacity to supply income from commercial and noncommercial nonwood forest products. Virtually all important nonwood forest products in the tropics, save rattan, can be harvested without cutting down trees. Commercial products that are already known number in the dozens and include nuts, oils, fibers, meat, cosmetic compounds, dyes, fruits, latex, edible bird nests, ornamental plants, spices, and pharmaceutical substances (Jacobs, 1987).

The harvest of these products can provide a perpetual annual stream of income for local people while leaving the natural forest largely intact. Logging and land clearing in the forest, however, generate essentially short-term economic returns. In the case of the type of selective logging practiced in the tropics, long-growing cycles for timber mean that the commercial value of a cutover stand cannot be replenished for more than half a century, if indeed ever. And in the species-rich, finely tuned ecosystems on poor soils, characteristic of many tropical forests, logging does three things to the ecosystem that harvest of nonwood products does not: It damages the canopy, damages the soils, and results in the removal of large quantities of minerals (Jacobs, 1987). In the case of clearcutting of tropical forest for resettlement projects (as in Indonesia and the Philippines) or for cattle ranches (as in Brazil and Central America), former forest lands often cannot even generate positive private economic returns without expensive governmental assistance. In the case of land clearing for pastures in Brazil, even heavy subsidies have proven insufficient to keep some ranchers in the black beyond six or seven years, and similar results are reported for Central America (Browder, 1988; Brown, 1988).

Selective logging as commonly practiced in tropical timber stands sharply curtails the forests' capacity to generate economic returns from use of nonwood resources (Gillis, 1988). It is not at all apparent that for a given forest parcel the economic value of this perpetual annual stream of income is exceeded by the economic value of logs extracted or land cleared. Several recent cases from Indonesia, the Philippines, and Peru in fact suggest that the potential economic benefits from keeping natural forests intact greatly exceed those that result from forest conversion. As late as 1938 the value of nonwood forest product exports in Indonesia was nearly as great as the value of timber exports (Jacobs, 1987).

Consider a much-simplified example, taken from Indonesian data.[6] Reliable information exists for export values of nonwood products but not for total production of such products. Exports of nonwood forest products in the early 1980s were perhaps slightly more than half the total of their annual production. In 1982 the value of exports of nonwood forest products reached $120 million, or 13.3 percent of the export value

6. The example is illustrative only, given the many simplifying assumptions employed. To begin with, it assumes that the ratio of exports to total production is equivalent for both types of harvest. But if anything, the ratio is probably lower for nonwood than for wood products. In addition, some logged-over timber stands are reentered within ten years, so that the assumption of no future harvests on cutover stands overstates the case against logging. Virtually all the other assumptions understate the case against logging. Reentry in Indonesia has caused even more serious damage to the residual forest than initial logging (Gillis, 1988a), and these costs are ignored in the present example. Moreover, whereas harvest of nonwood products is labor-intensive, logging is both capital-intensive and import-intensive, and not just because capital equipment in logging is imported. Thus, retained value for Indonesia is a much lower percentage of total export value for log exports than for exports of nonwood products (Gillis, 1988a). Finally, the harvest of nonwood forest products involves virtually no social costs in the form of environmental damage to soils, watersheds, habitat, and climate, whereas logging as presently practiced in the tropics involves abundant environmental costs not taken into account by logging firms. The present value formula used in these calculations is

$$PV = \frac{R_1}{(1 + r)} + \frac{R_2}{(1 + r)^2} + \cdots \frac{R_n}{(1 + r)^n}$$

where R_n = returns in year n, and r = discount rate.

of wood production. For convenience only, we will assume that on a per-hectare basis, gross nonwood product values form a similar fraction of gross wood product values for the tropical forest generally. The example initially ignores all the social and private costs of logging. We assume initially that no future harvests will take place on cutover stands and that residual stands left after logging can no longer furnish a flow of non-wood products (an assumption that will later be relaxed). Further assuming a 6 percent discount rate, the present value of the annual stream of income available from the harvest of nonwood forest products per hectare can be compared with the present value of the annual export of logs from each hectare affected. If the value of nonwood forest product exports per affected hectare is viewed as an annual perpetual return, then the net present value of this stream of income is 2.2 times greater than the net present value available from the gross value of log exports. Moreover, the discount rate required to equalize net present values of income from both activities is, not surprisingly, a high 13.3 percent. But at a discount rate about half as high, these results mean that for every hectare logged each year, Indonesia may give up twice as much future income, in present values, from nonwood products as it gains from logging. Suppose, however, that logging diminishes the nonwood productivity of cutover stands by only one-half. In that case, the present value of nonwood harvests is still 10 percent higher than if the same hectare were logged.

Under both sets of assumptions, all private and environmental costs of logging have been ignored. Because the private costs of logging are ascertained much more easily than the social costs, let us now consider what should be deducted from gross timber export earnings to find net returns to loggers. In Indonesia in 1982, logging and transport costs of logs to harbors have been estimated at close to half the gross value of timber export earnings (Gillis, 1988a; Repetto et al., 1988). Taking into account these costs, and still ignoring the environmental costs of logging, the present value of leaving the forest intact is again about twice as high as the present value of the return from logging.

Myers (1988) presents a similar example taken from the Bacuit Bay area of Palawan Island in the Philippines, involving a drainage basin of seventy-eight square kilometers with a mean slope of thirty degrees. Employing a discount rate of 10 percent, Myers finds that potential revenues from continued logging in the area (for the period 1987–96) would have a present discounted value of U.S. $8.6 million. Continued logging, however, will lead to a worsening of already serious problems for fishing and tourism arising from erosion, siltation, and bay sedimentation. In the absence of logging, the fishing and tourism industries in the area could generate revenues totalling $53.7 million, in discounted present value. With continued logging, the present value of revenues from fishing and tourism would be but $21.4 million. Logging, then, will destroy $32.3 million in economic values in fishing and tourism. Therefore, for each dollar gained from continued logging, four dollars will be lost in the fishing and tourism sectors. Moreover, the remaining timber resources would be totally exhausted by the year 2001, given continued logging, whereas both fishing and tourism would be adversely affected well into the next century.

Finally, a recent study for primary forest in Peruvian Amazonia indicates that the financial worth of the perpetual stream of nonwood forest products (primarily fruit and latex) is two to three times higher than for alternative land uses such as cattle ranching or plantation management (Peters et al., 1988). Moreover, the authors found logging to be a marginal financial option in this forest (near Iquitos). Net gains from selective logging, not clear-cutting, would be zero even if as few as 5 percent of the fruit and latex trees were damaged by logging. The authors also excluded the social and environmental costs of all three types of forest conversion. This study used a 5 percent discount rate and focused on net returns (after deduction of all harvesting and marketing).

These oversimplified examples suggest that during the past two decades environmentalists may have erred in focusing so strongly on the social and environmental costs of tropical deforestation, many of which are not easily measurable and which in any case have gone largely unheeded by governments. Economic arguments against present patterns of forest use are available, and they can be powerful even when the discount rate, so much maligned by many environmentalists, is deployed in the analysis.

Destruction of Equity Values

Many critics of environmental organizations, in industrial as well as tropical countries, have taken strong exception to what they view as environmental imperialism on the part of conservationists in wealthy countries, particularly insofar as tropical deforestation is concerned (Brown, 1988; Cohen, 1989; de Lama, 1989; Geld, 1989). To them, environmentalism is often viewed as a luxury of the rich. These critics see the need to overcome widely shared poverty in the short to medium term as overriding such longer-term issues as preservation of natural habitats and biological diversity. Moreover, as noted by Panuyouto (1987), conserving the environment is often viewed as depriving poorer socioeconomic classes of their free access to natural resources and therefore is seen as inimical to equity in income distribution.

These issues merit serious consideration, with respect to both present and future generations in tropical countries. Proposed solutions to deforestation that fail to take into account the needs of impoverished and landless rural dwellers are no solutions at all. Nevertheless, insofar as the current generation is concerned, it is not at all clear that deceleration of tropical deforestation is incompatible with greater equity in the distribution of income. Rather, a case may be made that the poor have been bearing a disproportionately high share of the costs and receiving a disproportionately low share of the returns from recent patterns of tropical forest utilization.[7] That being the case, accelerated conversion of tropical forest justified in the name of the poor would have led to a worsening, rather than an improvement, of the relative and the absolute impoverishment of the poor.

Costs to the Present Generation There is support for the assertion that poor people in poor countries are far more dependent upon soils, fisheries, and forests than are the wealthy (Brown, 1988). If so, then degradation of the resource base, particularly the portion that supports food production, involves more-serious immediate consequences for the poor than for the wealthy.

This is most obviously the case for the millions of people, typically cultural minorities, for whom tropical forests have been a traditional abode. In the Philippines, the numbers of these people are estimated at

7. Even as the poor bear a disproportionate share of the costs of forest depletion in the tropics, they may also bear a disproportionate share of the blame for it, as shifting cultivators. But quite apart from the fact that not all shifting cultivators are poor (Gillis, 1988a), shifting cultivation is not always the root cause of deforestation even in areas where shifting cultivators are most active. In many cases, large government highway projects (as in Thailand in the mid-seventies) have made natural forests accessible to loggers as well as to shifting cultivators. In many other cases in Asia, Africa, and Latin America, logging roads and resettlement programs have opened up previously inaccessible areas to shifting cultivators. In these cases, shifting cultivators merely administer the coup de grace to already vulnerable forest areas.

six million (Gillis, 1988b); and on the nearby island of Borneo, the forest-dwelling Dayaks and the Kenyah and Iban of Malaysia and Indonesia are together perhaps half as numerous. Liquidation of natural forest assets for wood or for the extremely limited agricultural potential of the soils lying beneath the forest canopy results in irreversible losses, including the destruction of what was formerly a perpetual stream of income from nonwood forest products. Cash income is lost, as well as materials for shelter and food in the form of meat, nuts, fruits, and fibers.

Tangible, immediate costs to generally poor forest dwellers extend well beyond these losses and include costs attendant upon increased erosion, greater difficulties in river transport, forest fires (Gillis, 1988c), and flooding that follow in the wake of deforestation. These same costs, particularly those of watershed damage, affect millions of marginal farmers downstream. As a result, in nations such as Thailand, both forestry and agriculture have become unsustainable in large areas in and adjacent to former forest lands (Panuyouto, 1987).

Costs to Future Generations The economies of many nations with significant remaining tropical forest endowments are strongly dependent upon these natural assets. This dependence is much more than a matter of the economic value of wood and nonwood forest products. The spatial dimensions of the protection furnished by intact forests extend not only to adjacent areas and local watersheds but also to faraway water systems and ultimately to seawater, the quality of which is so important to coral reefs and coastal fishing. Soil erosion, siltation, sedimentation, and disruption of water systems arising from deforestation take a heavy annual toll on productivity in agriculture and fisheries. In countries such as Indonesia, the Philippines, Thailand, Costa Rica, and Brazil, this toll also threatens the foundation of jobs and income in tourism, a labor-intensive industry in virtually all countries.

Sophisticated ethical systems are not required to assess the impact of deforestation upon future generations in economies that are now barely sustained by a shrinking natural resource base. Present dependency on these declining assets will either have to be replaced by future, and perpetual, dependency upon developed countries, or millions more of tropical citizens will have to migrate to developed countries.

In these circumstances, ethical systems, whether utilitarian, egalitarian, or libertarian, that might be used to help resolve questions of fairness in the use of natural resources across generations need not address the difficult problems of determining whether future generations in tropical countries will be wealthier or poorer than the present generation, but should address the matter of coping with future poverty arising from irreversible degradation of soil and water resources.

Returns If the poor may bear a disproportionately high share of the costs of deforestation in the tropics, perhaps this burden is counterbalanced by a disproportionately high flow of returns to them. After all, use of tropical forest endowments provides returns on capital invested in logging, ranching, and agricultural estates, as well as opportunities for labor income in these activities. Moreover, harvest of tropical wood provides returns over and above those necessary to attract labor and capital to extractive or land-clearing activities in the forest. These returns, called economic rents (Gillis, 1988a), are potentially quite large relative to total forest-related revenues and could be appropriated by governments and channeled to programs and projects for the benefit of lower-income groups.

Unfortunately, so far neither type of benefit has been sizable for the poor, whether in logging activities in Southeast Asia and tropical Africa or cattle ranching in Latin America. On the contrary, for the first two regions, employment gains for poor unskilled laborers in logging and timber processing have been quite limited (Gillis, 1988a, c, d). More important, in Asia and Africa, as well as Latin America, not only have very substantial rents been destroyed by commercial undertakings in natural forests,[8] but also a large share of those rents that were not destroyed through waste induced by government policies accrued primarily to the relatively wealthy rather than the poor.

Consider first the case of logging. Governments as forest owners and as sovereign taxing authorities have managed to capture only small

8. Three researchers have concluded that government policies toward use of the tropical forest in Southeast Asia resulted in the destruction of hundreds of millions of dollars of potential rents in the seventies and eighties. Fitzgerald (1986) concluded that in Indonesia, besides the capital costs of dozens of plywood mills erected in response to government incentives, Indonesians paid $956 million to become plywood exporters rather than log exporters. Gillis (1988a) estimated that these same incentive policies resulted in destruction of $547 million in timber rents over the period 1980–82 alone. This figure represented more than half the total amount of taxes collected by the government on all forest-sector activities. Finally, Boado (1988) estimated that similar policies in the Philippines between 1978 and 1982 resulted in the destruction of $500 million in potential resource rents from the forest.

fractions of available rents from logging. In Indonesia (1979–82) and Ghana (1971–74), governments captured through royalties and taxes only 38 percent of the total estimated rents in logging. The remainder accrued to investors in logging firms. Comparably low rent capture prevailed in logging in Liberia, the Ivory Coast, Cameroon, and Gabon (Gillis, 1988d). The outcome for the Philippines was even worse: From 1979 through 1982, 89 percent of available rents went to extractive firms, leaving only 11 percent to the government (Boado, 1988).

In Brazil, conversion to pasturage for cattle ranching had accounted for 72 percent of all the forest alteration detected by the Landsat satellite up to 1980. About 30 percent of this conversion was into several hundred heavily subsidized, large-scale cattle ranches, averaging fifty-five hundred hectares in size (Repetto, 1988). Without governmental subsidies, the typical large Amazonian ranch would have lost U.S. $2.8 million (in present value). The typical ranch also received tax and credit subsidies of $5.6 million (in present value). As a result, intrinsically uneconomic livestock operations were rendered very profitable indeed. Total costs of these subsidies for 460 ranches by 1983 was estimated at $2.6 billion (Browder, 1988). These benefits were received primarily not by the very poor or even the moderately poor in the affected Amazon but by investors based in the more prosperous South.

The Brazilian case is not atypical. Virtually all tropical countries have provided sizable tax incentives for logging and timber processing and land clearing in the forests, in some cases coupled with credit subsidies (Gillis and Repetto, 1988). Inasmuch as the beneficiaries of these subsidies tend strongly to be in the upper quartile of the income distribution, those who bear the brunt of the immediate costs of deforestation receive little in the way of material benefits.

Destruction of Other Values

Other values even less tangible and measurable than equity are corroded by deforestation. Tropical rain forests stabilize climates and serve as habitat and food sources for wildlife, as pools of plant species valuable for medical compounds and genetic material of now-unknown uses, as a matrix for evolution, as a source of knowledge, and as a medium for education and recreation (Jacobs, 1987). That many of these values are unquantifiable using present technology in no way diminishes their significance.

These values are treated in rich detail in a number of readily accessible sources and in other chapters of this book.[9] Many of these values are also ultimately economic in character when a long view is taken, especially the values pertaining to climate, genetic diversity, and recreation. That being the case, here again we may speak of a clash between the economic values derived from forest destruction and the economic values available from intact forests.

Finding Solutions

The foregoing discussion may seem to suggest that economic, ecological, and ethical goals are not at all incompatible, insofar as tropical forest issues are concerned. Bad economics that has formed the basis for policy making has contributed immeasurably to tragic consequences for ecology and income distribution in virtually all nations where tropical forest cover was extensive as late as 1950. This section sketches the principal features of a sensible approach for using good economics to curtail needless destruction of the world's tropical forests. The main features of this approach are stress upon the role of prices in resource conservation; reaffirmation of the importance of discounting in projects encroaching upon natural forests; accentuation of the public-goods nature of tropical forests, from a worldwide point of view; and swift and widespread incorporation of resource accounting within national income accounting frameworks.

The Role of Prices

Economists use the term *elasticity* to summarize the response of economic agents to changes in relative prices of goods and services. Elasticities are applied to a variety of types of behavior, such as consumption, supply of labor effort, propensity for risk taking, and production. Those

9. Woodwell et al. (1978) and Jacobs (1987) provide general sketches. Barney (1980) discusses the role of the rain forest in climate stabilization. The importance of useful plant species from the tropical forest is dealt with by Holloway (1977) and Myers (1980, 1984, 1985). Ashton (1976) describes the importance of the vast pool of genetic material found in the forest and suggests how the great genetic diversity of the Malaysian rain forests is partly due to adaptation to the diversity of soils on which they grow. Finally, new knowledge arising from study of the rain forest has laid the foundation for a tropics-centered botany, radically changing old concepts of climax vegetation, architecture of all woody plants, life-forms of monocotyledons, the significance of animals as seed dispensers, and the role of fungi in converting nutrients for trees (Jacobs, 1987).

who believe that consumers, producers, savers, and investors tend to be largely unresponsive to price signals may be called elasticity pessimists. Those who instead see a major role for prices in guiding economic behavior may be called elasticity optimists.

For much of the first quarter-century after World War II, particularly in the numerous countries that adopted national economic planning in the fifties and sixties, economic policies were strongly influenced by elasticity pessimism, which seemed to derive significant support from economists' demonstrations of market failures, in which prices were absent or dysfunctional, and from economic model-building exercises (Taylor, 1975). Most of these models were essentially short-term in focus and thus virtually ignored the role of prices in resource allocation. Many of the models were based on misapplications of input-output analysis, in which output was based on fixed coefficients of labor and capital inputs in production by industry services and agriculture. Labor, capital, and material inputs were seen as unsubstitutable even in the face of major changes in their relative prices, not only in the short run, when the scope for adjusting to price signals is very limited, but also in the long run, when decision makers could adjust to new price conditions.

Incalculable damages to economic welfare, to income distribution, and, above all, to the environment resulted from policies founded on elasticity pessimism. Price controls on foodstuffs led to widely known disasters such as feeding bread instead of grain to livestock in Poland and Russia, and to the stagnation of agricultural production in Peru, Bangladesh, and Tanzania (Lele, 1986). Underpricing of water in the American Southwest and in southern Russia gave rise, as we have seen, to well-documented waste of this valuable resource. Undervalued exchange rates, coupled with high tariffs on consumer goods and low tariffs on capital goods—all typical of policies infused with elasticity pessimism— led to adoption of capital-intensive technology in capital-poor nations such as Indonesia, Tanzania, Honduras, and the Ivory Coast (Gillis et al., 1987). Artificially cheap, subsidized credit spawned both resource waste and income distribution inequities in dozens of countries, including almost all of Africa and Latin America.

The influence of elasticity pessimism has generally waned in the past decade or so, owing to wider recognition of the consequences of policies founded upon it. But this waning has been less true for policies affecting the environment than for agricultural, credit, and foreign exchange policies. As late as 1974, governments and oil companies in industrial and developing countries routinely published projections of oil consumption based on the assumption of near-zero demand elasticity for energy. In the influential report of the Club of Rome in the early seventies (*Limits to Growth*), the role of prices in resource conservation was almost nonexistent. Deregulation of oil prices in the United States and curtailment of heavy subsidies on the use of gasoline and kerosene in Indonesia, Colombia, Bolivia, and Venezuela were delayed for years by false assertions about the inefficacy of higher prices in fostering energy conservation. We have seen that virtually all of the elaborate schemes proposed to save the Aral Sea failed to consider the role of higher prices for irrigation water in conservation.

Nowhere in environmental policies has the role of prices in conservation been more neglected than in policies affecting the use of tropical forests. In nearly all countries, governments as owners have consistently sold wood resources at prices well below their commercial and social value. Timber royalties, or stumpage fees, have typically been small fractions of wood value, and taxes on wood products, especially products used in local sawmills and plymills, have been even less substantial than royalties (Gillis and Repetto, 1988). License fees, or charges based on size of timber concession areas, have been similarly low in tropical nations. In Brazil and other countries where forests have been cleared for ranches, incentives for clearing have extended well beyond artificially low land prices, to subsidized low-interest rates for investments in land clearing and negative, rather than positive, taxes on cattle operations.

Moreover, except for replanting deposits required of loggers in Indonesia in the early 1980s (Gillis, 1988a), few, if any, costs of environmental degradation have been included in the prices charged to loggers or to plantation operations requiring large-scale land clearing. Although some of these costs are not easily measured, others are. Relatively good documentation of the loss of agricultural productivity from the removal of forest cover, in the form of erosion and siltation, is now available (Myers, 1988).

The Discount Rate

The concept of present value lies at the core of economic analysis of private as well as public projects and policies involving streams of benefits and costs in future periods. Economists have debated for decades the criteria for setting discount rates used in present-value calculations (Marglin, 1963; Gramlich, 1981). But the debate centered upon whether the social opportunity cost of capital or the marginal rate of time preference was the appropriate basis for choosing a particular discount rate, not whether using a discount rate in cost-benefit analysis was legitimate. Over the past two decades, however, several economists and environmentalists have called into question any use of the present-value criterion, and indeed the role of cost-benefit analysis itself, in decisions affecting the environment (Mishan, 1967; Daly, 1977; Page, 1980).

Environmental critics have attacked the present-value criterion on at least two grounds. First, they contend that use of any positive discount rate involving long-lived projects biases decisions in favor of present generations, for two reasons: (1) The current generation tends to be myopic about the future and therefore tends to use excessively high rates of discounts on future streams of benefits, and (2) the present-value criterion, as used in cost-benefit analysis, does not allow the next generation to have a time preference (discount rate) different from our own (Page, 1980). Second, environmental critics argue that use of the present-value criterion leads to irreversible actions such as global warming and species extinction.

This chapter does not attempt to resolve the debates about myopia, differing rates of time preference, irreversibility, and the appropriate role of cost-benefit analysis. My point here is that formal methods of project analysis in general, and the discount rate in particular, are not necessarily the enemies of tropical forest conservation. Arguably, more damage has been done to the tropical forest by discount rates that have been too low rather than high enough.

To understand this assertion, as applied to tropical forests, two facts must be remembered. First, the overwhelming proportion of tropical forests are owned by governments. Second, a very large share of the responsibility for forest destruction has been attributable to government infrastructure, electric power, and resettlement projects with putative benefits stretching over several generations. The lower the discount rate, the more attractive these forest-encroaching projects appear to the current generation of policymakers. The higher the discount rate, the less economical such projects are perceived to be. At zero rates of discount, the case for these public projects can easily be made compelling.

Particularly within the past decade, dozens of government projects have made large incursions into the tropical forest. The $4 billion Trans-Gabon railway was intended primarily to open up more than four million hectares of previously inaccessible forest land (Gillis, 1988d). In Sarawak vast areas of tropical forest would be submerged by a $3.3 billion project involving two dams on the Rajang River (Gillis, 1988c). As a result, 83 percent of the population above the catchment areas would have to be resettled into other forest areas, where additional deforestation would be expected from increased shifting cultivation. In peninsular Malaysia, a scheduled government project involves the clearing of a 350-square-mile swath of forest along the Penang-Kota Bara road. In Thailand the lower northeastern region was covered by undistributed forest as late as 1973; then the area was made accessible to loggers and shifting cultivators by construction of a major highway, resulting in the destruction of one million hectares of forest land in only four years (Panuyouto, 1987). The transmigration program of the Indonesian government, underwritten for so long by the World Bank, was responsible for four to five times as much deforestation as was logging in the mid-1980s (Setyono et al., 1986). In the Philippines, government-promoted fish ponds have come to occupy 100,000 hectares where mangrove forests once stood (Boado, 1988). In Brazil several huge hydroelectric projects have submerged vast areas of forested land. The $4 billion Tucurui project alone has flooded 2,160 square kilometers, and similar-sized projects are under construction near Manaus and Porto Velho (Browder, 1988). In all of these cases, higher, rather than lower, discount rates in cost-benefit analysis of the projects would have been in the interest of conservation.

Environmental critics of the use of the present-value criterion in social-cost benefit analysis may have also helped to redirect attention away from a much more fundamental problem in all decision making affecting ecology and the environment. Good economics requires that all real costs and all real benefits be considered in decision making on public projects. Undervaluation of future costs and overvaluation of future benefits in infrastructure projects encroaching upon tropical forest endowments have played major roles in decisions by governments and aid donors to proceed with many of these projects. Siltation in hydroelectric projects in deforesting areas provides an excellent example. In Brazil, India, the Dominican Republic, and many other countries, unexpectedly high rates of siltation have led to massive unforeseen costs in hydroelectric projects and to sharp constriction in not only the estimated life of dam projects but also in power production during the shortened life of such projects (Brown, 1988). In the Philippines (Myers, 1991), siltation has cut the operational lives of major hydropower reservoirs by one-half or more. Mistakes in forecasting future costs and benefits in such projects were a consequence not of the use of cost-benefit analysis per se but of the use of poor-quality scientific information regarding erosion and siltation over the affected watersheds. When a dam has a projected life of fifty years, and heavy siltation reduces that to seven years, the choice of a high or low discount rate becomes almost inconsequential in decisions to undertake the project.

The Public-Goods Nature of Tropical Forests

Public-goods theory in economics provides several concepts helpful in approaches to deforestation curtailment in the tropics. Particularly valuable, when applied on an international scale, are the concepts of pure public goods, externalities, and free riders.

We have seen that an intact tropical forest provides a large number of productive as well as protective services or benefits. Many of these benefits are divisible and appropriable by individuals and firms, such as food gatherers, loggers, and plantation owners. Such benefits are internalized to firms and individuals; other parties are excluded from partaking of them. But many forest services have characteristics of pure public goods, in that the benefits are neither divisible nor appropriable by any single person. The benefits instead are indivisible: No one can be excluded from enjoying such benefits whether they actually pay for them or not. Moreover, the benefits are nonrival; that is, consumption of these services by any one person or groups of persons does not diminish possibilities for consumption by others. Examples include stabilization of local climate, maintenance of pools of genetic materials, watershed protection, and regulation of runoff. Many of these benefits are localized, to one region of a country or to an area as large as an entire country.

Some of the services provided by forests have international dimensions, however. Forest endowments in the tropics have significant effects on the stabilization of global atmosphere and upon desertification over wide areas. Around the world, agriculture, medicine, and even some aspects of industry depend in varying degrees on the richness of known genetic resources in tropical forests, which contain from 50 to 80 percent of all species on earth (Myers, 1991). Thus, certain characteristics of intact tropical forests may be seen as pure public goods open to all global citizens, independent of who pays for them. To the extent that citizens in nontropical countries derive such benefits, they may be called free riders.

Free riders in industrial countries include owners and employees of wood-product, pharmaceutical, and cosmetic enterprises based on tropical forest resources, and citizens of industrial countries who benefit from the climatic, water, and wildlife protection provided by the forest. Worldwide interests are clearly furthered when Brazil, Indonesia, or Gabon sets aside new areas in parks and forest reserves. It is therefore apparent that the constituency for tropical conservation is worldwide. But because most of this constituency consists of free riders, who cannot be excluded from these benefits (so long as they last), free riders have little incentive to pay for the benefits and may even be unaware they are partaking of the benefits.

The foregoing constitutes a strong argument for joint financing activities and policy reforms directed toward conservation in the tropics, shared between tropical and industrial nations. Particularly suitable for joint financing are programs of research on critical determinants of healthy forest ecology, including ecosystem structure and function, fruiting patterns, regeneration, obstacles to transplantation, and flora-fauna symbiosis in the moist forest. Joint financing is mandatory for support of expanded forest preserves. Above all, joint finance is essential for rural development projects that provide poverty-stricken rural dwellers with alternatives to destructive forms of shifting cultivation and with incentives to maintain, not destroy, the forest capacity for supplying nonwood products and protective services of worldwide value.

The Role of Resource Accounting

The terms *gross national product* (GNP), *national income, depreciation,* and *personal income* are familiar to persons with only a modicum of economic literacy. Movements in the variables these terms represent are closely watched by all governments and by most private-sector decision makers. The ultimate test for many government policies has been their impact upon the rate of growth of these variables.

The conceptual framework from which these macroeconomic measures spring is called national income accounting. The basic purpose of national income accounts is to enable analysts to measure the performance of the economic system. Although traditional estimates based on national income accounting, such as gross investment, aggregate consumption, and total exports, have always been subject to significant measurement errors, the margin of error has diminished steadily since the first U.S. national income accounts were published in 1942. They do a reasonably good job of measuring, considering what they attempt to measure.

The system of national accounts in use by most countries, however, suffers from a major flaw that has serious implications for environmental policies: The system greatly distorts the role of natural resources in economic processes. Although the depreciation of man-made capital equipment and infrastructure is recognized in the national income accounts, the depletion of soils, minerals, hydrocarbons, and forests is not. The result is a perilous asymmetry in the way we measure, and therefore the way we think about, the value of natural resources (Repetto et al., 1988). This asymmetry gives rise to patently anomalous, and uneconomic, practices. On the one hand, expenditures for cleaning up an oil spill involving millions of gallons, such as that in Prince William Sound in Alaska in 1989, add to the nation's gross national product, even though the affected waters and sea life are severely harmed. On the other hand, a country could exhaust all of its forest resources and, in the process, silt up its rivers and harbors, but measured national income would not be reduced as these resources vanished.

Consider a country that for a few years had greater depreciation of its man-made capital stock than it added in new investments in physical capital. That country would soon suffer a decline in its measured GNP, because physical assets would wear out at a faster rate than they were being replaced. Policymakers would have a clear signal that something was seriously amiss. But a country that year after year draws down on its natural resource base—by mining, drilling, or logging, for example— may enjoy high rates of GNP growth for long periods, even in the absence of any new investments in sustaining the stock of these natural assets. Under prevailing systems of natural income accounting, the economy's health would appear robust during the drawdown. Therefore, the liquidation of man-made assets shows up in the national income accounts as economic decline; the liquidation of productive assets provided by nature shows up as economic growth.

This grossly defective system of information provides false signals to policymakers, leading them to destroy, or at best, ignore economic values of the environment to secure illusory or unsustainable short-term gains in measured income that register as additions to GNP.

Clearly, a high premium should be placed upon incorporation of concepts of natural resource accounting in the national income accounting frameworks of all nations, tropical or otherwise. The technology for doing so is known, the data requirements far from daunting, and the implementation problems manageable. Moreover, the concept of resource accounting has been widely accepted by such institutions as the Organization for Economic Cooperation and Development and the World Commission on Environment and Development and by a wide range of academic experts (Repetto et al., 1988). Nevertheless, to date, neither the United Nations Statistical Office nor the World Bank nor any industrial or developing country governments have agreed to make depletion accounts for natural resources an integral part of the overall national income accounting framework. These authorities take the position that depletion accounts should be calculated, but kept separate from the main national income accounting tables. Thus policymakers, official aid agencies, and economic analysts will continue to view GNP growth, unadjusted for resource depletion, as the prime measure of economic performance.

Data from Indonesia, a major producer of tropical timber, indicate how resource accounting might alert policymakers and environmental groups to the costs of deterioration in natural resource assets and might point to the need for policy changes. For the decade 1971–81, Indonesia's economic performance, by conventional measures in national income accounting, was widely regarded as successful: Gross domestic product (GDP) growth averaged just under 8 percent per year, or nearly three times the rate of other middle-income developing countries during the same period (Gillis, 1990). A substantial part of Indonesian economic growth, however, was fueled by liquidation of several natural resource assets, including oil, hard minerals, and natural tropical forests. By 1980, Indonesia exported more tropical timber than all of Africa and Latin America combined (Gillis, 1984). An exhaustive study by Repetto et al. (1988) indicates, however, that use of conventional measures of GDP substantially overstated Indonesia's income growth. For the period 1970–84, roughly coterminous with the period of nearly 8 percent GDP growth, 4 percent of the recorded annual growth was generated not by a sustainable productivity increase but by the drawdown of natural endowments of oil, soils, and forests.

Although there is nothing inherently wrong in drawing upon natural resource assets to finance economic growth, there is something wrong in using systems of information that ignore the real economic costs of such actions. Incorporating resource accounting concepts directly into existing systems of national income accounts therefore supports economic, ecological, and ethical goals of all societies. Failing to do so will result in continued overestimation of the development potential of nations.

Deploying Economic Arguments for Conservation

Tropical forest conservation is not a matter that can be fully settled by economic determinancy. Powerful economic arguments can be mustered, however, in favor of sharp curtailment of tropical deforestation. Moreover, these arguments are not only consistent with but also highly supportive of many conservation positions founded primarily upon ecological or ethical grounds.

The economic arguments have been infrequently marshaled by environmentalists. This has been doubly unfortunate, because ecological and ethical arguments for tropical conservation often have not been communicated to policymakers in the language most intelligible to them: the short-run as well as long-run economic costs of ecological degradation. Inasmuch as government policies have been directly and indirectly responsible for a sizable share of tropical deforestation, these policies must be reformed in short order to avert a worldwide shortage of tropical forests. Economic arguments are essential for reinforcing biological and ethical arguments if this is to occur.

Appropriate use of prices, discount rates, public-goods theory, and resource accounting could have forestalled much of the irreversible destruction of the earth's endowment of tropical forests over the past quarter century. It is not by any means too late to deploy these tools in the interests of tropical conservation. Another decade of delay, however, will render the effort moot.

INCENTIVES FOR CONSERVATION 11

William A. Butler
The environment is currently much in the news. Heat and drought, beach pollution and dying dolphins, forest fires in Yellowstone, too much urban ozone and too little stratospheric ozone, the greenhouse effect and the destruction of tropical rain forests, acid precipitation, radon, groundwater pollution—all are widely featured in the media. And now the United States has a president who proclaims himself an environmentalist, an Environmental Protection Agency administrator whose career has been as a professional environmentalist, and a Congress with a Senate majority leader who says he is prepared to move on a broad environmental agenda and who engineered the reauthorization of the Clean Air Act. But how can we be sure with the complexity of the current environmental problems that any new corrective actions will be the right solutions?

Environmental Regulation by Command and Control

Currently, environmental law in the United States emphasizes command and control: laws, regulations, deadlines, and penalties. Undeniably in the past two decades, this approach has had a significant measure of success. Progress is slowing, however, and comes at ever greater expense. Among the problems of this approach are the continued use of the legal system, with its attendant delays and costs; the technological basis of the approach, with the government dictating the use of "best available technology"; the establishment of unrealistic goals and unrealistic deadlines by which to accomplish them, a process that breeds cynicism; the difficult practical problems posed by enforcement; and the ever more complicated nature of the statutes and implementing regulations, which few people can be expected to understand.

Many people have concluded that the United States is poised at the beginning of a new approach to attacking environmental problems. They assert that the time has finally come for a greater emphasis upon market orientation and economic incentives to control pollution, approaches that economists and their sympathizers have long championed but that to date have been largely rejected by Congress and the environmental community.

Using Market Forces to Protect the Environment

In December 1988 a public policy study entitled *Project '88—Harnessing Market Forces to Protect Our Environment: Initiatives for a New President* made the case more persuasively than ever before that it is time for a market-based incentive approach to pollution control.[1] The study was nominally aimed at the then new Bush administration, which had already given it a favorable reception, but it was also aimed at Congress, the regulated community, environmental groups, and the Environmental Protection Agency (EPA).

The authors of the report were drawn from academia, the government, public interest law, think tanks, industry, and the world of practical politics. The theme of the report is that in our search for pollution control and environmental quality, we must harness market forces by providing incentives for business and individuals to go beyond what regulators require.

1. "Project '88—Harnessing Market Forces to Protect Our Environment: Initiatives for a New President." A public policy study sponsored by Senator Timothy E. Wirth (Democrat of Colorado) and Senator John Heinz (Republican of Pennsylvania). Washington, D.C., December 1988 (hereafter cited as "the report"). Contributors to and reviewers of the report are listed in its introduction at pp. iii–v. Most of them have written elsewhere on the report's thesis, and those writings are extensively footnoted throughout the report.

In a sense the report is old wine poured into a new bottle, putting a new emphasis on ideas that have been around for some time but were not ripe until now.[2] It stresses greater use of economic incentives rather than command and control regulations to achieve environmental goals. An array of tradable credits and permits, pollution charges, swaps, refunds, and deposits is proposed. Many of the ideas go several steps beyond current EPA programs under the 1970 Clean Air Act for trading emissions credits. The idea is to promote cost-effective solutions to very complex environmental problems. Drawing upon the report and other sources, I will examine this proposed change in regulatory approach.

The proposal is that economic incentives, at least initially, would only supplement and not supplant most of the existing system of laws. Eventually, a set of new initiatives would be developed that are politically more achievable than the next generation of expensive command and control regulations. The proposed approach looks at a variety of interrelated public policy issues, attempts to find a common goal among suggested solutions in different areas, and recognizes the potential of market forces as a means of achieving that goal.

The report is perhaps the most careful exposition yet of the proposed new regulatory emphasis upon economic incentives. Far from being academically abstract, it applies these concepts to sixteen major environmental and natural resource issues. The authors stated that they did not intend to let economic standards set environmental standards; that is, they did not propose putting a price on the environment. In fact, the report does not discuss specific environmental goals but instead focuses on better mechanisms for achieving whatever goals or standards are set by Congress or the EPA—in short, cost-effective (least-cost) compliance.

Proponents of economic incentives generally acknowledge the political difficulty of removing market barriers that promote inefficient resource use and eliminating unwarranted subsidies to environmentally destructive actions, but they also stress the importance of attempting to remove these barriers. They emphasize the innovative deployment of economic forces to achieve heightened protection of the environment at lower cost to society than command and control measures currently require. They are pragmatic in seeing that, especially with the current U.S. budget crunch, the government cannot simply throw money at

2. What follows draws upon the report's summary at pp. 1–5 and upon sources cited therein.

problems. Furthermore, in today's competitive world economy, the government cannot saddle the economy with unnecessary costs that hobble technological advances and sustainable management of natural resources.

Among the questions illustrating such observations are these: Is the solution practical? Is it cost-effective? informative? easy to monitor? flexible? self-motivating? comprehensible? feasible and practical politically? Will it result in an equitable distribution of costs and benefits?

Summarizing the beneficial effects of a regulatory system that stresses economic incentives, the report concludes that insofar as major environmental problems are interrelated, effective policies can help solve several problems simultaneously.[3] Energy efficiency, for example, helps lessen the problems of global warming, acid precipitation, local air pollution, and national energy security.

Conventional regulatory approaches, though modestly effective in the past, are increasingly less so and need to be supplemented. Methods are needed to ensure that producers and consumers face the full social costs and consequences of their actions. Hence the emphasis on least-cost solutions.

Incentive-based approaches have the benefit of making environmental debate more understandable to the general public, by allowing the public to focus on appropriate goals instead of technical questions about how to achieve those goals. Yet the report suggests that we adapt, not abandon, present programs, because market-based policies do not fit every problem, and in any effective regulatory system there is a need for what is both practically and politically feasible.

Air Quality Issues

The principles outlined above can be applied to specific problem areas in the environment. Among these are domestic air-quality issues. The approaches described below are not radically new, but most of them are not yet fully utilized.

We have, for example, the problem of stationary-source air pollution, notably from coal-burning utilities.[4] The Clean Air Act of 1970 established ambient air quality standards for such pollutants as sulfur dioxide,

3. See esp. the report at pp. 6–8.
4. See the report at pp. 24–30 and sources cited therein.

particulates, carbon monoxide, and ozone. The act's general approach was to require the EPA and the states to create plans to achieve standards for pollutants by specified deadlines, which have been extended repeatedly and have not yet been met in numerous regions of the country. The current remedy for this problem is to cut off government funding or prohibit new growth, options that are certainly difficult politically and harmful economically. Solving the real problem—the pollution—involves many small sources and a need for technological innovation. Creating the incentives necessary for devising many small fixes, however, has been difficult, especially in the case of small businesses. Smaller sources, with limited resources and a variety of air pollution problems, may have trouble applying technological changes that have been effective with large industries.

A partial solution is marketable emissions permits and a trading program building on the existing 1970 Clean Air Act offset program. Under the current offset program, which the EPA began in 1976, firms wishing to establish new facilities in areas that do not meet ambient air standards must offset their new emissions by reducing existing emissions by a greater amount. This reduction can be accomplished with their own facilities or through agreement with other firms, and under the concomitant "banking" program, firms may store emission credits for future use, allowing either for internal expansion or a sale of credits to other firms.

To promote greater use of emissions trading and to eliminate uncertainties among firms reluctant to participate, the report recommends four major steps. The first is to develop an accurate emissions baseline as the basis for issuance of initial permits. The second is for states to develop systems for overseeing and monitoring exchanges and sales of permits among firms. The third is to establish and enforce fixed target reductions over multiyear periods. The number of permits issued would decline with the volume of pollution allowed as the years progressed. Steep fines would ensure enforcement; if fines were less than the costs of permits, the system would not likely work. Fourth, the federal government, assisted by the states, must guarantee the liquidity and security of the emissions trading market.

By following this procedure, a pollution source can choose whether to reduce its emissions in accordance with a schedule or to purchase additional permits from firms that have managed to reduce their emissions faster than required. New sources of pollution would have to acquire permits from existing sources, and firms that did not reduce their emissions would have to compensate by buying credits. Regulators would no longer be in the business of evaluating different pollution control technologies, because firms would do that themselves, driven by the price of continued pollution. Regulators would instead manage the permit system, keeping track of each source's current permit level, monitoring emissions trading, reviewing proposed sales of permits, and ensuring enforcement.

Acid rain has caused environmental damage in the United States and also poses an international problem.[5] Because of the cost of remedying it, congressional gridlock developed, blocking reauthorization of the Clean Air Act until late 1990. The real problem is unregulated midwestern utility plants built before 1970 and the huge expense required to retrofit them. To assure the continuing competitiveness of high-sulfur coal, the 1977 Clean Air Act Amendments effectively ruled out fuel switching, which otherwise would have been a cost-effective strategy to reduce sulfur dioxide pollution at many plants. The amendments instead required expensive SO_2 reduction technology, in practice usually scrubbers, for new major coal-burning pollution sources such as utilities. Such new sources not only had to meet SO_2 emission standards set for their airshed but also had to demonstrate, through best available technology, a significant reduction of SO_2 emissions over what would have been spewed forth without such technology, regardless of the kind of fuel burned. Low-sulfur western coal therefore lost a potential competitive advantage because passage of the act required congressional support from states producing high-sulfur coal. The imposition of such high-cost technology on new plants had an unanticipated effect, however: It created a toxic-sludge disposal problem. And by ruling out cost-effective fuel switching as a compliance strategy, the act created a further disincentive to retire old plants or to explore new methods of reducing SO_2 and nitrogen oxides.

The report promotes a new credit program for acid rain reduction, making use of marketable emissions trading on a regional or national basis. The government would set acceptable levels regionally or nationally for SO_2 or NO_x emissions. Firms able to reduce such emissions faster than required would generate permits that could be banked or traded with firms that were unable or unwilling to invest in emission

5. On the subject of acid rain, see the report at pp. 30–34 and sources cited therein.

control equipment. An initial auction for obtaining permits would raise some of the money necessary for concurrent research and development. States and utilities would choose the most efficient and economical way to meet or better the standards: scrubbers, low-sulfur coal, fluidized-bed technology, or another approach or combination of approaches. This system might begin within companies and then be expanded within an airshed and then nationally.

The Bush administration's proposed Clean Air Act amendments dealing with acid rain provided for pollution permits that could be sold by utilities to cut their SO_2 or NO_x emissions and could be bought by plants with pollution problems whose solutions were more costly than buying others' permits. The amendments proposed to cut urban smog by allowing automobile manufacturers to select from a variety of emission control measures so long as they met overall emissions reduction levels. Both proposals for utilities and automobile manufacturers were to be phased in. In the acid rain reduction program, for example, 107 electric utilities would be involved in Phase 1, which would be restricted to in-state emissions trading; Phase 2 would involve national trading.

The administration's proposed Clean Air Act amendments would have eliminated the 1977 Clean Air Act's percentage pollution reduction requirements that led to scrubber use for utilities. (Economists have described scrubbers as ridiculous solutions because other cheaper alternatives are available, although they may not protect coal miners' jobs in areas with high-sulfur coal.) Congress would set the pollution reduction goals, but the means to achieve the goals would remain open to the regulated community in order to spur innovation, investment, and initiative.

Congressional reaction and that of the regulated community illustrate some of the problems faced by proponents of greater regulatory use of economic incentives. Among the questions skeptics asked were broad ones of law versus economics. Should pollution be viewed as a crime, or a necessary evil to be regulated through economic incentives? Should the government endorse what could be viewed as a license to pollute? Is it possible to make pollution control programs strict enough to enforce emission cuts for electric utilities and auto manufacturers while giving companies the flexibility to trade pollution permits among themselves? How can we best, if at all, combine new market incentives with traditional pollution control methods? If short-term emission-reduction limits on SO_2 and NO_x produced by utilities are too strict, can the free market provisions work, given that plant owners will have little opportunity to weigh the cost of cutting pollution against the cost of buying pollution permits from other firms? Is there something wrong with a market incentive system that theoretically allows a company to increase its pollution emissions? Would a system of emission fees be easier to implement than federal pollution permits?

Have we actually reached the limits of effectiveness of command and control regulations? Are we likely to obtain poorer results at higher costs by sticking with command and control regulations? Is a system allowing the banking of pollution credits necessary for the overall market-based scheme? How can compliance planning and enforcement provisions be made sufficiently strict to ensure against cheating? Are present monitoring systems sophisticated enough to ensure that the new system actually reduces pollution? How much time should be allowed to phase in the system commensurate with necessary flexibility and opportunity to find trading partners? What about contradictory state programs, still operating under a command-and-control theory? How does one avoid the double-counting of pollution or the possibility of a monopoly buy-up of emissions permits?

Such questions illustrate that many people remain skeptical that market incentives will in the long run be the most efficient and least costly method of dealing with pollution. The result for the Clean Air Act revisions proposed by the administration was for them to be so riddled with exceptions during subsequent committee negotiations as to lead some early supporters to fear that the final amendments would be worse than what they replaced.

The importance of market-based approaches to pollution prevention was most dramatically demonstrated when, in spite of all these questions and reservations, during the Congressional Clean Air Act Reauthorization debates in 1990 a plan for using a market-based system to cut sulfur dioxide emissions broke the logjam of thirteen years and enabled adoption of a cost-effective approach for tackling the acid rain problem.

The Act as adopted utilizes market mechanisms allowing trading in control credits designed ultimately to reduce dramatically acid rain precursors—a 10-million-ton annual reduction in SO_2 emissions and a 2-million-ton annual reduction in NO_x emissions—plus establishment of a permit system for emission sources with annual fees calculated per ton of emissions. The SO_2 reductions are to be achieved through a new and flexible market-based system under which power plants are to be allocated emissions allowances that will require them to reduce emissions by methods allowed by the states in which they are situated, or to acquire allowances (credits for having overachieved their SO_2 pollution reduction goals) from others in order to achieve compliance. Power plants will not be restricted to emitting specified levels of SO_2 as under traditional command and control approaches.

If they wish and as allowances are available, plants can buy SO_2 emission reduction credits from others so they can emit more of these pollutants than initially authorized under the allocation scheme, and other plants can sell unused allowances that result from their reducing emissions beyond what is necessary under the initial allocation formula. A steadily diminishing national SO_2 emissions cap has been established to ensure that the desired pollution reductions will be achieved over the next decade.

Sulfur dioxide pollution allowances from EPA will also be available through a limited annual auction, and direct purchase for use by new plants. To reduce NO_x emissions, the Act adopts the more traditional command and control approach of imposing mandatory emissions standards on individual sources.

In certain portions of the country, indoor radon is another serious air pollution threat.[6] Radon is a natural decay product of radium, and high human exposures occur when radon gas from soil with a high radium content enters a building through cracks or openings in the foundation. Exposure over long periods can lead to cancer, and the EPA has identified radon as one of the most serious environmental risks facing the nation.

One problem with radon is that it occurs naturally, with a regionally high incidence. The current safety program depends upon information access, because radon danger is primarily in private homes. The ability of homeowners to make judgments about its threat frequently is not high.

Radon poses a regulatory problem that is only partially amenable to economic incentives and requires a series of approaches. These approaches might include tax incentives and subsidized loans to encourage homeowners to test for the problem and correct it where it occurs; the establishment of model construction codes for new housing that provide

6. For a discussion of radon, see the report at pp. 35–39 and sources therein cited.

for venting where necessary; soil testing and land-use planning as part of the building permit process; improved certification to eliminate unreliable testing; mitigation requirements for radon as a prerequisite for real estate transactions; and improved homeowner information to promote voluntary compliance. Proponents of greater use of economic incentives in regulation acknowledge that a mix of economic incentives and traditional command and control requirements, as is illustrated by these proposals, is necessary at times.

The ozone and carbon monoxide problem caused by automobiles will probably also not respond as well to the market approach as some other problems will.[7] Nonetheless, a variety of regulatory and incentive-based approaches is possible. As the state of California has done, a regulatory authority could promote stricter emission standards nationally by requiring devices on gas pumps to capture and recycle vapors during refueling, encouraging reduction of gas volatility, and promoting fleet conversion to cleaner fuels. The report promotes fleet-wide mileage averaging and goes so far as to suggest the transferability of emission reduction credits from mobile sources to a manufacturer's stationary sources.

In fact, when dealing with motor vehicles and their fuel, the Clean Air Act Amendments of 1990 have focused more on technology-based command and control provisions than on market-based ones, but not exclusively. The Amendments call for a further tightening of emission standards applicable to motor vehicles, as part of the ozone and carbon monoxide pollution abatement program. They also require oil companies to produce alternative fuels for motor vehicles, and for the automobile industry to produce vehicles capable of using such alternative fuels for sale to fleet operators in designated areas failing to meet certain clean air standards. The Amendments establish a California pilot program to evaluate production of even lower polluting vehicles than those produced for other states. Within this framework, however, the affected parties are free to allow market considerations to guide their choices on how to attain the statutory goals.

Moving from purely domestic air pollution problems, one can apply regulatory concepts stressing economic incentives to the even more intractable problems of international air pollution: global warming and stratospheric ozone depletion.[8] Many scientists conclude that global

7. See the report at pp. 40–42.
8. International air pollution questions are dealt with in the report at pp. 9–23, in turn citing a voluminous literature.

warming—the greenhouse effect—is the single most important environmental threat facing the world today. The report's authors suggest increased efforts to prevent or at least retard global climate change while easing adaptation to global warming should it occur anyway. In addition to promoting research into efforts to control global warming, the United States can promote energy efficiency and alternatives to fossil fuels, whose burning contributes to carbon dioxide in the atmosphere. Energy-efficiency measures would include the promotion of energy efficiency in appliances, encouragement of the use of insulation, and utility promotion of and payment for these practices. Many of these ideas are familiar to the American public and are being used in some areas, but in the past, low oil prices have slowed their progress.

At the multilateral and international levels, where economic incentives to mitigate environmental problems are just beginning to appear, potential solutions to the greenhouse effect include the prevention of tropical deforestation through debt-for-forest swaps, currently under way in some countries; an international treaty on greenhouse gases; and improved family-planning efforts to reduce population pressures that cause conversion of forested areas to agriculture. These suggestions provide a mix of market-oriented and command and control solutions.

Yet another important global air pollution problem is stratospheric ozone depletion, causing increased ultraviolet radiation to reach the ground with attendant adverse health and ecological effects. Many people are familiar with the U.S. decision to reduce such potential ozone depletors as CFCs, the agreement under the Montreal Protocol of 1987, and the strengthening measures agreed to in Paris in 1990 for a near-total elimination of CFC production within the decade. The United States has already implemented a phase-out regulatory system for CFCs based on the idea that those most in need of CFCs will pay the most for their use and that as CFC costs get higher, substitutes will appear and be preferred in the marketplace. Also, incentives to recover and reuse potential ozone depletors, to develop alternatives, and to label potential ozone-depleting products so that the public can react and avoid them in the marketplace are all possible approaches.

The 1990 Clean Air Act Amendments provide for a year 2000 phase-out of production and sale of CFCs and several other chemicals thought to contribute to destruction of the stratospheric ozone layer, advancing the schedules set by the Montreal Protocol. The EPA by regulation will presumably continue its marketable permit system for production and use of the steadily declining total of CFCs available during the phase-out period. The Amendments also mandate recapture and recycling when CFCs are replaced.

Land and Water Issues

Proponents of greater use of economic incentives in regulation, including the authors of the *Project '88* report, do not restrict specific examples of such incentives to those involving air pollution. Concerning public land management, for example, a number of current U.S. institutional obstacles discourage economically wise management of public land.[9] Among the obstacles are strong institutional incentives to emphasize commercial development and use of resources as commodities at the expense of recreational uses, despite statutory requirements stressing multiple use of public lands. Few current institutional incentives promote nonmarket use of public land, and the market value of public land for recreational use is more difficult to calculate than is its use for, say, timber or minerals. Politically motivated subsidies further distort markets and emphasize resource use, the classic example being below-cost timber sales in various parts of our country. Also, federal spending for recreational land acquisition has been reduced.

Market-oriented solutions to these problems include alteration of management policies to reflect the growing economic impact of tourism and recreational use of public lands, a change requiring government regulators to manage public lands for long-term rather than short-term economic benefits; the elimination of government incentives for use of public commodities, such as below-cost timber sales; and the reinvestment of revenues from the use of nonrenewable resources (such as oil) into recreational and environmental assets (such as new national parks)—the concept behind the existing but only partly implemented Land and Water Conservation Fund.

Another land-use problem is the need for improved protection of wetlands. The current conundrum is that wetlands are valuable environmentally but their owners are not the ones who reap the environmental benefits. Furthermore, federal policies are contradictory. Some of them, like certain public works projects and agricultural policies, encourage the

9. For the report's discussion on public land management issues, including wetland preservation, see pp. 58–67.

destruction of wetlands, and others, such as the Clean Water Act, seek to protect wetlands.

Helpful market incentives can reflect wetland values. Suggested solutions include ending subsidized construction of federal flood control and drainage projects, eliminating favorable treatment of wetland conversion to agricultural and other uses, and enforcing cross-compliance linked to receipt of federal support programs. The 1985 Food Security Act, for example, prevents the payment of federal subsidies to those who illegally drain wetlands. The 1990 Farm Act furthered economic incentives, both positive and negative, for farmers not to drain wetlands by allowing them to sell conservation easements to the federal government and by creating penalties for draining and filling wetlands by excluding those who do so from participating in other agricultural benefit programs.

Other ideas include modifying the federal acts to allow excise taxes on fishing tackle and hunting equipment to be used for wetland acquisition and restoration, and creating a sport fishing conservation stamp like the federal duck hunting stamp as a revenue source for purchasing wetlands.

Inefficient allocation of water supplies and poor water quality are also problems to be addressed.[10] Water supply problems encompass water scarcity, pollution, federal water development policy, and Bureau of Reclamation and Corps of Engineers policies that provide cheap water at federal expense, policies viewed by many as outdated. Proponents of a regulatory approach stressing economic incentives suggest that barriers to water markets be removed to create economic incentives for water conservation and voluntary trades for the right to federally supplied water. The report illustrates such a suggestion with descriptions of nascent water markets and trading of water rights currently beginning in the American Southwest, especially Southern California, where drought has caused a water-supply crisis requiring allocation mechanisms.

As for water quality, nonpoint source pollution is an example of what is currently a seemingly insoluble political problem. The report's authors propose some combination of both regulatory (command and control) and market policies for nonpoint water pollution control. They emphasize the salutary effect of water markets on the protection of wildlife

10. Problems of federal water policy, both quantitative and qualitative, are discussed in the report at pp. 47–57 and in sources cited therein.

refuges such as Kesterson in California. If water costs more, farmers will allow less runoff, and therefore there will be less pollution from the mineral salts and pesticides it contains. Providing incentives and support for environmentally sound farm practices like integrated pest management is also encouraged, which in turn results in less water pollution from less pesticide use. The opportunity also exists for greater experimentation with tradable discharge permits for point sources to reduce water pollution efficiently in a least-cost method analogous to the permit trading system for air pollution.

The EPA has begun seriously exploring options for using permit trading, deposit systems, and other market-based approaches to tackle water pollution, laying the groundwork for possible consideration of such proposals during the upcoming reauthorization of the Clean Water Act. Among the ideas being considered are a federal program of effluent fees for controlling industrial toxics; requirements for agribusinesses to post bonds based on potential nonpoint source runoff damages from their property; deposit/refund programs to reduce nonpoint source pollution from agricultural sources by requiring farmers to pay a deposit on fertilizers and pesticides purchased, with refunds conditioned on adoption of land management practices preventing water pollution by the use of these chemicals; and a permit trading program between point and nonpoint pollution sources to control water pollution on a watershed basis.

The Future for Marketplace Incentives

The above examples illustrate some of the many ways proponents of greater use of market incentives in the regulatory context apply market-based concepts in practical terms. Economic, ecological, and ethical use of environmental law requires a greater consideration of market incentives and less reliance on command and control strategies. The report's authors conclude that it is time to experiment more with market incentives as a method of controlling pollution because the marginal utility of ever-more-complex command and control regulation is declining, and the costs, both economic and political, of the current regulatory system are increasing. Because environmental problems are so complex, future regulatory systems should maximize innovation, incentive, and variety of solutions.

The groundwork has already been laid. Encouraged by the example of at least limited acceptance of incentive-based regulation by Congress during the Clean Air Act reauthorization process, the Environmental Protection Agency has established an agency-wide task force to give concerted attention to economic incentives as a supplement to the agency's current regulatory strategy. The EPA is gradually accepting the notion that the best available technology (BAT) system can actually create barriers to innovative solutions for pollution control. The alternative to BAT may be economic incentives and performance goals, not dictated technological solutions.

The EPA has also been instrumental in establishing an advisory group of environmentalists, industrial representatives, and academics to promote innovative technology. The National Advisory Council for Environmental Technology Transfer (NACETT) is viewed by the EPA as a source of additional ideas for EPA implementation that will promote marketplace incentives.

The EPA, in a major new report entitled "Economic Incentives: Options for Environmental Protection" released by its Office of Policy, Planning and Evaluation in March, 1991, identifies dozens of market-based incentives to tackle land, water, and air pollution problems. The EPA has made developing such incentives a top priority, the report explains, because market-based incentives potentially achieve the same or better environmental results at far lower cost to industry and the public than do command and control regulations.

The report deals with four broad categories of problems. Under municipal solid waste incentives, the EPA addresses the problem of communities generating ever more solid waste with ever fewer places to put it by suggesting volume-based pricing of municipal waste management services, and incentives to encourage recycling of scrap tires, used oil, beverage containers, auto batteries, and newspapers. A separate section on global climate change incentives suggests a fee based on the carbon content of fossil fuels to encourage switching to less polluting fuels. Under water resource incentives, the report discusses proposals for changing the pricing of water to stop the inefficient use seen with the current low prices. To discourage toxic chemical pollution, the report suggests deposit/refund systems for pesticide containers and chlorinated solvents, and a system to charge fees for accidental releases of toxic chemicals from industrial facilities into the air or water.

There are other signs of increased congressional interest in marketplace incentives for pollution control. Senator Wirth and the late Senator

Heinz introduced the National Hazardous Waste Recycling Bill, which would create, among other things, a market for recycled oil. Recycling credits could be purchased if they were cheaper than meeting EPA minimum requirements for pollution control, as long as the total amount of recycling continued to increase.

Even without 1990's new Clean Air Act legislation, EPA points out that its emissions trading policy under the 1970 and 1977 versions of the Clean Air Act—such as the lead phasedown trading rules, the New Source Performance Standard compliance bubble concept, the rules by which automobile manufacturers may average testing results for all models they produce to demonstrate compliance with the EPA miles-per-gallon auto fuel efficiency standards, some of the CFC controls, and effluent discharge trading rules—already uses market incentives. Recycling and waste minimization initiatives based on marketplace incentives are also being seriously considered.

As a mechanism to mend the rift among ecology, economics, and ethics, the use of market incentives to promote pollution control is moving to center stage. It should become at least a primary method, if not *the* primary method, of future regulatory action.

CHEMICAL PROSPECTING: A PROPOSAL FOR ACTION

12

Thomas Eisner

In this chapter I urge that chemical prospecting, the exploratory process by which new, useful natural products are discovered, be substantially intensified. I shall focus on why such intensification is needed and on how it might be implemented. Specifically, I put forward a plan for increased involvement of underdeveloped nations in the exploratory process, an involvement that in my view is warranted on economic and scientific grounds, and mandated if chemical prospecting is to remain viable in the long term.

The Problem

Species extinction—the death of birth, as it has been called—is the silent crisis of our time. Species are being lost at an ever-increasing rate, faster by orders of magnitude than rates of evolutionary replacement (Wilson, 1988). Even optimists concede that no reprieve is in sight. Human expansionist demands can be expected to wreak environmental deterioration and biotic destruction well into the next century.

I thank five friends: Carol Kautz for background research, and E. O. Wilson, Jerrold Meinwald, Ian Baldwin, and my wife, Maria, for useful discussions. My research on the biology of natural products is supported by NIH grant AI-02908 and New York State Hatch grants 191402 and 191405.

Although we are beginning to grasp that extinction is forever, we have yet to comprehend what we lose when species disappear. The point that cannot be overemphasized, and that is at the core of my argument here, is that biotic impoverishment is tantamount to chemical impoverishment. Loss of a species means a loss of chemicals that are potentially unique in nature, not likely to be invented independently in the laboratory, and of possible use. Aside from other measures of worth, species have chemical value.

Biochemistry and organic chemistry, the two disciplines that deal with the chemistry of nature, have succeeded in giving us a comprehensive view of what life is about in molecular terms. Biochemistry has concentrated on the fundamentals—the molecules and molecular pathways that have come to be viewed as primary in metabolism—that became established early in evolution and are now attributes of life in all its forms. Organic chemistry, because of its interest in molecular structure per se, has focused more on secondary metabolites, those myriads of compounds, often aberrant in structure, that are produced by specialized metabolic pathways unique to individual species or species groups. Secondary metabolites are secondary in name only. They are the chemical marks of distinction of individual species, and in the biotic world they are as diverse as life itself. To the organisms that produce them, secondary metabolites are adaptive keys to survival. And to humans, who are so frequently able to put such compounds to use, they are ready-made aids to progress on a diversity of technological and chemical fronts, including most importantly medicine. Secondary metabolites are the gems of the treasury of nature, a treasury upon which we have come to depend and which is threatened with depletion.

Drugs from Nature

The implications of species loss to medicinal chemistry are staggering. Humans have always engaged in the search for drugs from nature, and the quest has a long history of paying off. The antimalarial properties of the bark of the cinchona tree from which quinine was isolated were known to the Incas, and cardiotonic preparations from foxglove plants, the source of digitalis, were used in medieval times. Most important, however, is that the search for natural medicinals is continuing to pay off to this very day. Miracle drugs only relatively recently isolated include the anticancer agent vincristine (from the Madagascar periwinkle, *Ca-*

tharanthus roseus), the immunosuppressant cyclosporin (from Norwegian Fungi Imperfecti), and the anthelminthic agent ivermectin (from a Japanese actinomycete). Immeasurable benefits have accrued from the use of these medicinals, in treatment of Hodgkin's disease and leukemias, prevention of organ rejection after surgical transplants, and treatment of helminthic diseases in humans (river blindness), cattle, and domestic animals (Noble et al., 1958; Adamson et al., 1965; Borel et al., 1976; Campbell et al., 1983; Aziz, 1986; Walsh, 1987; Byrne, 1988; Eckholm, 1989).

The financial returns from the marketing of pharmaceuticals are substantial. Sales worldwide for 1980 totaled more than $70 billion (Pradhan, 1983). Cyclosporin, although only in its fifth year on the U.S. market, is reaching $100 million in annual sales (Byrne, 1988). Also worth noting is that drug discovery is still very much a matter of serendipity. Ivermectin and cyclosporin came to light in the course of routine activity screenings of microorganisms; in fact, study of the fungal source of cyclosporin was almost dropped when it failed to show the antibiotic potency for which it was initially assayed (Byrne, 1988). The antitumor properties of *Vinca* were discovered incidentally during testings of the plant for antidiabetic action (Noble et al., 1958).

Drugs from nature make up a large fraction of our pharmaceutical arsenal. In the United States alone, upwards of one-quarter of all medical prescriptions involve formulations based on plant or microbial products or on derivatives or synthetic versions thereof (Farnsworth, 1988). Although biotechnology can be expected to bring about revolutionary progress in vaccine development and many aspects of therapeutics, no one expects these advances to obviate our need for conventional medicinals and especially for new drugs from nature.

How much of nature's chemical treasury has so far been uncovered? Precise figures are hard to come by, but data pertaining to one major group of secondary metabolites, the alkaloids, convey some idea of the incompleteness of our knowledge. Alkaloids are extraordinarily diverse in structure and biological activity. Thousands have been characterized chemically, of which hundreds proved active in useful ways. They include anesthetics, analgesics, narcotics, vasoconstrictors and vasodilators, respiratory stimulants, muscle relaxants, anticholinergic and cholinergic agents, insecticides, and parasiticides, to mention but a few. Yet only about 2 percent of flowering plants—5,000 of the estimated total of 250,000 species—have so far been examined for alkaloids. The bulk of these compounds, and for that matter of secondary metabolites generally, have yet to be discovered (see Eisner's testimony in U.S. Congress, 1982).

Plants are but a fraction of what remains unexplored in the organic world, however. Microorganisms, in their infinite variety, are still very much a chemical unknown, and that vast plurality of animals, the invertebrates, which include so many little-known marine and soil-dwelling forms, are often not even included in screening programs. The species themselves in these groups remain largely undiscovered.

Does species extinction really matter, given that one might be able to compensate, through chemical inventiveness, for whatever chemical gems might be lost through species extinction? As regards development of new medicinal products, I would say that it does indeed matter. Drug synthesis, as a rule, is not a purely inventive process. Drugs are commonly modeled after natural products, because natural products often provide the first clues to the therapeutic possibilities of given molecular structures. Nature, therefore, is the ally of organic chemists and a frequent source of their inspiration. What we risk losing in chemical knowledge through extinction is doubtless in large measure irreplaceable.

The Need for Increased Chemical Screening

The search for medicinals, as for natural products generally, is essentially a two-stage process. First, organisms or parts of organisms are screened for chemical or biochemical activities, and second, active components from these sources are isolated and characterized. The first stage involves use of bioassays, tests by which the natural materials, usually in the form of chemical extracts, are assessed for effects on selected organisms, cell cultures, or other target systems. The second stage, more purely chemical in approach, involves fractionation and purification techniques, followed by spectrometric and other analytical procedures. The first stage is technique-oriented and often relatively labor-intensive; the second is technology-intensive and dependent on sophisticated (and costly) apparatus. The two stages, screening and characterization, are frequently undertaken at the same academic, governmental, or industrial establishment. Biologists and chemists work in collaboration in these efforts, which are undertaken nowadays chiefly in the industrial world.

The question that comes to mind is whether such an arrangement is ideal. Given that chemical prospecting needs to be intensified, how can the intensification best be implemented? In my judgment, what is primarily needed is a vast expansion of the screening effort, of that initial exploratory probing for biological activities, as well as a substantial shift of that effort to the parts of the world where mass extinctions are taking place, the underdeveloped nations in the tropics. I am proposing not a curtailment of screening efforts now under way in established settings (quite the contrary, some of these should themselves be expanded) but the creation of additional screening laboratories, mostly in the Third World and specifically dedicated to the chemical testing of organisms from threatened and vanishing habitats. These screening efforts could be undertaken in conjunction with conservation programs in these nations and could with time become an integral part of the supporting structure of the programs.

Screening Laboratories in the Third World

Conservation programs are now gaining momentum in underdeveloped nations. A major component of these efforts is what can be called biological inventorying: the cataloging of the biological resources of areas slated for preservation, including a listing, to the maximum extent possible, of all inhabiting animals and plants. The latter task is formidable, but essential if some measure of biotic worth is to be assigned to environmental preserves. Biologists worldwide, including ecologists, systematists, and environmentalists, are increasingly responding to the need to undertake these efforts. What I propose is that chemical screening, in itself a form of inventorying, be undertaken as part of the biological cataloging process. In my view, major benefits will derive from the linkage of these programs.

First, the screening process itself will benefit. Take, for example, the establishment of a screening laboratory at a tropical site. Although the laboratory would not need to be established in the proximity of environmental preserves, it would profit from being within the overall region and accessible to the sites. This placement would make it possible for fresh biological samples to be tested, potentially in minimal amounts and, given that chemical activities may be seasonally or sporadically variable, at different times of the year. Ongoing biological monitoring at the preserves would also make possible the study of morphological and ecological variants of the source organisms. In fact, the possibility that the screening personnel could collaborate with biologists in the area could be profitable in many ways. The rationale for sample selection could be affected, for example. Rather than being screened strictly by random selection, organisms could be chosen for chemical study on the basis of biological leads. Plants notably free from insect-inflicted injury could be screened for insect repellency or toxicity. Others with zones of inhibition around their stem or with surface structures conspicuously unencumbered by mycelial growth could be tested for allelochemics or antibiotics. Soil arthropods noted to guard or mouth their eggs could be screened for antifungal agents, and so forth. Screening programs attached to marine or limnological conservation efforts could similarly profit from such biological input.

Nations that established the screening laboratories would also gain advantages. Regional socioeconomic needs could be involved in the setting of priorities for screening. Medical needs might dictate, for instance, that particular emphasis be given to the search for antifungal and antiparasitic agents. Most important, the information obtained through screening could have economic value for the Third World country involved. The inevitable follow-up to the discovery of chemical uses of selected organisms would be the establishment of working linkages with universities and industries—initially, perhaps, mostly in developed nations—that would undertake the characterization and synthesis of the active chemicals uncovered. At that stage, proprietary arrangements could be made to insure that profits derived from the eventual commercialization of the new chemicals revert in fair measure to the nations that did the screening.[1]

Although it may be premature at this stage to delineate how the proposed screening laboratories might be financed, I suggest that they could be established through what has become known as the debt-for-

---

1. Two further advantages would pertain to the nations undertaking the screening. First, screening laboratories would create appropriate professional opportunities for biologists, biochemists, and chemists from underdeveloped nations who receive advanced, specialized training in industrial nations. Currently, these scientists frequently lack such opportunities when returning to their homeland. Screening laboratories would thus strengthen the science establishment in these nations. Second, chemical prospecting is essentially noninvasive. The usual sequel to the discovery of a biological activity is not the harvesting of the source organism but the identification of the chemicals responsible, and their eventual production by laboratory synthesis. Thus, chemical exploration is compatible with biological conservation.

nature swap program (Lovejoy, 1984). By this arrangement, debtor nations are allowed to convert their indebtedness to local-currency investments, a strategy that is already proving useful in the implementation of Third World conservation programs, including the creation of preserves. To establish screening laboratories under such auspices makes sense, because in time they would become functional components of the conservation effort. Moreover, they might be particularly useful additions to such programs, because they have the potential of becoming self-sufficient and profitable. In a most fitting way, chemical exploration could become part of biological conservation. The study of our chemical treasury would be linked to the preservation of the biotic world in which it is embodied.

CONCLUDING REMARKS VI

13 CLOSING THE CIRCLE: WEAVING STRANDS AMONG ECOLOGY, ECONOMICS, AND ETHICS

We initiated this book because we were convinced that the crushing environmental problems of our time would be difficult or impossible to address effectively if we were unable to reconcile and integrate the perspectives of ecology, economics, and ethics. The various contributors to this volume have provided important insights regarding this complex relationship. Substantial gaps in our understanding remain, however, and the many drifting pieces of the broken circle are still unconnected.

Stephen R. Kellert and F. Herbert Bormann

The fundamental assumption nonetheless remains apparent and compelling. Our capacity to address global environmental problems will necessitate a better understanding of the environmental deficits humans are inflicting on the planet, a recognition of the need to deal with these problems in ecological as well as economic terms, and a cognizance that an effective response will require a shift in our ethical terms of reference.

We are sobered by the immensity of the task and profoundly challenged to plan for a future marked by the potential of large-scale deterioration of our basic life-support systems. Some of the contributing authors paint a grim picture of accelerating biological and ecological impoverishment and declining quality of human life. We are left wondering how our seemingly unique moral and thinking species can consciously control its future to any great extent. Has any creature ever had the capacity to plan rationally for an essentially unknown future?

Do we really have a choice? Despite the uncertainties, the next quarter century appears unique in confronting humanity with the prospect of making dangerously flawed decisions that could leave a legacy of environmental degradation so severe that future generations would judge our period as a dark age in which the very foundations of the planetary ecosystem were seriously weakened.

What are the symptoms of the global environmental deficit? How can we better diagnose it? What are the remedial and therapeutic alternatives? These themes represent recurrent threads woven through the various chapters. In reviewing them, we begin to discern hopeful and positive understandings, with at least a better definition of the problem if not the measure of its solution.

One perspective of the current ecological impact is Wilson's allusion to the four horsemen of the environmental apocalypse, which, in various guises, nearly all of the authors touched upon. The first rider, toxics, is discussed to various degrees by Jackson, Pimentel, Connett, Goldfarb, Likens, and others. Collectively they describe a rain of contaminants and human waste leading to the widespread toxification of air, water, and food chains and a legacy of long-lived effects on a wide range of species and habitats.

The second and third horsemen of the environmental apocalypse are forms of atmospheric degradation such as stratospheric ozone depletion, global warming associated with the buildup of carbon dioxide and other "greenhouse" gases, and increasing acidification of rain. Such problems are critical aspects of the presentations of Myers, Likens, Butler, and others.

The fourth horseman—the pale rider called Death—is the extraordinary scale of contemporary species extinctions, discussed by Wilson, Myers, Ehrenfeld, Rolston, and Eisner. Each author reflects on the tragic possibility of hundreds of thousands, or more than a million, extinctions during the coming decades if current rates of habitat destruction continue. The death of birth, as Eisner describes this scale of species extinction, is the silent crisis of our time. It has the potential to affect profoundly the feedback relationship between the biosphere and various planetary life-support systems, with largely unpredictable and perhaps irreversible consequences for humankind.

The understanding of ecological problems and their causes is prerequisite to identifying alternatives to destruction. In some situations, modest behavioral and institutional adaptations, with a primary reliance on engineering and technical ingenuity, are sufficient for partially dealing with these problems. The scope and diversity of our current environmental malaise, and the realization that its causes are interwoven into the fabric of our modern enterprise, inevitably lead to the recognition that effective solutions require consideration of socioeconomic and cultural forces. From this perspective, environmental mitigation and remedial response become extraordinarily more complex and politically risky. We are no longer suggesting a few judicious adjustments to existing mechanical levers; instead we are suggesting fundamental alterations to the economic and ethical building blocks of our contemporary social order.

At the very least, the authors recognize the necessity of curbing human population growth as a means of placing far less demands on our planetary ecosystems. Even more important, many of them acknowledge the need to reduce our consumption of space and materials and to achieve far greater efficiencies in our use of resources. As Connett so provocatively remarks, "When some people look into a trash bag, they see things like plastic, paper, metal, and food waste. I see our whole world being thrown away."

Significant socioeconomic remedies are suggested. Although the contributors cover a wide range of possibilities, three particular recommendations emerge: improving our current economic accounting practices to include environmental impacts in their calculation, providing greater opportunities for deriving economic benefits from resource conservation, and enhancing our reliance on existing market mechanisms to achieve predetermined environmental goals. Underlying each approach is Gillis's assertion that the prevailing tension between ecology and economics is an artificial consequence of a relatively recent economic narrowness rather than an inevitable conflict of perspectives: "Good economics not only is good ecology but indeed is required for good ecology. The dichotomy that many perceive to have arisen between economics and ecology is false and has persisted primarily because of bad economics."

As an initial step away from the prevailing "bad economics," Gillis suggests installing better economic accounting procedures for measuring the true environmental costs of our collective actions, particularly those involving major depletions and degradations of natural resources. This effort would require a vastly improved method for incorporating the depreciation impacts of exploiting renewable resources beyond their sustainable limits and of reducing biological carrying capacity through environmental destruction.

To encourage in decision makers and politicians a better appreciation of the economic value of wisely managed biotic and other natural resources, Eisner, Myers, and others recommend a greater emphasis on the opportunities provided by nature to generate commodity benefits. Eisner innovatively suggests establishing chemical screening laboratories in areas rich in genetic resources, such as the moist tropical forests of many Third World countries. The resulting partnership with technologically sophisticated industries of the developed world could lead to a range of beneficial products generating profits for both participants and thereby enhancing the perceived economic value of species and their associated ecosystems.

A more immediate basis for providing incentives for conservation through economic self-interest is described by Butler. Rather than having governments promote environmental improvements through coercive regulatory laws—what he refers to as the conventional command-and-control strategy—Butler calls for establishing overall conservation goals that the private sector is then given considerable discretion to pursue. In the case of air pollution, for example, an overall level of air quality might be set for a particular nation or region, with industries permitted to trade allowable amounts of pollution, depending upon their relative capabilities, so long as they collectively complied with the overall environmental goal. Although such a scheme may appear to reward some industries for polluting, the initial setting of an environmental standard and then its gradual tightening could assure continued improvements in overall air and water quality. Most of all, it could encourage environmental progress within an economic incentive system that makes sense to both the business sector and the public in capitalist-oriented societies.

On the other hand, both Goldfarb and Likens stress that mending the broken circle cannot be left solely in the hands of industry and government. It must also involve the development of a new view of the individual's personal responsibility toward the environment. Goldfarb further stresses the need for remodeling our educational system so we are better prepared to see matters holistically.

Despite the economic and ecological insights offered, most of the contributors eventually conclude that neither economics nor ecology by itself can provide a sufficient basis for coping with the scope of our current environmental crisis. Each author in his own way additionally argues for fundamental alterations in how we, as a species, perceive the natural world and, as individuals, act in an ethically responsible fashion.

This concern for noneconomic and nonecological values as an additional guide to a more sustainable relationship to nature assumes various expressions. Jackson looks to nature's inherent wisdom, citing Milton's insight: "She, good cateress, / Means her provision only to the good / That live according to her sober laws / And holy dictate of spare Temperance." Jackson encourages us to view nature as a model for behavior rather than as an adversary to conquer and refashion as so much malleable clay awaiting a higher and more refined use. In seeking nature's wisdom, we find both the means to a more satisfactory life and to a less environmentally destructive existence. Such a change is not likely to occur if we assume the need to continue consuming at our current levels of excess and waste. "I think most of us are fighting against things we do not wish to destroy," argues Jackson. "All of us treat nature as a coolie to provide the things that once possessed cannot be done without."

A major impediment to this altered and more benign relationship to nature is a lack among most people of a basic affinity for and personal identification with the environment. Aldo Leopold (1968 [1949]) suggested a generation ago that the emergence of an individually meaningful and powerful environmental ethic stems from one premise: "The individual is a member of a community of interdependent parts. . . . An ethic, ecologically, is a limitation on freedom of action in the struggle for existence. . . . No important change in ethics was ever accomplished without an internal change in our intellectual emphasis, loyalties, affections, convictions. . . . We can be ethical [only] in relation to something we can see, feel, understand, love." Leopold suggested, in effect, that an environmental ethic limiting individual short-term wants for the sake of long-term needs of the natural community will come only from developing a profound affection for and personal identification with nature.

Developing this new attitude toward nature will require no small change in consciousness, difficult under the most ideal circumstances but especially problematic when it involves many obscure species and biotic processes of little obvious relationship to most people. Rolston, nonetheless, argues that this level of appreciation and awareness is possible and essential if the current scale of massive extinctions is to be stopped: "The species too has its integrity, its individuality, its right to life. . . . Every extinction is an incremental decay in [a] stopping of life. . . . Every extinction is a kind of superkilling. It kills forms . . . beyond individuals. It kills essences beyond existences, the soul as well as the body. . . . It kills birth as well as death."

It seems doubtful that a profound shift in ethical consciousness can be achieved unless humans develop a far greater sense of humility, respect, and even awe toward nature. Not only do we need to forgo the mentality of conqueror and remodeler of nature, but as Ehrenfeld proposes, we also require far less stress on the importance of an environmental management or stewardship perspective that assumes complete knowledge to manipulate and readjust nature to our ends. This point of view is not offered as a denial of modern scientific resource management. Modern society has left few landscapes unscathed and many needing remedial attention. Yet the idea of managing nature can carry with it the seeds of its own defeat if it is not reluctantly and humbly applied. A tradition of condescension in human manipulation of nature frequently leads to grotesque mistakes. Environmental intervention is unavoidable today, but not in the grand Western tradition of assuming the capacity to remake an imperfect world (Kellert, 1984).

As Wilson suggests, we need to come to the humbling realization of our limits. "The truth is that we never conquered the world, never understood it. We only think we have control." Perhaps what we require is an attitude more of studentship than of stewardship, a view of nature as teacher and us as apprentices to its mysteries and methodologies. This posture would not relinquish the need for greater scientific research and even environmental manipulation but instead would temper our actions with a spirit of caring and humility.

The emergence of an environmental ethic could lead to the realization that efforts on behalf of respecting and sustaining nature are really creative ventures on behalf of ourselves (Kellert, 1988). The most compelling reasons for environmental conservation are not material enhancements or altruism or the acceptance of scientific knowledge but the personal conviction that nature is as much a place for nurturing human fulfillment as it is for raising crops or generating harvestable commodities. As Wilson remarks, humanity is exalted not because we are so much above nature but because knowing nature elevates the concept of ourselves.

Adamson, R. H., R. L. Dixon, M. Ben, L. Crews, S. B. Shohet, and D. P. Rall. 1965. Some pharmacological properties of vincristine. *Archives Internationales de Pharmacodynamie et de Therapie* 157:299–304.

Akesson, N. B., and W. E. Yates. 1974. *The use of aircraft in agriculture.* Rome: Food and Agriculture Organization.

———. 1984. Physical parameters affecting aircraft spray application. In *Chemical and biological controls in forestry,* ed. W. Y. Gardner and J. Harvey, 95–115. Washington, D.C.: American Chemical Society.

Altieri, M. A., M. K. Anderson, and L. C. Merrick. 1987. Peasant agriculture and the conservation of crop and wild plant resources. *Conservation Biology* 1:49–58.

Arrington, L. G. 1956. *World survey of pest control products.* Washington, D.C.: U.S. Government Printing Office.

Arrow, K. J. 1973. Rawl's principle of just saving. *Swedish Journal of Economics* 51(3).

Ashton, P. 1976. Factors affecting the development and conservation of tree genetic resources in Southeast Asia. In *Tropical trees: Variation, breeding, conservation,* ed. J. Burley and B. T. Styles. London: Academic Press.

Astin, A. W., K. C. Green, and W. F. Korn. 1987. *The American freshman: Twenty-year trends, 1966–1985.* Los Angeles: Cooperative Institutional Research Program, University of California.

Aziz, M. A. 1986. Chemotherapeutic approach to control of onchocerciasis. *Infectious Diseases Reviews* 8:500–504.

Bailey, R., and P. Connett. 1986. *Recycling in Germany.* Canton, N.Y.: Video Active Productions. Videotape.

———. 1987a. *Joe Garbarino: The only way to go.* Canton, N.Y.: Video Active Productions. Videotape.

———. 1987b. *Millie Zantow: Recycling pioneer.* Canton, N.Y.: Video Active Productions. Videotape.

———. 1987c. *Recycling in the USA: Don't take no for an answer.* Canton, N.Y.: Video Active Productions. Videotape.

————. 1987d. *Skamania County, Washington: A materials recovery center.* Canton, N.Y.: Video Active Productions. Videotape.

————. 1988a. *How Rodman recycles.* Canton, N.Y.: Video Active Productions. Videotape.

————. 1988b. *Zoo doo and you can too.* Canton, N.Y.: Video Active Productions. Videotape.

————. 1989a. *Recycling's missing link: Fillmore County, Minnesota.* Canton, N.Y.: Video Active Productions. Videotape.

————. 1989b. *Waste management as if the future mattered.* Canton, N.Y.: Video Active Productions. Videotape.

————. 1990. *Europeans mobilizing against trash incineration.* Canton, N.Y.: Video Active Productions. Videotape.

Barney, G. O. 1980. *The global 2000 report to the president.* Washington, D.C.: U.S. Government Printing Office.

Bentham, J. 1948 [1789]. *The principles of morals and legislation.* New York: Hafner.

Berry, W. 1990. A practical harmony. In *What are people for?* San Francisco: North Point Press.

BioCycle staff, ed. 1989. *The BioCycle guide to composting municipal wastes.* Emmaus, Pa.: J.G. Press.

Boado, E. 1988. Incentive policy and forest use in the Philippines. In *Public policies and the misuse of forest resources,* ed. R. Repetto and M. Gillis, 180–186. New York: Cambridge University Press.

Bok, D. 1988. *The president's report, 1986–87.* Cambridge: Harvard University.

Borel, J. F., C. Fever, H. V. Gubler, and H. Stahelin. 1976. Biological effects of cyclosporin A: A new antilymphocytic agent. *Agents and Actions* 6:468–475.

Bormann, F. H. 1972. Unlimited growth: Growing, growing, gone? *BioScience* 22(12): 706–709.

————. 1990. The global environmental deficit. *BioScience* 40:74.

Bormann, F. H., and G. E. Likens. 1967. Nutrient cycling. *Science* 155:424–429.

————. 1979. *Pattern and process in a forested ecosystem.* New York: Springer-Verlag.

Braithwaite, R. W., and W. M. Lonsdale. 1987. The rarity of *Sminthopsis virginiae* (Marsupialia: Dasyuridae) in relation to natural and unnatural habitats. *Conservation Biology* 1:341–343.

Brewer, G. 1987. European plastics recycling, part 1. *Resource Recycling,* May/ June.

Brodeur, P. 1986. Annals of chemistry in the face of doubt. *New Yorker* (June): 70–87.

Browder, J. 1988. Public policy and deforestation in the Brazilian Amazon. In *Public policies and the misuse of forest resources,* ed. R. Repetto and M. Gillis, 260–266. New York: Cambridge University Press.

Brown, J. W. 1988. Poverty and environmental degradation: Basic concerns for U.S. cooperation with developing countries. Paper presented at the Michigan

State University Conference on Cooperation for Sustainable Development, East Lansing, May 15–18, 1988.

Brown, L. R., W. U. Chandler, A. Durning, C. Flavin, L. Heise, J. Jacobson, S. Postel, C. P. Shea, L. Starke, and E. C. Wolf. 1985. *State of the world, 1985.* New York: Norton.

Brown, M. H. 1987a. *The toxic cloud.* New York: Harper and Row.

———. 1987b. Toxic winds. *Discover* (November): 42–49.

Brown, W. M. 1986. Hysteria about acid rain. *Fortune* 113:125–126.

Brundtland, G. 1987. *Our common future.* New York: Oxford University Press.

Byrne, G. 1988. Cyclosporin turns five. *Science* 242:198.

Campbell, W. C., M. H. Fisher, E. O. Stapley, G. Albers-Schhonberg, and T. A. Jacob. 1983. Ivermectin: A potent new antiparasitic agent. *Science* 221:823–828.

Carson, R. 1962. *Silent spring.* Boston: Houghton Mifflin.

Cohen, R. 1989. U.S. complaints on Amazon's destruction spur Brazil's resentment and defiance. *Wall Street Journal,* February 17.

Commoner, B., M. Frisch, J. Quigley, A. Stege, D. Wallace, T. Webster, and T. Luppino. 1988. *Final report: Intensive recycling feasibility study for the city of Buffalo.* Flushing, N.Y.: Center for the Biology of Natural Systems, Queens College.

Commoner, B., M. Frisch, H. A. Pitot, J. Quigley, A. Stege, D. Wallace, and T. Webster. 1989. *Intensive recycling pilot project in East Hampton, N.Y.* Flushing, N.Y.: Center for the Biology of Natural Systems, Queens College.

Cramer, C. 1988. 222-bushel corn—without chemicals. *New Farm* 10:12–15.

Dale, J. E. 1980. The rope-wick applicator: Tool with a future. *Weeds Today* 11(2): 3–5.

Daly, H. 1977. *Steady-state economics.* San Francisco: W. H. Freeman and Co.

de Lama, G. 1989. Brazil resists campaign to save rain forests. *Chicago Tribune,* March 12.

Dregne, H. E. 1983. *Desertification of arid lands.* New York: Hardwood Publishers.

Driscoll, C. T., J. N. Galloway, J. F. Hornig, G. E. Likens, M. Oppenheimer, K. A. Rahn, and D. W. Schindler. 1985. *Is there scientific consensus on acid rain? Excerpts from six governmental reports.* Millbrook, N.Y.: Institute of Ecosystem Studies.

Eckholm, E. 1976. *Losing ground.* New York: Norton.

———. 1989. River blindness: Conquering an ancient scourge. *New York Times Magazine,* January 8.

Ehrenfeld, D. 1981. *The arrogance of humanism.* New York: Oxford University Press.

———. 1986. Thirty million cheers for diversity. *New Scientist* 110:38–43.

Ehrenfeld, J. 1983. The effects of changes in land-use on swamps of the New Jersey Pine Barrens. *Biological Conservation* 25:353–375.

Ehrlich, P. R., and J. Roughgarden. 1987. *The science of ecology.* New York: Macmillan.

Eisenberg, J. F. 1980. The density and biomass of tropical mammals. In *Conservation biology: An evolutionary-ecological perspective,* ed. M. E. Soulé and B. A. Wilcox, 35–56. Sunderland, Mass.: Sinauer Associates.

Environmental Defense Fund. 1987. *Summary of all available EP toxicity testing data on incinerator ash.* Washington, D.C.

———. 1988. *If you are not recycling you are throwing it all away.* Washington, D.C.

Environmental Protection Agency. 1986. *Test methods for evaluating solid waste: Physical/chemical methods.* 3d ed. EPA/SW846. Washington, D.C.

———. 1987. *Municipal waste combustion study: Assessment of health risks associated with municipal waste combustion emissions.* EPA/530-SW-87-021g. Washington, D.C.

———. 1989. *The solid waste dilemma: An agenda for action.* EPA/530-SW-89-019. Washington, D.C.: Office of Solid Waste.

Farman, J. C., B. G. Gardiner, and J. D. Shanklin. 1985. Large losses of total ozone in Antarctica reveal seasonal ClO_x/NO_x interaction. *Nature* 315:207–210.

Farnsworth, N. R. 1988. Screening plants for new medicines. In *Biodiversity,* ed. E. O. Wilson and F. M. Peter, 83–97. Washington, D.C.: National Academy Press.

Federal Register. 1981. February 5, 11,128.

Federal Register. 1982. March 26, 32,284–32,285.

Feinstein, M. S., F. C. Miller, J. A. Hogan, and P. F. Strom. 1987. Analysis of EPA guidance on composting sludge. Parts 1–4. *Biocycle,* January–April.

Fish, H. 1988. What goes up . . . *Adirondack Life,* January/February.

Fitzgerald, B. 1986. An analysis of Indonesian trade policies. CPD Discussion Paper no. 1986-22, July 22. Washington, D.C.: World Bank.

Flavin, C., and A. B. Durning. 1988. Building on success: The age of energy efficiency. World Watch Paper no. 82. Washington, D.C.: World Watch Institute.

Forcella, F., and M. J. Lindstrom. 1988. Movement and germination of weed seeds in ridge-till crop production systems. *Weed Science.* 36:56–59.

Ford, R. J. 1986. Field trials of a method for reducing drift from agricultural sprayers. *Canadian Agricultural Engineering* 28(2): 81–83.

Forman, R. T. T., and B. A. Elfstrom. 1975. Forest structure comparison of Hutcheson Memorial Forest and eight old woods on the New Jersey Piedmont. *William L. Hutcheson Memorial Bulletin* 3(2): 44–51.

Franklin Associates, 1986. *Characterization of municipal solid waste in the United States, 1960–2000.* Prairie Village, Kans.

Frans, R. 1985. *A summary of research achievements in cotton.* Washington, D.C.: Cotton Integrated Pest Management, Integrated Pest Management of Major Agricultural Systems.

Frisbie, R. 1985. *Regional implementation of cotton IPM*. Washington, D.C.: Cotton Integrated Pest Management, Integrated Pest Management of Major Agricultural Systems.

Fürst, P., C. Krüger. H.-A. Meemken, and W. Groebel. 1989. PCDD and PCDF levels in human milk: Dependence on the period of lactation. *Chemosphere* 18:439–444.

Futuyma, D. 1973. Community structure and stability in constant environments. *American Naturalist* 107:443–446.

Gamlin, L. 1987. Rodents join the commune. *New Scientist* 115:40–47.

Geld, E. 1989. Will farming destroy Brazil's Amazon? *Wall Street Journal*, January 13.

Gilbert, L. E. 1980. Food web organization and conservation of Neotropical diversity. In *Conservation biology: An evolutionary-ecological perspective*, ed. M. E. Soulé and B. A. Wilcox, 11–34. Sunderland, Mass.: Sinauer Associates.

Gilbert, L. E., and P. H. Raven. 1975. *Coevolution of animals and plants*. Austin, Tex.: University of Texas Press.

Gillis, M. 1984. *Environmental and resource management issues in the tropical forest sector of Indonesia*. Development Discussion Paper no. 142. Cambridge: Harvard Institute for International Development.

———. 1988a. Indonesia: Public policies, resource management and the tropical forest. In *Public policies and the misuse of forest resources*, ed. R. Repetto and M. Gillis, 43–105. New York: Cambridge University Press.

———. 1988b. The logging industry in tropical Asia. In *People of the tropical rain forest*, ed. J. Denslow and C. Padoch, 321–327. Berkeley: University of California Press.

———. 1988c. Malaysia: Public policies and the tropical forest. In *Public policies and the misuse of forest resources*, ed. R. Repetto and M. Gillis, 115–198. New York: Cambridge University Press.

———. 1988d. West Africa: Resource management policies and the tropical forest. In *Public policies and the misuse of forest resources*, ed. R. Repetto and M. Gillis, 299–342. New York: Cambridge University Press.

———. 1990. Tax reform and the value-added tax. In *World tax reform*, ed. M. Boskin and C. E. McLure, 227–232. San Francisco: Institute for Contemporary Studies.

Gillis, M., and R. Repetto. 1988. Conclusion: Findings and policy implications. In *Public policies and the misuse of forest resources*, ed. R. Repetto and M. Gillis, 385–394. New York: Cambridge University Press.

Gillis, M., D. Perkins, D. Snodgrass, and M. Roemer. 1987. *Economics of development*, pp. 220–225. New York: Norton.

Goldfarb, W. 1984. *Water law*. 1st ed. Chelsea, Mich.: Lewis.

Goodman, D. 1975. The theory of diversity-stability relationships in ecology. *Quarterly Review of Biology* 50:237–266.

Gramlich, E. 1981. *Benefit cost analysis*. Englewood Cliffs, N.J.: Prentice Hall.

Greenpeace. 1988. *Stepping lightly on the earth: Everyone's guide to toxics in the home*. Vancouver, British Columbia.

Halvorson, H. 1988. Address to the forum on biotechnology. Cook College, Rutgers University, New Brunswick, N.J., April 8.

Hartwick, J. 1977. Intergenerational equity and the investing of rents from exhaustible resources. *American Economic Review* 6(5): 973–975.

————. 1978. Substitution among exhaustible resources and intergenerational equity. *Review of Economic Studies*, 347–354.

Havas, M., T. Hutchinson, and G. E. Likens. 1984. Red herrings in acid rain research. *Environmental Science and Technology* 18(6): 176A–186A.

Helfrich, H. W., Jr., ed. 1970. *The environmental crisis: Man's struggle to live with himself*. New Haven: Yale University Press.

Helmers, G. A., M. R. Langemeir, and J. Atwood. 1986. An economic analysis of alternative cropping systems for east-central Nebraska. *American Journal of Alternative Agriculture* 4:153–158.

Holloway, H. L. O. 1977. Seed propagation of *Dioscoreophyllum cumminsii*, source of an intense natural sweetener. *Economic Botany* 31:47–50.

Hubert, M. K. 1971. Energy resources. In *Environment: Resources, pollution and society*, ed. W. W. Murdock. Stamford, Conn.: Sinauer Associates.

Hunter, M. L., Jr., G. L. Jacobson, and T. Webb. 1988. Paleoecology and the coarse-filter approach to maintaining biological diversity. *Conservation Biology* 2:375–385.

Hyslop, J. A. 1938. Losses occasioned by insects, mites, and ticks in the United States. Washington, D.C.: U.S. Department of Agriculture.

Jacobs, M. 1987. *The tropical rain forest*. New York: Springer-Verlag.

Janzen, D. H. 1975. *Ecology of plants in the tropics*. London: Arnold.

————. 1982. *The relationship of basic research to the development of the technologies that will sustain tropical forest resources*. Washington, D.C.: Office of Technology Assessment.

Jordan, T. N., H. D. Coble, and L. M. Wax. 1987. Weed control. In *Soybeans: Improvement, production, and uses*, ed. J. R. Wilcox, 429–457. Madison, Wis.: American Society of Agronomy.

Kahaner, L. 1988. Something in the air. *Wilderness* 52(183): 18–27.

Kalamazoo (Mich.) *Gazette*. 1990. Paper industry sets recycling goal. February 14.

Kania, J. J., and B. B. Johnson. 1981. *An impact assessment model of limiting crop pesticide usage in agriculture*. Lincoln, Nebr.: Department of Agricultural Economics, University of Nebraska.

Kellert, S. R. 1984. Wildlife values and the private landowner. *American Forests* 90(11): 27–28, 60–61.

————. 1988. *Social and psychological dimensions of an environmental ethic*. Proceedings of the International Conference on Outdoor Ethics. Washington, D.C.: Izaak Walton League.

Kidder and Peabody and Co., Inc. 1988. *A status report on resource recovery as of December 31, 1987.* New York.

King, A. D. 1983. Progress in no-till. *Journal of Soil and Water Conservation* 38:160–161.

Kneese, A., et al. 1983. The ethical foundations of benefit-cost analysis. In *The ethical foundations of benefit-cost analysis,* ed. A. Kneese, S. Ben-David, and W. D. Shulze, 73. Washington, D.C.: Resources for the Future.

Koch, T. C., J. Seeberger, and H. Petrik. 1986. *The ecological handling of trash: A handbook for optimized concepts for waste handling.* Karlsruhe: C. F. Müller.

Kondrat'ev, K. Y., A. A. Grigorev, and V. F. Zhalev. 1985. Comprehensive investigation of dust storms in the Aral Sea area. *Meteorologiya Gidrologiya* 4:32–38.

Kovach, J., and J. P. Tette. 1988. A survey of the use of IPM by New York apple producers. *Agriculture, Ecosystems and Environment* 20:101–108.

Kroll, G. 1985. Mandatory recycling in the village of Hamburg, New York. *Journal of Resource Management and Technology* 14:4.

Kulp, L. 1987. *Interim assessment: The causes and effects of acidic deposition.* Washington, D.C.: National Acid Precipitation Assessment Program.

Lanley, J. P. 1982. Tropical forest resources. National Technical Information Service, Tropical Forestry Paper no. 30. Rome: Food and Agriculture Organization.

Larkin, P. A. 1977. An epitaph for the concept of maximum sustained yield. *Transactions of the American Fisheries Society* 106:1–11.

Latham, S. B., J. W. Allen, T. Goldfarb, J. Morris, and W. M. Vukoder. 1988. *A nonincineration solid waste management and recycling plan for the town of North Hempstead, New York.* Sea Cliff, N.Y.: New York Coalition to Save Hempstead Harbor.

Lele, U. 1986. Phoenix or Icarus? In *World economic growth,* ed. A. He ᵒerger, 159–196. San Francisco: Institute for Contemporary Studies.

Leopold, A. 1933. *Game management.* New York: Charles Scribner's Sons.

———. 1968 [1949]. *A Sand County Almanac.* New York: Oxford University Press.

Lichiello, P., and L. Snyder. 1988. *Plastics: The risks and consequences of its production and use.* Los Angeles: School of Architecture and Urban Planning, University of California.

Likens, G. E. 1983. A priority for ecological research. *Bulletin of the Ecological Society of America* 64(4): 234–243.

———. 1985a. *An ecosystem approach to aquatic ecology: Mirror Lake and its environment.* New York: Springer-Verlag.

———. 1985b. An experimental approach for the study of ecosystems. *Journal of Ecology* 73:381–396.

――――. 1989a. *Long-term studies in ecology: Approaches and alternatives*. New York: Springer-Verlag.

――――. 1989b. Some aspects of air pollution on terrestrial ecosystems and prospects for the future. *Ambio* 18(3): 172–178.

Likens, G. E., and F. H. Bormann. 1974. Acid rain: A serious regional environmental problem. *Science* 184:1176–1179.

Likens, G. E., F. H. Bormann, N. M. Johnson, D. W. Fisher, and R. S. Pierce. 1970. Effects of forest cutting and herbicide treatment on nutrient budgets in the Hubbard Brook watershed-ecosystem. *Ecological Monographs* 40(1): 23–47.

Likens, G. E., F. H. Bormann, and N. M. Johnson. 1972. Acid rain. *Environment* 14(2): 33–40.

Likens, G. E., F. H. Bormann, R. S. Pierce, J. S. Eaton, and N. M. Johnson. 1977. *Biogeochemistry of a forested ecosystem*. New York: Springer-Verlag.

Lipsett, B., and D. Farrell. 1990. *Solid waste incineration status report*. Arlington, Va.: Citizen's Clearinghouse for Hazardous Wastes.

Lockeretz, W., G. Shearer, and D. H. Kohl. 1981. Organic farming in the corn belt. *Science* 211:540–547.

Lovejoy, T. E. 1984. Aid debtor nations' ecology. *New York Times*, October 4.

Mackenzie, J. J., and M. T. El-Ashry. 1988. *Ill winds: Airborne pollution's toll on trees and crops*. Washington, D.C.: World Resources Institute.

Margalef, R. 1963. On certain unifying principles in ecology. *American Naturalist* 97:357–374.

Marglin, S. 1963. *Public expenditure criteria*. Cambridge: Harvard University Press.

Marlatt, C. L. 1904. The annual loss occasioned by destructive insects in the United States. In *Yearbook of the Department of Agriculture*, 461–474. Washington, D.C.: U.S. Government Printing Office.

Mason, E. 1982. The Harvard economics department from the beginning to World War II. *Quarterly Journal of Economics* 3:383–434.

Matthews, G. A. 1985. Application from the ground. In *Pesticide application: Principles and practice*, ed. P. T. Haskell, 93–117. Oxford: Clarendon Press.

May, R. M. 1973. *Stability and complexity in model ecosystems*. Princeton, N.J.: Princeton University Press.

Mazariegos, F. 1985. The use of pesticides in the cultivation of cotton in Central America. In *Industry and Environment* (July/August/September): 5–8. A United Nations Environment Program publication.

McNeely, J. A. 1988. *Economics and biological diversity*. Gland, Switzerland: International Union for the Conservation of Nature and Natural Resources.

Micklin, P. 1988. Desiccation of the Aral Sea: A water management disaster in the Soviet Union. *Science* 241:1170–1172.

Miller, J. T. 1988. *Living in the environment*. Belmont, Calif.: Wadsworth.

Mishan, E. J. 1967. *The costs of economic growth*. London: Staples Press.

Molina, M. J., and F. S. Rowland. 1974. Stratospheric sink for chlorofluoromethanes: Chlorine atom–catalysed destruction of ozone. *Nature* 249:810–812.

Myers, N. 1975. *The cheetah* Acinonyx jubatus *in Africa*. IUCN Monograph. Gland, Switzerland: International Union for the Conservation of Nature and Natural Resources.

———. 1980. *Conversion of moist tropical forests*. Washington, D.C.: National Academy of Sciences.

———. 1983. *A wealth of wild species: Storehouse for human welfare*. Boulder, Colo.: Westview Press.

———. 1984. *The primary source: Tropical forests and our future*. New York: Norton.

———. 1985. Tropical deforestation and species extinction. *Futures* 17(5): 451–463.

———. 1988. Environmental degradation and some economic consequences in the Philippines. *Environmental Conservation* 15(3): 205–213.

———. 1991. Tropical forests: Present status and future outlook. In *Climatic change* (special issue on tropical forests and climate). In press.

National Academy of Sciences. 1987. *Regulating pesticides in food*. Washington, D.C.: National Academy Press.

———. 1989. *Alternative agriculture*. Washington, D.C.: National Academy Press.

National Board of Agriculture. 1988. *Action program to reduce the risks to health and the environment in the use of pesticides in agriculture*. Stockholm: General Crop Production Division, National Board of Agriculture.

New York Times. 1987. Incinerators held to pose ash hazard. September 30.

———. 1988. Pay-by-bag trash disposal pays, New Jersey town discovers. November 24.

Noble, R. L., T. T. Bee, and J. H. Cutts. 1958. Role of chance observations in chemotherapy: *Vinca rosea*. *Annals of the New York Academy of Sciences* 76:882–894.

Norton, B. G. 1987. *Why preserve natural variety?* Princeton, N.J.: Princeton University Press.

———, ed. 1986. *The preservation of species*. Princeton, N.J.: Princeton University Press.

Noss, R. F. 1987. Corridors in real landscapes: A reply to Simberloff and Cox. *Conservation Biology* 1:159–164.

Odèn, S. 1968. *The acidification of air and precipitation and its consequences on the natural environment*. Uppsala: Swedish National Science Research Council, Ecology Committee.

Odum, E. P. 1969. *Fundamentals of ecology*. Philadelphia: Saunders.

Office of Technology Assessment. 1979. *Pest management strategies*. Washington, D.C.

Oka, I. N., and D. Pimentel. 1976. Herbicide (2,4-D) increases insect and pathogen pests on corn. *Science* 193:239–240.

Page, T. 1980. The severance tax as an instrument of intertemporal equity. In *Economics, ecology, ethics,* ed. H. Daly, 306–323. San Francisco: W. H. Freeman.

Paine, R. T. 1966. Food web complexity and species diversity. *American Naturalist* 100:65–75.

Panuyouto, T. 1987. Economics, environment and development. Development Discussion Paper no. 259. Cambridge: Harvard Institute for International Development.

Partridge, E., ed. 1980. *Responsibilities to future generations: Environmental ethics.* Buffalo, N.Y.: Prometheus Books.

Perrow, C. 1984. *Normal accidents: Living with high-risk technologies.* New York: Basic Books.

Peters, C., A. Gentry, and R. Mendelsohn. 1989. Valuation of an Amazonian rainforest. *Nature* 339:655–656.

Pimentel, D. 1961. Species diversity and insect population outbreaks. *Annals of the Entomological Society of America* 54:76–86.

———. 1976. World food crisis: Energy and pests. *Bulletin of the Entomological Society of America* 22:20–26.

———. 1986. Agroecology and economics. In *Ecological theory and integrated pest management practice,* ed. M. Kogan, 299–319. New York: John Wiley and Sons.

Pimentel, D., and L. Levitan. 1986. Pesticides: Amounts applied and amounts reaching pests. *BioScience* 36:86–91.

Pimentel, D., and C. A. Shoemaker. 1974. An economic and land use model for reducing insecticides on cotton and corn. *Environmental Entomology* 3:10–20.

Pimentel, D., and D. Wen. 1990. Technological changes in energy use in U.S. agricultural production. In *Agroecology,* ed. C. R. Carroll, J. H. Vandermeer, and P. M. Rosset, 147–164. New York: McGraw Hill.

Pimentel, D., C. Shoemaker, E. L. LaDue, R. B. Rovinsky, and N. P. Russell. 1977a. *Alternatives for reducing insecticides on cotton and corn: Economic and environmental impact.* Washington, D.C.: Environmental Protection Agency.

Pimentel, D., E. C. Terhune, W. Dritschilo, D. Gallahan, N. Kinner, D. Nafus, R. Peterson, N. Zareh, J. Misiti, and O. Haber-Schaim. 1977b. Pesticides, insects in foods, and cosmetic standards. *BioScience* 27:178–185.

Pimentel, D., J. Krummel, D. Gallahan, J. Hough, A. Merrill, I. Schreiner, P. Vittum, F. Koziol, E. Back, D. Yen, and S. Fiance. 1978. Benefits and costs of pesticide use in the U.S. food production. *BioScience* 28:772, 778–784.

Pimentel, D., D. Andow, R. Dyson-Hudson, D. Gallahan, S. Jacobson, M. Irish, S. Kroop, A. Moss, I. Schreiner, M. Shepard, T. Thompson, and B. Vinzant. 1980a. Environmental and social costs of pesticides: A preliminary assessment. *Oikos* 34:127–140.

Pimentel, D., E. Garnick, A. Berkowitz, S. Jacobson, S. Napolitano, P. Black, S. Valdes-Cogliano, B. Vinzant, E. Hudes, and S. Littman. 1980b. Environmental quality and natural biota. *BioScience* 30:750–755.

Pimentel, D., L. McLaughlin, A. Zepp, B. Lakitan, T. Kraus, P. Kleinman, F. Vancini, W. J. Roach, G. Selig, W. Keeton, and E. Graap. 1991. Environmental and economic benefits of reducing U.S. agricultural pesticide use. In *Handbook of pest management in agriculture,* vol. 1, 2d ed., ed. D. Pimentel, 679–718. Boca Raton, Fla.: Chemical Rubber Company Press.

Pimm, S. L. 1984. The complexity and stability of ecosystems. *Nature* 307:321–326.

———. 1991. *The balance of nature?* Chicago: University of Chicago Press.

Piore, M. J., and C. F. Sabel. 1984. *The second industrial divide: Possibilities for prosperity.* New York: Basic Books.

Platt, B., C. Doherty, A. Broughton, and D. Morris. 1990. *Beyond 40%: Record setting recycling and composting programs.* Washington, D.C.: Institute of Local Self Reliance.

Pradhan, S. B. 1983. *International pharmaceutical marketing.* Westport, Conn.: Quorum Books.

President's Science Advisory Committee. 1965. *Restoring the quality of our environment.* Environmental Pollution Panel, President's Science Advisory Committee, The White House, Washington, D.C.

Rawls, J. 1971. *A theory of justice.* Cambridge: Harvard University Press.

Repetto, R. 1988. Overview. In *Public policies and the misuse of forest resources,* ed. R. Repetto and M. Gillis. New York: Cambridge University Press.

Repetto, R., and Gillis, M., eds. 1988. *Public policies and the misuse of forest resources.* New York: Cambridge University Press.

Repetto, R., M. Wells, and F. Rossini. 1988. Natural resource accounting. Draft manuscript. World Resources Institute, Washington, D.C.

Ricklefs, R. E. 1987. Community diversity: Relative roles of local and regional processes. *Science* 235:167–171.

Ridgway, R. 1980. Assessing agricultural crop losses caused by insects. In *Crop loss assessment,* proceedings of the E. C. Stakman Commemorative Symposium, Agricultural Experiment Station Miscellaneous Publications, no. 7, 229–233. St. Paul: University of Minnesota.

Robbins, L. 1935. *An essay on the significance of economic science.* 2d ed. London: Macmillan.

Roush, R. T., and J. A. McKenzie. 1987. Ecological genetics of insecticide and acaricide resistance. *Annual Review of Entomology* 32:361–380.

Rowland, F. S. 1989. Chlorofluorocarbons and the depletion of stratospheric ozone. *American Scientist* 77:36–45.

Rowland, F. S., and M. J. Molina. 1975. Chlorofluoromethanes in the environment. *Review of Geophysical Space Physics* 13:1–35.

Seattle Solid Waste Utility. 1988. *Recycling potential assessment and waste stream forecast.* Seattle.

Sen, A. K. 1987. *On ethics and economics.* New York: Basil Blackwell.

Setyono et al. 1986. A review of issues affecting the sustainable development of Indonesia's forest land. Washington, D.C.: International Institute for Environment and Development. Unpublished.

Shaunak, R. K., R. D. Lacewell, and J. Norman. 1982. Economic implications of alternative cotton production strategies in the lower Rio Grande Valley of Texas, 1923–1978. Texas Agricultural Experiment Station, B-1420:25. College Station, Tex.

Shea, C. P. 1988. The chlorofluorocarbon dispute: Why Du Pont gave up $600 million. *New York Times*, April 10.

Shields, E. J., J. R. Hygnstrom, D. Curwen, W. R. Stevenson, J. A. Wyman, and L. K. Binning. 1984. Pest management for potatoes in Wisconsin: A pilot program. *American Potato Journal* 61:508–517.

Simberloff, D., and J. Cox. 1987. Consequences and costs of conservation corridors. Conservation Biology 1:63–71.

Skinner, N. [pers. com., Berkeley City Council, 2180 Milvia Street, Berkeley, Calif. 94704.]

Smith, R. A. 1872. *Air and rain: The beginnings of chemical climatology.* London: Longmans, Green and Co.

Solow, R. 1974. Intergenerational equity and exhaustible resources. *Review of Economic Studies*, 29–46.

Spears, J. 1979. Can the wet tropical forest survive? *Commonwealth Forestry Review* 57(3): 1–16.

Stegner, W. 1953. *Beyond the hundredth meridian.* Boston: Houghton Mifflin.

Sumarkova, V. V., and G. M. Degtyarev. 1985. Water demand of agricultural crops: Runoff of irrigation in the Amudar'Ya basin. *Meteorologiya Gidrologiya* 11:93–102.

Taylor, L. 1975. Theoretical foundations and technical implications. In *Economy-wide models and development planning*, ed. C. R. Blitzer, J. R. Tanner, and L. N. Price, 140–148. London: Oxford University Press.

Temple, S. A. 1987. Predation on turtle nests increases near ecological edges. *Copeia* 1987:250–252.

Terborgh, J. 1986. Keystone plant resources in the tropical forest. In *Conservation biology: The science of scarcity and diversity*, ed. M. E. Soulé, 330–344. Sunderland, Mass.: Sinauer Associates.

Terborgh, J., and B. Winter. 1980. Some causes of extinction. In *Conservation biology: An evolutionary-ecological perspective*, ed. M. E. Soulé and B. A. Wilcox, 119–134. Sunderland, Mass.: Sinauer Associates.

Tew, B. V., M. E. Wetzstein, J. E. Epperson, and J. D. Robertson. 1982. *Economics of selected integrated pest management production systems in Georgia.* University of Georgia, College of Agriculture Experiment Station, Research Report 395.

Thomas, L. 1989. Memorandum from the Society of the Plastics Industry to its members, December 22. Washington, D.C.

Thorne, E. T., and E. S. Williams. 1988. Disease and endangered species: The black-footed ferret as a recent example. *Conservation Biology* 2:66–74.

Tye, Larry. 1988. Effects of acid rain seen as widening. *Boston Globe,* July 14.

U.S. Bureau of the Census. 1971. *Statistical abstract of the United States, 1970.* 92d ed. Washington, D.C.: U.S. Department of Commerce, Bureau of the Census.

———. 1988. *Statistical abstract of the United States, 1987.* 108th ed. Washington, D.C.: U.S. Department of Commerce, Bureau of the Census.

U.S. Congress. House. 1982. *Endangered Species Act: Testimony at congressional hearings.* 97th Cong., 2d sess. Serial 97-32, pp. 129–133.

U.S. Department of Agriculture (USDA). 1936. *Agricultural statistics, 1936.* Washington, D.C.: U.S. Government Printing Office.

———. 1954. *Losses in agriculture.* Washington, D.C.: Agricultural Research Service.

———. 1961. *Agricultural statistics, 1961.* Washington, D.C.: U.S. Government Printing Office.

———. 1965. *Losses in agriculture.* Washington, D.C.: U.S. Government Printing Office.

———. 1975. *Farmers' use of pesticides in 1971: Extent of crop use.* Washington, D.C.: Economics Research Service.

———. 1986. *Agricultural statistics, 1986.* Washington, D.C.: U.S. Government Printing Office.

U.S. General Accounting Office. 1986. *Rangeland management: Grazing lease arrangements of Bureau of Land Management facilities.* Washington, D.C.

Urban, D. L., R. V. O'Neill, and H. H. Shugart. 1987. Landscape ecology. *BioScience* 37:119–127.

Usher, M. B., and M. H. Williamson, eds. 1974. *Ecological stability.* New York: Halstead Press.

van den Bosch, R., and P. S. Messenger. 1973. *Biological control.* New York: Intext Educational Publishers.

Van Dobben, W. H., and R. H. Lowe-McConnell, eds. 1975. *Unifying concepts in ecology.* The Hague: W. Junk.

Vol'futsen, I. B. 1986. Variation of the annual flow of the Amu-Dar'Ya and Syr-Dar'Ya. *Meteorologiya Gidrologiya* 4:32–38.

von Neumann, John, and Oskar Morgenstern. 1953. *Theory of games and economic behavior.* Princeton, N.J.: Princeton University Press.

Walker, R. H., and G. A. Buchanan. 1982. Crop manipulation in integrated weed management systems. *Weed Science* 30, Supplement 1:17–24.

Walsh, J. 1987. Merck donates drug for river blindness. *Science* 238:610.

Ware, G. W., W. P. Cahill, P. D. Gerhardt, and J. M. Witt. 1970. Pesticide drift, 4: On target deposits from aerial application of insecticides. *Journal of Economic Entomology* 63:1982–1983.

Waste-to-Energy Report. 1986. Industry concern growing over EPA proposal to classify ash as hazardous. September 16.

Wax, L. M., and J. W. Pendleton. 1968. Effect of row spacing on weed control in soybeans. *Weed Science* 16:462–464.

Webb, R. E. 1976. *The accident hazards of nuclear power plants.* Amherst, Mass.: University of Massachusetts Press, pp. 197–198. Copyright © 1975, 1976 by Richard E. Webb.

Weiss, E. B. 1988. *In fairness to future generations: International law, common patrimony, and intergenerational equity.* London: Transnational.

White, L., Jr. 1967. The historical roots of our ecological crises. *Science* 155:1203–1207.

White, P. S., and S. P. Bratton. 1980. After preservation: Philosophical and practical problems of change. *Biological Conservation* 18:241–255.

Williams, N. H., and R. L. Dressler. 1976. Euglossine pollination of *Spathiphyllum* (Araceae). *Selbyana* 1:349–355.

Wilson, E. O. 1988. The current status of biodiversity. In *Biodiversity,* ed. E. O. Wilson and F. M. Peter, 3–20. Washington, D.C.: National Academy Press.

Wilson, H. P., M. P. Mascianica, T. E. Hines, and R. F. Walden. 1986. Influence of tillage and herbicides on weed control in a wheat (*Triticum aestivum*)—soybean (*Glycine max*) rotation. *Weed Science* 34:590–594.

Woodwell, G. M., E. C. Conrad, and J. F. Phillips. 1978. The biota and the world carbon budget. *Science* 199:141–146.

Work on Waste, USA, staff. 1988. In Austria a county of 100,000 recycles 67% of its waste. *Waste Not* no. 9, 1. Canton, N.Y.

CONTRIBUTORS

F. Herbert Bormann
School of Forestry and
Environmental Studies
Yale University
New Haven, Connecticut

William A. Butler
Dickstein, Shapiro, Morin
Washington, D.C.

Paul H. Connett
Department of Chemistry
Saint Lawrence University
Canton, New York

David Ehrenfeld
Department of Environmental
Resources
Cook College
Rutgers University
New Brunswick, New Jersey

Thomas Eisner
Section of Neurobiology
and Behavior
Cornell University
Ithaca, New York

Malcolm Gillis
Dean and Vice Provost
Duke University
Durham, North Carolina

William Goldfarb
Department of Environmental
Resources
Cook College
Rutgers University
New Brunswick, New Jersey

Wes Jackson
The Land Institute
Salina, Kansas

Stephen R. Kellert
School of Forestry and
Environmental Studies
Yale University
New Haven, Connecticut

Gene E. Likens
Institute of Ecosystem Studies
Cary Arboretum
New York Botanical Garden
Millbrook, New York

Norman Myers
Consultant in Environment
and Development
Oxford, England

David Pimentel
Department of Entomology
Cornell University
Ithaca, New York

Holmes Rolston III
Department of Philosophy
Colorado State University
Fort Collins, Colorado

Edward O. Wilson
Museum of Comparative
Zoology
Harvard University
Cambridge, Massachusetts

INDEX